The Teaching and Learning of Argument in Sixth Forms and Higher Education

The University of Hull
School of Education
Centre for Studies in Rhetoric

The Teaching and Learning of Argument in Sixth Forms and Higher Education

A project funded by The Leverhulme Trust

Final Report

Sally Mitchell

1994

Acknowledgements

- So now to write the Acknowledgements. This should be an easy task – there are so many people who come readily to mind.

- Difficult too – how will you include and do justice to them all? Where on earth will you start?

- In the three years of this project many teachers and students have been involved. It's their work which fills the pages of this report – I'll start with them.

- They *are* absolutely central.

- Well, yes, this project couldn't have happened without their co-operation and openness. Some, like Dave Kenyon, have even been co-researchers. I really must thank them all.

- But hold on, just go back a bit. Isn't it the Leverhulme Trust who should come first? After all, it was they who recognised the need for a look at argument in sixth forms and higher education ...

- ... and very generously funded the project. Yes, you're right.

- And that, of course, brings us on to Richard Andrews, the director of the project, whose brainchild it was originally.

- Oh, there's a great deal that I can say about him. His enthusiasm for one, encouragement and support, another. And then, his generosity, good humour, ideas, extensive knowledge and lively interest in the development of argument on all fronts... I could go on.

- Well, you could, but I suspect you have others to thank and we've only just so much space and a deadline to meet.

- Right then, how about the support team that Richard gathered around me?

- Do you mean Audrey Rusling, the project secretary?

- Oh, most definitely Audrey – an invaluable person! But I was thinking as well of the steering committee: Judith Atkinson, Jerry Booth, Martin Brooks, Stephen Clarke, Paul Drew, Alan McClelland and Patsy Stoneman. Being steered was a real pleasure – I'm not sure how straight our course was, but the dialogue was good.

- You really valued that, didn't you – the chance to talk, be part of what you would call a 'discourse community'?

- Oh yes! Absolutely vital, and I'm very grateful for all the opportunities I've had to do that, at talks, conferences and workshops – not least the Argument Conference in York, which was hosted by the Esmée Fairbairn and Leverhulme projects. Patrick Costello and I are publishing a book from that – I mustn't forget to mention Patrick!

- And then there were your trips to Denmark; another way of broadening your perspective thanks to the Danish Association of Teachers of English and the British Council.

- Definitely, definitely! But what about all those odd informal conversations that have often been so formative, isn't there a way of acknowledging them?

- Do you think this is the place to do so? Shouldn't you first acknowledge all the journals who have agreed to publish the fruits of your labours?

- Of course I was getting round to that. Let's see: *English in Education, Curriculum, ETUDE, The English and Media Magazine, Literacy Learning: secondary thoughts.* Then there's Heinemann/Boynton Cook for a chapter in a book on genre edited by Aviva Freedman and Peter Medway.

- And let's not forget this report, too, for which thanks are due to the printing services at Hull University and to Ulla Wiberg for the final touches.

- Right that must be it? Can we go now?

- Not quite. I'm thinking again of those times when, especially of late, the nature of argument and the conundrums of teaching and learning it, have dominated, seemingly, all my conversations and thoughts. What about the people who've had to put up with that and more, have joined in, encouraged and enlightened me? What about them?

- Okay then. I know there are several people we've already mentioned who have done that. Who are these others you'd like to include?

- Mark Reid, Steve Burwood, other friends and family.

- Ah yes, of course – people who almost go without saying. Will that do?

- Yes, finally, that will have to do.

Foreword

How to Use This Report

This report is intended as a resource to be used in thinking about the nature and place of argument in teaching and learning at sixth forms (16-19), higher education and possibly other levels, and in a wide range of disciplines (not only those explicitly mentioned here). In this sense, I hope that the report will be an agent for reflection and the consolidation and improvement of practice. Though it includes some practical suggestions for use in teaching situations, these are not intended to represent final outcomes. The research has been more nearly the exploration of a problem (or rather a matrix of problems) than the statement of a solution and the report reflects this. I hope that exploring the problem may be the stimulus for readers to put together strategies and solutions suited to their own particular situations and goals. My aim that the report be a prospective tool as well as, inevitably, a retrospective account rests on a dialogic principle, which, appropriately enough, as I go on to suggest, is a key to the generation of argument.

Contents

Introduction

At the outset of this project the following objectives were stated:

- to identify the existing practice in sixth forms and higher education regarding the teaching of argument
- to identify the needs for spoken and written argument in education and in the 'real world'
- to look at the relationship between spoken and written argument
- to locate gaps in the teaching of argument
- to forge links between sixth forms and tertiary institutions for the purpose of collaboration in this field
- to take positive approaches in the teaching of argument
- to devise materials for use in each of the levels of education
- to trial these materials
- to report the findings

Behind these objectives lies an interest in, and indeed concern about, the ability of students in conducting argument at all levels of education. Many researchers have seen argument in this regard as a language issue and to a great extent therefore it has been seen as the concern of English teachers and language educators. The role and functions of argument are, however, far more extensive than this focus suggests, and particularly so when students enter academic contexts: in learning to argue students are engaged with far more than formal issues, in many cases they are staking claims to identity within the discipline itself. The ability to argue is intimately tied up with the ability to recognise and operate within appropriate parameters, to understand the 'decorum' of a discourse, to display sufficient knowledge, to know how to activate that knowledge in novel yet situated ways. For these issues to be properly understood it is necessary to look more widely than language and the contexts of English classrooms; nonetheless it is language and language use that have provided one of the initial impetuses to this research.

Reports produced over recent decades, for instance, have highlighted the problems encountered by students in writing argument (Gorman et al 1988; Britton et al 1975 amongst others):

> Pupils proceeded to write their descriptions in an additive way rather than by logical selection, producing an unfocused listing of similarities and differences without benefit of an overview. (Britton et al. 1975, p. 132)

> At times problems in argumentative structure were caused by the volume of subject matter, but more typical of 'breakdowns' was the sudden appearance of illogically placed information, gaps in knowledge, wildly exaggerated statements, or passages of semi-confusion possibly hinging upon the misuse of a word or phrase. (Gorman et al. 1988, p. 146)

Although these studies do not address the levels with which this project has been concerned, there is continuity between the problems they highlight and those experienced at sixth form and higher education levels.

The reports do however identify development in argumentative ability. Gorman et al., for instance, were able to distinguish between the abilities of 11 and 15 year olds, noting that the latter were better versed in writing argumentative prose and could draw on journalistic modes amongst others; whilst the former often retained features of spoken argument in their written work: 'outbreaks of dramatic dialogue in the midst of standard prose paragraphs.'(p. 148).

It is worth noting here that development is seen as a movement way from the spoken. This very powerful model of argumentative literacy is continued and strengthened at sixth form and higher education levels where the forms in which students write become, on the whole, increasingly restricted and determined by convention. The movement away from speech is perhaps exemplified in the prevalent notion of academic objectivity in writing. Argument becomes, ostensibly at least, less and less related to the personal and to the speaking voice and more concerned with disciplinary procedures. The difficulties of understanding disciplinary arguments (usually in the form of authoritative texts which need to be correctly quoted and referenced) can produce the same 'additive' descriptions and 'breakdowns' as are noted in the earlier years of schooling.

Speech does, however, remain an important medium for learning and developing argument, though the connections between it and writing are not always clear or capitalised upon. Gubb (1987), who was one of Gorman's team, noted, for instance, a disjunction between what was generated in discussion and what was subsequently recorded in writing:

> Breakdowns occur in logic, grammar gets forgotten; changes of topic take place with disconcerting abruptness and passionately expressed views are reduced to trite one-line opinions ... Discussion suddenly seems to have little connection with discursive writing. (p. 163)

This project has noted similar disjunctions between spoken and written argument and has considered the various ways and contexts in which speech is used to develop argument and conversely the kinds of argument that contexts make possible – in writing as well as speech. The remit of the project to examine the forms and functions of argument not in one subject area, but across a range of disciplines makes the influence of context upon argument a particular area of interest.

As I've suggested the project has augmented its grounding in these earlier studies with explorations of the role and nature of argument in particular disciplinary discourses. This has led to a consideration of the place of argument in the transformation of knowledge and the achievement of 'expert' or 'insider' status within discourses.

In addition to the concern with educational contexts, there has over recent years been growing interest in the relevance and transferability of skills acquired in such contexts to the world of employment and other 'real' world environments. The project has noted and explored the implications for argument of recognising the overlaps, disparities and transitions between education and other spheres of life. Its primary focus has, however, remained with the sense in which academia itself constitutes a world.

x

1. Methodology

The methodology of this project has been broadly ethnographic; that is, it has taken various singular and local situations or instances of argument and attempted to understand and describe these as particular practices, rather than, for instance, as abstractions or generalities. The methodology involved observations in teaching and learning situations, taping of oral data, collecting of written data and interviewing the participants. Questions which were raised as part of this approach have addressed such areas as the participants' beliefs and concepts about their practices, the way and the occasions on which they express these (if indeed they do outside the context of a research project), what their actual practices consist in, for what purposes and under what conditions. These are questions about the way concepts (such as 'argument') are defined and manifested within various frames of reference – individual frames, classroom frames, institutional frames, for instance – and within various cultural and linguistic forms, such as, in speech; the small group, the seminar, the debate and, in writing; the essay, review, report.

Centred around the relatively abstract idea of 'argument', the approach described here is what Geertz (1993) has described as 'an ethnography of thought'. It is worth including some of his descriptions here, because they form a suggestive backdrop to the work of this project. The ethnography of thought is based on:

> the belief that ideation, subtle or otherwise, is a cultural artefact. Like class and power, it is something to be characterised by construing its expressions in terms of the activities that sustain them. (p. 152)

Sustaining these activities are:

> such muscular matters as the representation of authority, the marking of boundaries, the rhetoric of persuasion, the expression of commitment and the registering of dissent. (p.153)

These matters are likely to be described in an ethnography of thought. Similarly it will have things to say about the following:

> ... translation, how meaning gets moved, or does not, reasonably intact from one sort of discourse to the next; about intersubjectivity, how separate individuals come to conceive, or do not, reasonably similar things; about how thought frames change (revolutions and all that), how thought provinces are demarcated ("today we have naming of fields"), how thought norms are maintained, thought models acquired, thought labour divided. (p. 154)

This list of possible discoveries has resonated throughout the work of this project. It covers what occurs in classroom discourse, the roles taken by teachers and students in learning, the way their talk and writing can produce consensus or difference, the way arguments that are adequate in one area of learning are inadequate in another, the way narrative works to conserve what argument works to change.

The kinds of questions and issues raised and addressed in the ethnographic approach have resulted in a number of 'case studies' of work in particular disciplines at both sixth form and higher education levels. Some of these are included in this report. The Interim Report of the project (Mitchell 1992b) contains case studies of subjects at A level.

The case studies are informed by and inform a theoretical context, in which I include the findings of other researchers. The theory element of this research did not pre-date nor remain unaffected by the empirical fieldwork; neither were my observations 'innocent' of theoretical perspectives and interpretative tools. Rather theory and practice were mutually informing. In this sense the research method approximates to what Glaser and Strauss (1967) term 'Grounded Theory'. Here theory is conceived as emerging from the collection of data and the immersal of the researcher in the field. It is then tested and refined in the light of further collection and observation. There were aspects of the present project which militated against the testing of theory by further observation in the same field. This was largely a result of the wide scope of the project which meant that after the first year's study of practice at sixth form level, the focus was switched to higher education. Whilst this prevented thorough consolidation in the single field, it nonetheless provided a basis for the identification of similarity and difference across levels. Further research would be valuable to examine in greater depth the characteristics of each level and indeed of individual disciplines.

What can be claimed as *generalisable* theory from the case study approach is to an extent limited and its value needs instead to be seen in terms of the *relatability* of the findings. Bassey (1981) states that the merits of the case-study should be judged on:

> the extent to which the details are sufficient and appropriate for a teacher working in a similar situation to relate his decision making to that described in the case study. (p. 85)

Among the questions that a teacher reading the study might ask are, he suggests:

> How was the procedure introduced to students?
> *Could I do it?*
> What were the students like in the experiment?
> How far were they motivated to learn?
> *Would it be suitable for my students?* ...

These questions suggest the pedagogical orientation which can derive from the case study approach and which is important to the present project. The singularity of case studies makes them suggestive rather than prescriptive, enlightening in so far as they resonate with the experiences of others. In this way they are *usable*, suitable tools for reflection. This, for me, is a crucial aspect of this research; that it should enable individuals – both teachers and students – involved in similar situations and practices to recognise what is familiar, notice what is different and to make connections with or distance themselves from what is described. I hope that in this way the report may be a catalyst for improvement. As Bassey (1983) comments, in pedagogical research:

> theory is created in pursuit of improvement and for the achievement of that improvement, not as the ultimate purpose of the research. (p. 111)

Summary of the Research

Year One

- set up contacts with teachers in two sixth forms

- observe one 'unit of study' in nine subjects at A level: History, Politics, Sociology, Communication Studies, English, Theatre Studies, Biology, Mathematics, Physics

- analyse data, including written work

- questionnaire to sixth form students gauging attitude to argument in sixth form subjects

- write Interim Report

Year Two

- establish contacts with departments in three universities

- undertake major studies of Sociology, English, Fine Art

- undertake smaller 'snapshot' studies and work with staff introducing innovations in EFL work, Applied Biology, Electronic Engineering, Dutch Studies, Financial Accounting, Philosophy

- write second Interim Report (unpublished)

Year Three

- devise material and undertake teaching and marking for induction module on argument with undergraduate students

- observe practice in Danish Sixth Form College (Gymnasium) for purpose of comparison

- write Final Report

2. Theoretical Discussion: Key Words and Ideas

In this section of the report I want to introduce and explore certain terms and ideas which have informed my thinking about argument in sixth forms and higher education. Many of the terms are overlapping and mutually informing, but it is not my intention to collapse them into or strictly mark them out from one another, rather to see them as tools for thinking about this area, each offering a slightly different approach.

I will begin with **argument** itself, but will not at this stage claim to say anything like enough about it. It will be the briefest of introductions to a term which, I think, becomes richer and more complex in the light of the succeeding ideas I will introduce. So at the end of this section I will return to argument again and reflect on the dimensions it has acquired through being placed in the light of the other clustering ideas and perspectives. The discussion can be divided into roughly two major sections: Argument in Contexts; Argument as Cognitive Processes.

Argument

To begin with a highly conventional way of understanding argument: the definitions supplied by the OED. Already argument is not one thing but several:

1) proof, evidence

2) (in astronomy and mathematics), the angle, arc or other mathematical quantity from which another required quantity may be deduced

3) a statement or fact advanced for the purpose of influencing the mind; a reason urged in support of a proposition

4) a connected series of statements or reasons intended to establish a position (and hence refute the opposite); a process of reasoning, argumentation

5) a statement of reason for and against a proposition; discussion of a question, debate

6) subject matter of discussion or discourse in speech or writing; theme, subject

7) the summary or abstract of the subject matter of a book; a syllabus, the contents

Notice that argument is both singular (proof, evidence, subject, theme) and connected, dynamic and a process: statement but also debate. There is a sense in which argument seems to take into account alternative positions, whether in the mathematical definition where what is known suggests a way of discovering what is not yet known or in the notion that a statement of reasons intended to establish a position also carries with it the intention to refute the opposite.

4

These definitions provide useful starting points and are embedded in much of what is described in this report. Nevertheless there is a certain static quality, a formality to these definitions; they tell us little about where argument takes place, how it is experienced and by whom, what functions it performs, what different forms it might take.

They also have little to do with the way argument is commonly thought of in everyday life. Look at the way sixth form students defined argument in a questionnaire we used. According to them, argument is 'an angry replacement for discussion', 'a strong expression of disagreement, often purposely caused through boredom'; it 'enables you to get what you want', 'can be used to show many kinds of self-feeling – to demonstrate love, hate and so on' and is 'used when it's a last resort'.

These comments wrest the definition of argument away from the domain of abstract reasoning, which is, in the disembodied form of dictionary definitions, cool, academic and formal and show it to perform powerful social and personal functions, many of which are anything but reasonable.

In the educational situations with which this project is concerned these different senses of argument raise important questions. What kinds of argument are fostered and valued in the process of becoming educated? What kinds of reasons or statements are legitimate in establishing a position? Is becoming educated also becoming reasonable, and if so, what does 'reasonable' mean? Does it have room for passion or 'self-feeling'? Is argument connected to persons or to propositions? Does argument mean and do different things in different domains? If so, who is it that decides what counts as meaningful and appropriate?

These are questions which relate to issues of power, **control** and **identity**. Our questionnaire to the sixth formers provides a first example of these issues and the problems they raise in terms of understanding argument. The structured part of the questionnaire was based on a definition of argument which we supplied, either explicitly, as in this introductory paragraph:

> When you write an essay setting out a point of view or looking at several points of view and deciding which you agree with, you are usually conducting an argument. You also engage in argument when you discuss an issue or topic with others, or when you try to explain your ideas or why you think something is right or wrong. Argument is more than just a row, although, of course this is part of its meaning.

or inexplicitly through the kinds of specific questions we asked, such as, for example:

> Which of these forms of argument are used in your subject?
> a) making points related to previous points
> b) raising questions related to previous points
> c) supplying evidence as proof
> d) persuading someone of your point of view
> e) seeing both sides of an issue or question
> f) weighing up the arguments of others

The students complied with our requirements to the point where (at the end) we asked for their 'own ideas about what argument is and how and where it is used' and here our control over the definition and the language it was couched in was undermined and thrown into perspective.

Power determines what can be argued, how and by whom. Although our intention in inviting students to respond to the questionnaire was to find out what they thought and what their experiences were, it was we who set the parameters for what it was possible to say – though there were some ways, as I've suggested, in which they could subvert or resist this control.

Early on in this project I looked at the role played by questions in classroom discourse (see Mitchell 1992a). I discovered that questions had an important part to play in determining who was powerful and who constrained within a particular context: that is, who could make and validate meaning and who must adopt meanings or remain silent. Although it was generally teachers who held power through their domination of the question form, some questions also held the potential for new and shared meaning and so could be seen not only as powerful but also as empowering. Giving students the licence to question, even if this means requiring them to do so ('Write down three questions about the text you've just read') is a way of sharing power. Questioning 'is a way of putting into language what has not yet been thought and of giving to absence the potentiality of presence.'(p. 39) But this power is always subject to further constraining criteria: 'good question, but not one to be dealt with here', 'all questions are equal but some are more equal than others'.

The ability to argue – which shares qualities with the ability to question – can be similarly empowering, but also similarly constrained. In all institutional contexts and particularly perhaps at A level and beyond, the sense in which some questions and some arguments are more and some less equal than others is a constant factor in the learning that takes place. The balance between the relative open- and closedness of argument (both terms which are used to describe questions) is a theme which has runs through this report, as it affects both the processes of learning and its outcomes.

Context

Argument already seems to be different things in different situations: in mathematics, it is an angle used to deduce another quantity, in formal schooling situations (or idealised schooling situations?) it is, perhaps, a process of reasoning (often developed, as our questionnaire definition suggested, in the essay form) and influencing the mind (but perhaps not the heart), and in other situations it is angry, an outer manifestation of inner feeling, beyond the bounds of reason and discussion.

In *The Uses of Argument* (1958), Stephen Toulmin made an important distinction between a notion of logic as somehow universal – both as a science, uncovering the laws of right reasoning and an art, offering tips on how to argue rightly – and a more situated approach to logic or argument, which looks at the ways in which cases are made in the furtherance of certain purposes. He suggested that:

> ... validity is an intra-field, not an inter-field notion. Arguments within any field can be judged by standards appropriate within that field, and some will fall short; but it must be expected that the standards will be field dependent, and that the merits to be demanded of an argument in one field will be found to be absent (in the nature of things) from entirely meritorious arguments in another. (p. 255)

This way of thinking about argument has been important to this project, which has taken place in a wide range of different fields (disciplines) at different stages in the educational process and has needed to take account of the different ways in which argument is conducted and indeed valued both as a disciplinary activity and as a way of learning at various stages.

What sort of things make up a context? There seem to me to be a number of ways in which context comes to bear. All of them can be seen as ways in which an action is framed; some, like ideology, are very extensive and indeed difficult to see beyond, others, like form, are more limited (or can be made to seem so) and so can be more closely addressed. They can also be the means by which to uncover ideology.

Ideology is very much an all embracing term (and idea), which describes the invisible structures and beliefs by which we operate and which appear as natural unchallengable ways of doing things. Ideologies are associated with dominant forces and positions within our culture, which nonetheless keep the conditions and premises upon which domination rests invisible, precisely because they are seen to be natural. Ideologies are thus seen to be normative, conservative and also context-free. Challenges to ideology come often from marginal groups within it, which seek to overturn its assumptions by making them visible. So, for instance, feminists have critiqued the dominant ideology of patriarchy and this has included, incidentally, a critique of academic argument and discourse as patriarchal (see Lamb 1991, Meyer 1993). Meyer names the impersonal authoritative and objective stance associated with writing a formal academic essay as an 'illusion' and characterises the 'for and against' notion of argument as polarising and aggressive. Like Lamb, she wants to challenge the way we think of 'argument' and her critique is therefore not only of practices but also of definitions.

Ideological approaches are those which seek to name and undermine the forces of ideology, rather than to uphold it. Brian Street's (1984) approach to literacy, for example, is ideological because it seeks to supplant the 'autonomous ' model which suggests that literacy is not affected by social context with an approach in which what counts as literacy varies between situations and according to the value and position accorded to it by ideology. His critique emerges from attention to what has been named as *other* within the dominant ideology, in this case, those who have been named as illiterate (the passive tense is no accident here) and considering the possibility of alternative interpretations and namings.

It is virtually impossible to be free of ideology in some form or other and I take it to frame in more or less evident ways all the examples of argument I have came across.

Discourse is really the mouthpiece of ideology. It describes the way language is used, the way its components are organised to create knowledge and relationships. It allows things to be said, but also contains what can be said: it enables and constrains the kinds of meanings we can make about the world. Foucault (1972) said of its determining role: 'one cannot speak of anything at any time; it is not easy to say something new...' (p. 64). Michael Billig (1991) has also made this point by commenting that when we hold an attitude or opinion about something we are indicating both something personal about ourselves and at the same time locating ourselves within a wider controversy. Our opinion is a 'dual expression' (p. 43) which owes as much to current debate as our own thinking.

Discourse can also be more widely defined than as a particular form of language use and this is useful to bear in mind:

At any moment we are using language we must say or write the right thing in the right way while playing the right social role and (appearing) to hold the right values, beliefs and attitudes. Thus what is important is not language, and surely not grammar, but *saying (writing)-doing-being-valuing-believing combinations*. These combinations I call "Discourses", with a capital "D" ("discourse" with a little "d", to me, means connected stretches of language that make sense, so "discourse" is part of "Discourse"). Discourses are ways of being in the world; they are forms of life which integrate words, acts, values, beliefs, attitudes, and social identities as well as gestures, glances, body positions and clothes. (Gee 1989 p. 6-7)

There is not just one discourse; there are discourses; different ways of using language and creating meanings which vary according to context. Academic discourse, for example, construes the world differently from everyday discourse and, within academia, different **disciplines** (Toulmin's term is fields) operate with different discourses. Disciplines therefore also constitute contexts. Concepts which enable meaning to be formulated in, say, sociology, are different (though there will be overlaps) from those in, say, psychology (see section on speech). So whilst a discourse may allow communication within one field, it may restrict the possibility of communication between fields (as is witnessed when people from a variety of disciplines come together to share a sense of what it is like to be within an academic community). In this sense, then, becoming part of one discipline (learning the operation and validity of its arguments) is also acquiring what has been called 'trained incapacity' to think outside the parameters of the field.[1] Again the way in which knowledge and learning are compartmentalised by institutional structures and discourses can be seen as a manifestation of ideology and has in fact been critiqued by such movements as (again) feminism which, in drawing from a number of disciplines, seeks as one of its aims to disrupt specialised disciplinary claims to knowledge (and, therefore, power). So what individuals do within and between fields may also change the nature of and shift the boundaries of that field.

Learning a discipline involves *learning* to speak and be heard in a particular discourse. Individuals are not simply located but become located. Neither do individuals come to learning discourse-free, but must manage transitions between discourses, learning what Sheeran and Barnes (1991) have called the **'ground rules'** – appropriate ways of speaking, writing, reading, thinking.

There are often tensions experienced in such transitions. A mature student on a Philosophical Methods course I observed hinted that the new ways in which she had been encouraged to consider the question of 'What is love?' had begun to alienate her from her family and friends; her identity, she felt, was somehow changing. Most people can be assumed to have something to say about love and find some relevancy for it in their own experience, but this 'common sense' discourse was not much help in the philosophy course or at least only in a limited way. The lecturer explained that in this course the topic of love was not a straightforward appeal to experience, though students should draw upon what they knew. This knowledge would not be personal or particular, but somehow general. From such general knowledge it would be possible to generate hypothetical or imagined examples, as distinct from actual lived experiences. At one step removed from experience, then, the

---

[1] The specialised nature of disciplinary discourse is a factor which militates against the transferability of skills between contexts and also against the practice of 'creative' thinking which is advocated as a problem-solving technique in business and industry, which requires the participants precisely to go beyond the bounds of normalised thinking.

approach becomes disinterested and cool. Philosophy demands that the question be looked at systematically and in a certain rigorous way. Succeeding attempts to define love are overturned and rejected, shown through a process of systematic reasoning to be merely synonymous with sexual desire or the 'will to live'. For all its rigour, though, the philosophical approach does not reach conclusions as to what love is: it removes certainty and replaces it with a relentless process of questioning. To adapt to this way of behaving, students either achieve a separation between the disinterested disciplinary approach and their own interested beliefs and experiences, or take over the philosophical approach altogether. Most academic disciplines have this type of enculturation – or at least the display of it – as an important aim.[2]

Physical setting, persons present, time allotted all have an impact on the kinds of argument that are possible. The size and layout of a room for instance affects the kinds of grouping and social interaction that are possible as does the contact time available. If short, the teacher may feel that she must pursue her own agenda more rigidly to ensure it is covered. Teachers tend to have different views about the kinds of space and groups size they like. Some, for instance, sense that their presence amongst a group of students may inhibit their contributions to discussion and dislike, for this reason, the enforced intimacy of tutorial groups – both because the group is thought to be too small to have a dynamic of its own and because the setting – the tutor's own office – is wrong. The role of the teacher in this setting is felt to be ambiguous and uncomfortable. Other teachers prefer the intimate arrangement as it allows the kind of discussion in which the teacher models for the students the kind of disciplinary discourse they need to learn. In this case the different dynamic and feel of a small group discussion from which the teacher is absent may not be thought to suit the purposes of disciplinary learning. The role and presence or absence or the teacher, both as 'expert' and 'authority' is a considerable factor in determining the type of argument which might take place. But the impact of the setting is open, to some degree, to the interpretation of those present, not only the teacher but the students as well. A teacher who asks a question in a lecture, for instance, in order to stimulate debate, may well be greeted with passive resistance by students who have understood the social rules of the situation differently. Similarly the impact of time on learning to argue will vary according to the value placed on the activity by the discipline, by the prevailing pedagogy and by the individual teacher.

Form and conventions might also be seen as part of the context for argument, though, like discourse and ideology, it is also intrinsic to what is produced. A form is an accepted way of doing something. In schooling, for example, written argument is generally seen as taking the form of an **essay** and again this form frames what can be argued and how. There is a nice example of this in a paper by Roz Ivanic and Denise Roach (1990), which tells the story of how when Denise first began her academic course as a mature student she answered an essay question directly with 'no', though she realised she would have to write more than this:

> With reference to the above question I could answer with namely one word *NO* – However for the purpose of this essay a deeper analysis is called for. (p. 14)

---

[2] An important argument against modularised degrees is that they do not allow sufficient experience within any particular discipline for a discourse to be adequately learnt. Students as a result learn something about the discipline (an outsider's point of view) without learning what is like to be within the discipline.

Noting the incredulous responses of her friends and after several redraftings the 'no' disappeared from the first paragraph to be replaced by the phrase 'is incorrect' in the *final* paragraph:

> So despite Firestone offering what she believes is a comprehensive analysis, her assumption that women's oppression is brought about through women's reproductive capacity is, as I argue, incorrect. (p. 15)

Denise's disagreement ends up, then, in the conventional place for the expression of opinion within the essay form – the conclusion – and is expressed in a cooler academic discourse. Ivanic and Roach pose this question: 'Is this superior argumentation, or is it a different set of discourse conventions for the same intellectual process?' (p. 15) The answer to this is complex, I think. When Denise answered the question with 'no', she was engaged in argument only in so far as she was expressing an opinion or making a statement. She was not however demonstrating the reasons *why* she arrived at that conclusion, nor giving any sense of alternative positions which might need to be taken into account and/or refuted in order to locate her opinion within a controversy. This is, however, a separate issue from the way she expressed her opinion and the place she gave to that expression in the essay. Education is only rarely about intellectual, as divorced from social processes, and in a sense, what Denise was intellectually capable of was not at issue here. Her first introduction was wrong because she did not understand the 'way of saying', the discourse which properly constituted the social practice she was engaged in; she did not understand what Bazerman (1988, p. 320) has called its 'decorum'.

There is, it seems, a distinction to be made between the mode of thinking that Denise needed to engage in (argumentative) and the form and discourse she needed to adopt for the 'valid' expression of this thinking (See Mitchell and Andrews 1994). This introduces a new key idea: **argument as a mode** – a 'way of doing', which can at some level be distinguished from its form of expression. Mode and form often *need to be* distinguished when learning to argue, in order for attention to be given to ways of generating argument as well as presenting it. It seems to me that an emphasis on argumentative *product* tends to fuse mode and form unhelpfully and can result in writing which though formally and rhetorically appropriate falls short in terms of argumentative content. This impression which leads me to separate mode and form is developed in later sections, particularly in regard to writing.

The point about the example above is that Denise was not simply being called upon to argue, but to argue in a certain way for a certain audience/readership. Her writing had, that is, a particular **rhetorical purpose**.

Rhetoric

The notion of rhetoric is closely tied to argument and argumentative contexts since it is concerned with the effectiveness of arguments and the way they persuade. Taking a rhetorical perspective on writing, for instance is to ask questions about *purpose* (see Andrews, 1992 and 1994) such as whom am I writing *for*? who am I writing *as*? for what *purpose*? what options are open to me to be effective? Asking such questions as these may denaturalise the processes of writing and bring them to a level of consciousness where they can be reflected upon. The rhetorical task may involve, or be perceived to involve, for instance, the construction of an impersonal objective stance, for the purpose of persuading a particular disembodied academic audience. Denise came to understand her writing task this way though she experienced it uneasily as 'fabricating a sort of detective story for the reader'(p. 15). Or, on another occasion in a different sort of context, it may involve speaking (as if) from the heart – as in the following example from a first year Biology undergraduate's speech to her tutor group. Below is the entire speech as Helen prepared it to speak. I'm including it here, ask it illustrates several of the points that have been made about argument so far, as well as others that will take the exploration further:

TO LIVE AND LET DIE

One of the basic human rights enjoyed by everyone of us is the right to live. Surely as death is part of life – we all die eventually (look at Fred – point at the skeleton) – the right to live also means the right to die.

But what does life mean to you?

(brief pause and audience response – probably nil)

To us (indicate group) life means:-
i   eating chocolate cake
ii   missing lectures
iii   the morning after the night before
iv   freedom of expression in all its forms
v   feelings and personality

What does death mean to you?

(brief pause and audience response – probably nil)

To us (indicate group) life (sic) means:-
i   a total lack of awareness
ii   becoming an object, a non-person
iii   having no purpose – you are useless
iv   no interaction with the community
v   being a temporary collection of organic ingredients, soon to be broken down and reassembled in another form

The medical definition of brain death includes the following criteria:-
1.   Apnoea – no spontaneous breathing (i.e. if respirator turned off)
2.   Unresponsivity – no movement to any stimulus
3.   Absence of cephalic reflexes (no pupil response, no eye movement when head is turned, no coughing when throat is stimulated)
4.   Flat EEG recording – electrocerebral silence
5.   Confirmation test of absence of cerebral brain flow for 30 minutes

The main subject on whom our case is based is Tony Bland.

Nearly 4 years ago he was crushed in the Hillsborough disaster. The result of this tragedy was that Tony suffered brain damage so severe that it left him in a permanent vegetative state – known as PVS. To all intents and purposes he became a living corpse. The person who was Tony Bland died that day at the Hillsborough stadium. The happy, vibrant, football loving young man has gone forever. All his family and friends have to remind them of Tony is a body which bears no resemblance to the former essence of his personality. This living corpse cannot comprehend its surroundings, cannot move, and is maintained by machines. Its vital signs are prolonged but it is in no way a prolongation of life. Tony can never be released from within this mound of flesh because Tony and all that he was has gone.

The only thing being preserved by his dependence on machines is his family's suffering. The essence of Tony has gone. Why preserve its mortal prison? It is time to allow Tony to die with his last dignity intact. If he had not had the operations and machines in order to maintain him he would have ceased to function that fateful day at Hillsborough.

His family could have laid his memory to rest and begun the grieving process along with the victims of the other tragic victims that died.

A doctor has a duty to sustain life where it is sustainable but has no duty – legal, moral or ethical – to prolong the distress of an incurable patient or their family.

Gastric tubes, intravenous infusions, antibiotics and respirators are all supportive measures for use in acute or subacute illness to assist toward recovery of health. To use such measures in the treatment of incurable patients is inappropriate as there is no expectancy of a return to health and therefore such practices can be considered bad medicine. When deciding whether to prolong a life, a doctor must take into account:

i   the patient's medical condition
ii their spiritual and emotional capacity
iii their religious convictions
iv the degree of interaction with friends and family
v   personal and social commitments of the patient and finally and perhaps m o s t controversial
vi the cost involved – what degree of care can be afforded on the patient's   behalf – by the family and the state

Doctor Howe – Tony's doctor – took all these points into consideration in his case and concluded that:-

'Medicine is not just a case of keeping people alive. We are not producing immortality'.

This was endorsed by one of the Law Lords involved in the historic ruling allowing Tony to die. He said:-

'It is lawful to cease to give treatment and care to a PVS (persistent vegetative state) patient considering that to do so involves invasive manipulation of the patient's body and which confers no benefit upon him'.

To end our presentation we decided to use a poem about death which we feel is appropriate to our case.

'Through vaults of pain,
Enribbed and wrought with groins of ghastliness,
I passed, and garish spectres moved my brain
To dire distress.
Where lies the end
To this foul way? I asked with weakening breath.
Whereon I saw a door extend –
The door to death
It loomed more clear:
At last! I cried. The all-delivering door!'

There are a number of ways in which this speech shows awareness of rhetorical purpose. At the beginning the instructions in brackets anticipate the context in which the words will be spoken (a skeleton she knows will be in the room, a group – her team for whom she is spokesperson, an audience). Rhetoric is in this instance literally pointing, but one might use this as a metaphor for the way it designates audiences through language. The nature of the audience (other members of the tutor group) is also constructed or anticipated in the choice of examples of what life means. They are a humorous appeal to shared experience and bridge the gap between the point of view of the speaker and that which she assumes her listeners to have. They range over several levels from the concrete and frivolous (chocolate cake) to the abstractly meaningful (feelings and personality). These examples are a form of cliché: they appeal to what is common. The second set of examples which refer to death(?) balances the first (there are the same number) and forms a contrast in tone. This contrast is an important part of the argument, which is based from the outset and throughout on the oppositional categories of life and death; 'feelings and personality' versus 'a temporary collection of organic ingredients'; 'the happy, vibrant, football loving young man', 'Tony Bland', the 'person' versus the 'living corpse' and the 'mound of flesh', 'he' versus 'it'. The opposition is built upon an appeal to (highly emotive) everyday definitions of what constitutes life and death.

Yet Helen is also a biologist speaking to biologists and indicates her awareness of this by bringing in the medical definition of brain death, which includes specialised terms and criteria. She also uses the opinions of experts to defend her view. This mix of discourses has to do, I think, with the context for which the speech was prepared. The tutor was concerned that his students were able to study biology successfully at university without grappling with its ethical and 'real world' implications and without experience of how to communicate their knowledge in other ways. He decided therefore to devote some tutorial time to 'for and against' debates on certain topical issues, which related to biology: "Drugs and Sport" and (this one) "When to turn off life support". Since the debates were taking place within the context of a tutorial rather than a seminar, lecture or laboratory session they were at the margins of disciplinary activity and this, it seems to me, contributes to making possible and legitimate the mix of the moral, ethical and commonsensical as well as clinical.

In addition the framing of the initiative as 'debate' with 'for and against' groups suggests that the topics may be treated in a general rather than specialised way and probably accounts for Helen's adoption of a 'public-speaking' type of form and tone. This carries with it certain interpretations of the audience. The students are invited to confront real world issues and they do so in real world terms (in which the spoken medium is certainly a factor). The framing sets up the topics as containing oppositions, two opposing points of view. What Helen produces conforms to this adversarial model of argument and may also account for the forcefulness of her rhetoric.

What can be made of the speech in terms of argument? The paragraph beginning 'Gastric tubes...' conforms closely to the definition from the OED: 'a reason urged in support of a proposition'. There are two reasons (or premises) here: the first is that gastric tubes etc. are measures to *assist recovery* of health; the second is that incurables have no expectation of recovery. The proposition (or conclusion) which derives from these is that using such measures is inappropriate (and therefore not good medicine). So here is a neatly formulated argument which fits our definition.[3]

Yet how much else is going on here in terms of argument with the purpose of influencing the mind (and heart)! The speech does all the following things in the service of argument: it lists, it conveys knowledge and asks questions, it establishes links with an audience, it tells a story (a very *current* one at the time), it uses authorities (quotes them), it employs a range of discourses, it appeals to emotion as well as reason and it concludes not with a statement

---

[3.] **Argument without context:**
Some views of argument are not concerned with context – aspects of the 'Critical Thinking' movement, for example, which are concerned with the formal structures of argument and the ability to recognise and use them. This is what Toulmin calls the logician's role in teaching the *'ars de penser, the ars conjectandi'* (p. 4). I think there is some value in this approach as a rigorous exercise according to a certain set of rules which may become a resource in other contexts, but such a view of argument and critical thinking is limited if it is excludes consideration of such factors as form, function and effect. Often too much is claimed for it as an approach: it lacks recognition of the role played by context and the symbiotic relation of context and individual, and so tends to exclude other ways of conceiving of argument.

but a poem. An understanding of argument within context and as effective (i.e. as having effects), has to take into account these extra dimensions.

Helen's argument for the turning off of life-support in cases such as Tony Bland's took place on an occasion where an argument was also made for the opposite view. Both her team and the opposing one also faced questions from the audience. As I've noted, several of the features of Helen's speech gesture towards this larger event of which it was a part. I think it's easy here to conceive of Helen's speech as an *action* contributing to an *event*, because of its obviously performative nature. But this is perhaps less easy to grasp when it is proposed for all acts of communication, written as well as spoken: an essay as performing an action as part of an event? Yet this idea is clearly a part of the rhetorical perspective and also behind other ways of characterising language use: 'literacy practices' and 'literacy events' as ways of understanding literacy (Barton 1994), Gee's definition of Discourse, and, for text, a notion of **genre**, understood as 'social action'.

Genre as Social Action

This idea was coined by Carolyn Miller (1984) in a highly influential article of the same name. Charles Bazerman (1988), using Miller's work, gives this summary:

> A genre consists of something beyond simple similarity of formal characteristics among a number of texts. A genre is a socially recognised, repeated strategy for achieving similar goals in situations socially perceived as being similar (Miller). A genre provides a writer with a way of recognising the kind of message being transmitted. A genre is a social construct that regularises communication, interaction and relations. Thus the formal features that are shared by the corpus of texts in a genre and by which we usually recognise a text's inclusion in a genre, are the linguistic/symbolic solution to a problem in social interaction. (p. 62)

Amy Devitt (1993) gives some concrete examples of how a sense of genre might help to solve such problems in social interaction:

> ... consider what we know when, as readers, we recognise the genre of a text. Based on our identification of genre, we make assumptions not only about the form but also about the text's purposes, its subject matter, its writer and its expected reader. If I open an envelope and recognise a sales letter in my hand, I understand that a company will make a pitch for its product and want me to buy it. Once I recognise that genre, I will throw the letter away or scan it for the product it is selling. If in a different scenario, I open an envelope and find a letter from a friend, I understand immediately a different set of purposes and a different relationship between writer and reader, and I respond/read accordingly. (p. 575)

Devitt goes on to argue that genre can play a mediating role with regard to traditional dichotomies which have dominated the way language use is understood:

> Genre is an abstraction or generality once removed from the concrete or particular. Not as abstract as Saussurian notions of *langue* or language system, genre mediates between *langue* and *parole*, between language and the utterance. Not as removed as situation, genre mediates between text and context. Not as general as meaning, genre mediates between form and content. Genre is patterns and relationships, essentially semiotic ones, that are constructed when writers and groups of writers identify different writing tasks as being similar. Genre constructs and responds to recurring situations, becoming visible through perceived patterns in the syntactic, semantic and pragmatic features of particular texts. (p. 580)

An important implication of this way of construing genre (as also of the rhetorical perspective which replaces the question 'what text is this?' with 'what persuasive action is this text performing?') is that it helps to collapse fixed boundaries which close off certain textual forms from others (the fact/fiction and literature/non-fiction divides would be examples). As Miller says of this understanding:

> It does not lend itself to taxonomy, for genres change, evolve, and decay; the number of genres current in any society is indeterminate and depends upon the complexity and diversity of the society. (p. 163)

But despite this flexibility, genres are recognisable and perform important communicative and identity-building functions. Thus as Swales (1990) has suggested the possession of one or more genres is one defining characteristic of a **discourse community**; a community, that is, which shares certain *saying (writing)-doing-being-valuing-believing combinations'* (Gee, 1989, p. 6).

What can be said about Helen's speech in terms of genre? The genre was not specified nor uniformly interpreted. Helen's speech conformed most to a recognisable public model (and was in fact highly thought of), but others were less carefully structured, less passionate or made more appeal to scientific discourses. These were closer perhaps to presentations than speeches. (My use of the term 'speech' itself indicates that I am distinguishing this text-type, from something more general such as 'talk', or more distinct, such as 'paper'.)

What type of generic situation was this, in fact? Was it about the communication of lay or scientific arguments to a lay or specialised audience? Who did the speakers see themselves as? Questions of this kind might have been used as part of this activity to bring the type of situation to a level of reflection and collaborative definition. A matrix such as the one below could be used as a focus for discussion:

AUDIENCE / SPEAKER(S)	LAY	SCIENTIFIC
LAY	Public speaking model? Ethical, common sense arguments?	Ethical, common sense arguments? Appeals to humanity?
SCIENTIFIC	Presentation, representation? Simplification of scientific arguments, plus ethics?	Paper, presentation? Scientific arguments and language? Objectivity?

The table is certainly both an oversimplification and overgeneralisation, but it prompts an awareness of differences as well as overlaps in types of forms and arguments employed in various situations. The matrix might be extended or adapted to include other kinds of speaker and audience. It is a way of introducing to students possibilities for constructing and presenting arguments, which might otherwise not be available to them. The boxes do not contain answers, 'correct' ways of categorising speakers and audiences and the forms of communication that exist between them, but rather create the possibility of choice. The idea here is that language should empower as much as construct the individual.

However, as I've suggested, individuals are differently empowered to bring about change within their environments, and some environments (those at the margins perhaps) are also more open to negotiation than others. The difference may depend on the ways in which knowledge and learning are conceived (differently by different groups), as well as the kinds of institutional structures which support and embody these conceptions.

Dialogue

A rhetorical view of argument implies in a sense that all argument is dialogic, in that it orientates towards a position beyond itself, and seeks to persuade. It operates therefore on a principle of **otherness**: the otherness of the person spoken to, other points of view, other positions. This otherness has in a sense been present in much of the discussion so far: the notion, for instance, that giving an opinion is a 'dual expression' (Billig 1991, p. 43). There are traces of otherness also in the dictionary definitions: 'a connected series of statements or reasons intended to establish a position (and hence refute the opposite)', 'A statement of reason for and against a proposition; discussion of a question, debate'. In the first of these definitions, the building of an established position carries with it an inbuilt defence mechanism, simultaneously a recognition and a warding off of alternative positions. The dialogism in this case is rather more implicit than in the second definition where more than one actual speaker is suggested. The definition from mathematics might also be understood as operating on a dialogic principle, since it describes how what is given or known ('the angle, arc or other mathematical quantity') is used to deduce or discover what is not given or known. This is rather like a dialogic understanding of the enthymeme (a syllogism with one premise unexpressed) which suggests that the omitted premise, rather than indicating an incomplete argument or an attempt to hoodwink the audience, represents rather a point of contact or dialogue with the audience: in order to understand the argument it must – and is trusted to – supply what is inexplicit.

The sense here is that the utterance is not meaningful in isolation but becomes meaningful in the context of its reception. This is what Bakhtin (1981) has called the 'activating principle':

> To some extent primacy belongs to the response, as an activating principle: it creates the ground for understanding, it prepares the ground for an active and engaged understanding. Understanding only comes to fruition in the response. Understanding and response are dialectically merged and mutually condition one another. (p. 282)

This description can be applied to actual situations in which words pass between individuals and is useful therefore in understanding what goes on in a spoken interchange and in reading texts. But for Bakhtin, language itself is dialogic, since it both carries with it a history of usage in different contexts and is again received and responded to in yet another context:

> ... actual meaning is understood against the background of other concrete utterances on the same theme, a background made up of contradictory opinions, points of view and value judgements – that is, precisely that background that, as we see, complicates the path of any word towards its object. Only now this contradictory environment is present to the speaker not in the object, but rather in the consciousness of the listener, as his apperceptive background, pregnant with response and objections. (p. 281)

16

This understanding of language suggests that words do not simply have meaning, but rather that they *make sense*, or fail to do so, within contexts. As the example of Denise's 'no' suggested, there is not really such a thing as plain talking. For Bakhtin a communicative act is not *about* a 'subject', as if the subject were somehow passive and inert, transferred intact from speaker to listener, but rather the subject, which he re-terms the 'hero', is a third active participant in the communication (see Schuster 1985).

It seems to me that argument can be dialogic in each of the senses that are raised here – implicitly, actually and/or as an internal feature of a single word or text. What, then, of Helen's speech? It appears to represent only one point of view and has a single speaker and thus to be a monologic utterance, yet it both anticipates and influences how others will respond by the kind of strategies it employs, and it is *actually* responded to by an opposing speech, by questions and by the assessment of peers. In these senses it is dialogic.

It also, as I noted before, includes a number of different voices within its internal structure, both those directly and indirectly quoted.[4] What Wertsch and Smolka (1993) contend is 'a basic question arising out of Bakhtin's work' can be applied quite straightforwardly to Helen's speech: 'This is the question, "Who is doing the speaking?" The Bakhtinian answer is "At least two voices"' (p. 74). Every word that Helen speaks is simultaneously spoken by another voice or combination of voices.

In learning to speak in the discourse of a discipline, students are engaging in specific dialogism of this kind; learning to make their voice heard through another voice:

> The word in language is half someone else's. It becomes 'one's own' only when the speaker populates it with his own intention, his own accent, when he appropriates the word, adapting it to his own semantic and expressive intention. Prior to this moment of appropriation, the word does not exist in a neutral and impersonal language (it is not, after all, out of a dictionary that the speaker gets his words!), but rather it exists in other people's mouths, in other people's concrete contexts, serving other people's intentions: it is from there that one must take the word, and make it one's own. (p. 293-4)

Students frequently encounter difficulty in both adopting the discourse (what Bakhtin calls the 'social language') and adapting it, making it their own. Denise's sense that she was fabricating by not simply saying 'no' is a good example. She felt very acutely that the language she was expected to use was not her own, that it was *more than* 'half someone else's'. Issues of power and access to power are implicated here; the population of language with one's own meanings is not straightforward and unrestricted. Gee's (1989) distinction between primary and secondary Discourses helps to clarify these issues.[5] Primary Discourse is that which 'we first use to make sense of the world and interact with others' (p. 7), whilst secondary Discourses are those which we acquire when we have access to social institutions and gain apprenticeships within them. However access to dominant social Discourses may

---

4. But the form is also **oppositional**; it seeks to close rather than open up debate, to persuade and co-opt rather than invite questions. Whilst in Bakhtin's definition, speaker and listener mutually influence each other, the form of the biology debate means that the possibilities for this are limited: Helen cannot easily revise her understandings, even in the light of questions. This argument might be said then to be, at some level, anti-dialogic. I think this needs to be remembered, that as well as operating upon otherness, argument can seek to subsume otherness, to coerce it into a position of sameness. It can be aggressive as well as playful. Amongst the dictionary definitions, this sense is certainly present. It returns us to the question of power with which this exploration started.

5. Gee actually seems to be borrowing an idea from Bakhtin (1986) here.

be restricted, 'the word' protected. This, Gee argues, is more likely to be the case for individuals whose primary Discourse is not close to a dominant secondary one, than for those for whom primary and secondary Discourses share affinities. Even where institutional access to 'the word' is gained, such individuals may have further to go in making it their own.[6] What emerges from Gee's analysis , for those involved in teaching, is the need to be aware of the constraints which can prevent the 'word' being appropriated and the dialogue being entered into. Dialogue between primary and secondary Discourses is an important way for transitions to take place – this is addressed in chapters 4 and 5 which look primarily at speech.

I should like here to note that Bakhtin's notion of dialogic understanding can also inform the conception of genre I introduced earlier. Anne Freadman (1988) develops the metaphor of a tennis game:

> Imagine a game of tennis, preferably, of course, (if you have any ball sense) singles. The players are not exchanging balls, they're exchanging shots [...] Player A plays a shot; player B plays it back. What is this 'it'? It is not useful to say '"it" is the ball'; and manifestly inaccurate to call it the same shot. Player B is, let's say, the 'receiver', but to receive a shot s/he must return it, play, that is to say another. The same shot, then – Player A's serve – has a different value for each of the two players: a 'good shot' may win a point for its player, but, well-received, it may turn against s/him, its speed, its turn, or its angle enabling an unexpected return. (p. 91-3)

Freadman argues that, in her conception of genre as a game in which meaning is 'subject to play' and 'perpetual modification' (p. 93), it is important to move away from assumptions which concentrate on singularity and see a text '"in" a genre' and a genre '"in" a text'. Rather genre should be understood 'as consisting, minimally, of two texts, in some sort of dialogical relation.'(p. 97) Dialogue is conceived of here as an agent of change rather than replication.

The link between genre and dialogue provides a useful way of understanding the function and value accorded to students' texts in educational contexts. A piece of writing, for example, prepared by a student *prior* to a class and perhaps intended to be read or paraphrased there as a stimulus for discussion will be in a different dialogic relation (and therefore a different genre) than a piece which is written as the *outcome* of a class discussion and perhaps awarded a grade or a short comment by the teacher. In the first case the students' text can quite literally be thought of as part as a dialogue; it is also more likely that the more provisional, exploratory role of the writing will produce more dialogic aspects within the text itself, speculations and questions for example. In the second case, the writing is less likely to be used in an open dialogue, since a new topic of discussion will by that time have been introduced. In consequence of this the text itself may have a more monologic character, seeking to convey the authority and resolution of its utterance.

The differences I have suggested between these two pieces of writing are not always recognised and as a result the pedagogical potential of each is not exploited. The difficulty is compounded where different pieces of writing (in terms of dialogic relation and function) bear the same generic (in the more traditional sense of the word) name. The **essay** is the obvious example; in the British system, it embraces writing undertaken before and after

---

6. Gee suggests however that this need not be interpreted entirely negatively – there is something to be gained from outsider status. I consider this in the 'Exploring Ground Rules' chapter.

discussion, over varying periods of time – a week, a term, a pressurised examination hour – and in hugely varying conditions. The term is also used in a large number of disciplines in the Arts, Humanities and Social Sciences, and also , as I discovered, in A level Biology. Yet the criteria for 'essay' writing in these subjects is very different, in terms of structure, formal conventions and the argumentative (or other) content.

The ubiquitous use of the 'essay' means that the work students do in their writing appears to conform to some universal model, and, in a way, it not only appears to, it *does* conform, despite disciplinary variations. Writing, like speech, can, however, be freely adapted to context for a range of functions, processes and products. The potential of understanding genre, not as text-type, but as dialogue, is a diversification of contexts and forms employed as part of the learning process. Lev Vygotsky (1978) commenting that 'If one changes the tools available to a child, his mind will have a radically different structure' (p. 126) implies that contexts (relationships, environment, forms) have a determining influence on thought and thinking processes. If the context (say, the essay as outcome) is reproduced over and over without variation the thought patterns are likely to remain the same, but where they are varied (different forms of writing, different rhetorical tasks at different stages in the learning process) there is likely to be greater diversity of thought.

Mention of Vygotsky here brings my discussion to a consideration of argument as cognitive process.

Argument as Cognitive Process

There are close links between Bakhtin's theory of dialogue and Vygotsky's model of cognitive development, since both thinkers locate meaning in language and social interaction. For Vygotsky the development of the individual begins with the social: language structures are acquired in interaction and only later become internalised as 'inner speech' or thought. Thought, therefore, has a dialogic quality. Inter-mental processes provide a model for intra-mental ones (see Wertsch and Smolka 1993). Development, Vygotsky says, is dependent upon learning, by which he means guidance from or collaboration with others; it is not something which occurs independently. From this idea he derives the important notion of 'the zone of proximal development' (1978, p. 90), which indicates the difference between a child's mental ability in independently performed tasks and their ability when in interaction with an adult or more capable peers. Ability in interaction (learning) is in advance of development (which measures the internalisation of the socially learnt processes). If the zone of proximal development indicates the potential of interaction to extend the cognitive capacity of an individual, then the importance of dialogue in learning is clear. Beyond this, if argument is understood as dialogic process, it too takes a leading role in cognition and learning. As Billig (1991) puts it, 'the sound of argument is the sound of thinking' (p. 52).

Thinking can be broken down into a number of operations, which Bloom (1956), in seeking to formulate a taxonomy of educational objectives in the cognitive domain, listed as:

1 – knowledge
2 – comprehension
3 – application
4 – analysis
5 – synthesis
6 – evaluation

The objectives are hierarchically arranged, developing from simple to more complex operations. Operations like synthesis and evaluation are likely to make use of those found lower in the list. Something like this hierarchy appears to underlie most assessment at A level and undergraduate level. Put crudely, knowledge will receive a certain level of reward, which will be increased if it can be shown in relation to other knowledge or applied to some other situation, whilst the highest reward is reserved for the ability to take multiple sources of knowledge, show how they are related and critically evaluate them. If this is done in order to produce a new position or an 'original' argument (within the constraints of the discipline) then this will generally attract the highest grade. One way of thinking about the levels is in terms of the degree to which the material is dialogised, the degree to which otherness is assimilated and transformed into the 'own' voice of the student. One-sided (monologic) argument tends, perhaps for these reasons, not to be highly credited in the academic system: it does not show awareness of multi-voicedness.

The A level Cambridge History Project (CHP) provides a particularly useful example of the way cognitive skills are differentiated in assessment terms and of the high value placed upon argument which can be seen to result from a combination of the skills. Teaching and assessment are arranged according to domains of historical concepts and skills of analysis rather than content. The following extract from the syllabus of the 1992 pilot scheme suggests the increasing cognitive complexity required to move between levels 1 and 3:

Domain 5: Change and Development   **[Concept Domain]**

Levels   *Descriptors*

1. Demonstrates understanding of the ways in which significance may be attributed to events as trends and turning points, 'dead-ends' and 'false dawns' within a line of development through time.

2. Demonstrates understanding that lines of development are theories about as well as representations of the past, and that differing and competing lines of development may be advanced in order to describe and make sense of any part of it.

3. Demonstrates understanding of the reasons why and the ways in which different and competing lines of development may co-exist and be integrated within a single historical account.

Domain 6: Constructing Accounts   **[Skill Domain]**

Levels   *Descriptors*

1. Can select and organise material so as to construct developmental narratives.

2. Can select, organise and interpret material so as to construct alternative developmental narratives.

3. Can select, organise and interpret material so as to construct coherent narratives that make reference to concurrent sequences of events and different lines of development.

The Project director commented about the importance of the ability to argue within this syllabus:

> Candidates who do not put forward an argument and merely provide a narrative account are awarded level 0 on all domains.

Yet these criteria state that the highest achievement is the construction of 'coherent' **narrative**. The point is though that this narrative is developed out of an understanding of 'different and competing lines of development'; it is the outcome of a process of argumentation and it is new.

Novelty and Difference

The sense in which argument can be said to be about the creation of newness or novelty is an important one. Consider the following description of argument as contrasted with narrative and based around the idea of difference:

> All cultures need the categories of narrative and argument for dealing with two opposing, contradictory demands. On the one hand, a culture needs to provide institutionalised means of handling difference. Without difference there can be neither change nor new systems of values. Argument provides [...] the means for bringing difference into existence. At the same time, it provides conventionalised textual forms not just for maintaining and tolerating difference, but for culturally productive use of difference. Yet where there is only difference, the cultural group cannot attain stability, cannot reproduce itself or its values. Narrative [...] provides means of resolution of difference, of reproducing, in an uncontentious mode, the forms and meanings of a culture. Narrative serves as a major means of the reproduction of social and cultural forms and values.
>
> Narrative, in other words, is a form whose fundamental characteristic is to produce closure; argument is the form whose fundamental characteristic is to produce difference and hence openness. (Kress 1989, p.12)

Narrative in the CHP's scheme operates to close the process of argumentation, but the argument itself is still open to counter-argument (maybe in the form of competing narratives) and to change. The closure can be seen as a contingent moment in an on-going process. It is frequently tied up with written forms such as the essay (the primary vehicle through which the A level students express their argument) require resolution in the form and position of the 'conclusion'.[7]

'Bringing difference into existence' can be a difficult task: there is sometimes more than enough to do in trying to understand and reproduce – particularly when it comes to learning a new discourse. Academic essays and papers can often require students to take on the discourse of the discipline and additionally to manage the actual voices and meanings of others in the form of citations and references to existing writers within the field. Going beyond this to construct an argument out of and in response to these voices is not easy: how to appropriate the language and make one's own voice heard? How to produce a new and convincing account? Often the result of these demands is the suppression of the student's voice and the sense that it is 'other people' only who are speaking. The writing may contain the arguments of others, but is not itself fully argumentative. This, as I've suggested, will gain some credit in assessment terms, as the display of knowledge. In a subject such as philosophy, however, where citation and referencing is often not even a formal requirement, there is little escape from the need to argue – argument is here very much the thing itself. The problem is often compounded by the narrative form in which students are expected to write (the beginning, middle and end of the essay, for instance). The task for students trying to construct arguments (dialogic thinking) in writing (generally monologic forms) is to manage the structure and the form in such a way as to manage multiple points of view and generate dialogue (answer and response) rather than to suppress it, and, in addition, to make the meanings 'their own'. This is not a simple task.[8]

---

7. Two essays written for the CHP are discussed in the chapter entitled 'The Imposition of Structure'.
8. The chapters on writing address these issues in more detail.

David Kaufer and Cheryl Geisler (1989) have examined the idea of novelty in relation to academic writing and describe it as less 'a process of winning adherence for one's new ideas' than 'designing to be new'(p. 287). They outline four 'definitional propositions about authorial newness':

1. 'newness is less a property of ideas than a relationship between ideas and communities, and less an individual trait than a regularity of communal life and structure.'

2. 'authors in disciplinary communities rely on novelty claims to reference the complex processes by which they and their fellows learn and change through a shared epistemology'. Authorial contributions 'are carefully tied to and shown to grow out of existing knowledge'.

3. 'members of a disciplinary community refer to newness as a shorthand for the standards they must follow to contribute to this growth [...] Synthesising the literature they want a place in, authors lay the ground on which they hope to make their imprint. They manage to be new when the imprint they make fits the community standard and when they can make it before their competitors have a chance to make it theirs.'

4. 'the literature suggests that newness turns on a delicate balance between the inertia of the past and the drive to change it.' (p. 288-9)

These descriptions of how authors establish novelty add an intra-textual dimension to the sense in which argument is contextually embedded and exploitative of difference. The kinds of difference which can be successfully exploited are, in addition, dependent upon the aspects of existing accounts, knowledge and texts which are attended to within particular contexts. This presupposes that writers must have skills in identifying what counts as knowledge and discriminating how accounts differ.

In accordance with Bloom's hierarchy, Kaufer and Geisler suggest that novelty is developed out of a series of other operations upon texts. The first of these is the ability to 'inventory the stack of consensual knowledge in their target community' (p. 289-90). But it is not the case that there is just one inventory possible within any community: there are variations in what writers know. As a result when writers synthesise what they know, they also have to *persuade* their readers that this represents the consensual/communal knowledge. As Kaufer and Geisler point out, there is a combination of both the cognitive and social here.

How are these gaps or inconsistencies in the consensual knowledge represented? Kaufer and Geisler note that gaps can be characterised as either '"inherent" to the knowledge itself or an interpretative scheme (a "heuristic") that writers opportunistically impose upon knowledge to find something new to say.'(p. 290) The way in which knowledge is explored to uncover gaps must generally also be transparent, signalled as particular 'tools of analysis' or 'method', which are legitimate within the community. And novelty claims are also of different magnitudes, from claims against an isolated fact to the subversion of a dominant theory.

The understanding of and ability to produce novelty claims constitutes, according to Kaufer and Geisler, a significant difference between expert writers and student or novice writers.[9] They see the difference as in part due to the different status of these two groups within academic communities. The students do not have 'insider' status. They are generally taught 'to write an "original" essay', but by "original" is typically meant '"free of plagiarism" or

---

9. Their findings in this regard are discussed in chapter 6.

"in one's own voice" rather than new.' (p. 305) Students are not shown how to be 'poised in and against some intellectual community with the goal to talk back to it' (p. 306); how, that is, to be in dialogue.

The importance of goal and purpose highlighted here seems to me to be crucial; the overall focus of learning is not the acquisition and reproduction of knowledge (though these remain important process skills and may be a temporary focus). The 'lower' cognitive skills build towards or make a platform from which the higher, say, synthesis and evaluation can take place. But these operations are integrated with a purposeful (social) aim: the active manipulation of knowledge and the production of new knowledge (new narratives):

> ... learning a content may require more than traditional content (fact) learning. It may require considerable reading (summary and synthesis) skill as well. For novices seeking to be authors in some content, the focus on learning content should be a focus on learning consensus.
> Still, a common effect of too much stress on consensus is to diminish the novice's cognitive authority to question or change it. So the second front we must work on is mitigating the authority of consensus so that novices can practice staking claims against it ... (p. 307)

In this view the range of cognitive skills are not discrete but serve each other as part of the overall aim of 'talking back', having something to contribute newly to a dialogue[10].

Personal and Social Identity

Novelty is linked to the sense in which individuals can differentiate themselves from others whilst remaining part of a social context. This is represented by Rom Harré's model (1983) describing '**personal identity** projects'[11]:

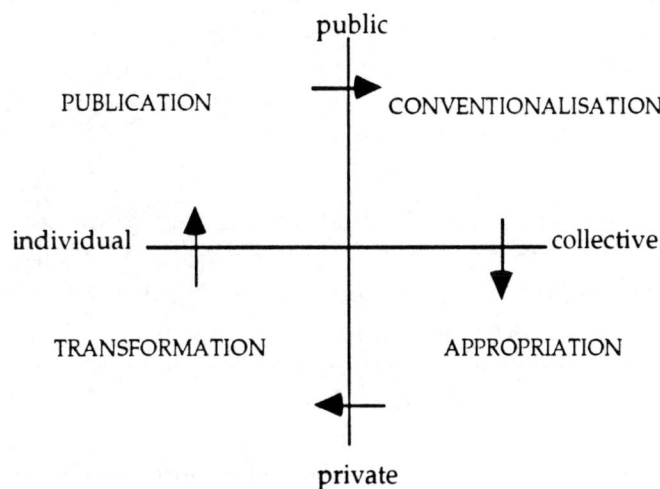

---

[10] Kaufer and Geisler develop their ideas here in a further paper (Geisler and Kaufer , 1989), which I used in the module on argument described in chapter 7.

[11] I was first introduced to this model when working at Exeter University with Malcolm Ross, Hilary Radnor and Cathy Bierton on assessment in arts education. See Ross et al, (1993) for an interpretation of the model in that context.

I see this as a model of discourse learning which pictures the relations between consensus and difference and therefore allows the process of learning to argue to be located. The model is constructed on two intersecting axes: public/private and individual/collective and describes four operations by which the individual moves between quadrants beginning in the public/collective and moving in a clockwise direction. The designation of the public/collective as the first quadrant accords with the Vygotskian view of cognitive development that thought is, in the first instance, social. The first quadrant should not be seen as a repository of static knowledge, but rather as a discursive arena; constituted by what Gee (1989) describes as: 'ways of being in the world; [...] forms of life which integrate words, acts, values, beliefs, attitudes and social identities.'(p. 6-7) As the individual traverses the quadrants she moves from a position of knowing about a Discourse, to knowing in a Discourse (Gee, 1987, p. 7, see also Goggin, 1994) This constitutes the difference between learning about, say, Linguistics, Sociology or Physics and becoming a Linguist, Sociologist or Physicist. It is a process of apprenticeship leading to enculturation. What the Harré model also suggests is that enculturation also involves differentiation, the development of personal as well as social identity.

Appropriation is the operation by which the individual takes on what is collective and public; this is the area of technical training, of learning methods, procedures, facts and information. It might involve, for instance, what Kaufer and Geisler term 'summary' and 'synthesis'. Such operations depend on particular ways of reading, writing and thinking, such as recognising and working with certain shared assumptions, concepts and ideas. Brian Street's description (1984) of the learnt nature of reading practices illustrates what Appropriation is about:

> rather than reading a text from the beginning to the end in the sequence in which the publisher has ordered it, they are urged to select using particular purposes from different parts of the text, using the contents page, index, chapter headings etc. and moving backwards and forwards within that text and to other texts. (p. 75)

Transformation is the crucial operation in terms of this discussion. This is where the individual, as Bakhtin put it, 'populates [the word] with his own intention, his own accent' (p. 293) It is where he begins to develop his own angle or insights, a personal contribution; as Harré puts it: 'the creation of distinctive personal being by the Transformation of one's social inheritance'(p. 257).

There is often felt to be between Appropriation and Transformation, where the individual does not feel equipped to transform until he has acquired sufficient knowledge from the public domain. The student in the following extract has just begun a degree in Sociology and has no previous experience in the subject. He expresses his uncertainty about attempting any form of argument (Transformation) with the knowledge he has so far acquired:

Roger: This first term hasn't really; it's not too much to do with argument. It's more the sort of assessing side of it at the moment because nobody really knows the topic well enough to put a case forward. I've noticed that in the seminars, there hasn't been, everybody's usually taken one side of the argument and ignored the other.

SM: So you think it's about understanding?

Roger: At the moment, yeah. I don't think anybody knows enough to argue. They're a bit wary of, because if you read a book and you see, think you see an argument, you'll think you're probably imagining it or you know it just feels very vague, you don't know where you are.

SM: Do you feel that in order to argue you need to have some kind of grounding or confidence, then?

Roger: To understand what you're arguing about, yeah. Which is a bit of a problem when you're only... if you read a book before the tutorial and you haven't done it before, you don't really have an awful lot of understanding. Perhaps after one tutorial, you could argue in another tutorial, but you need that tutorial to just to, I don't know, to note everything down, otherwise you don't know what you're talking about.

Roger's reticence is probably as much a learnt response in deference to the authority of the texts he has been presented with, as it is a necessary one. Students are not on the whole taught ways in which they can begin to make material their own, since the emphasis more often falls on covering material, than transforming it.

The process of differentiation (argument) is completed in the third operation: **Publication** where 'Idiosyncratic transformations can be brought out into the public arena' (p. 257) to be assessed against public criteria. In disciplinary argument, for instance, the individual's contribution would be judged, in part at least, by its intra-field appropriateness. To be successful it has to be new or idiosyncratic enough but not too much, since, as Harré puts it: 'depending on the reaction of that public, his personal innovations may earn him assessments running anywhere between "madman" and "genius"' (p. 257). Kaufer and Geisler make much the same point:

> Contributions that respect the past with too little change become tired and predictable [...]. Conversely, contributions that push change with too little rootedness are likely to remain unclassifiable rather than revolutionary. (p. 289)

Newness, that is, is dependent on orientation and Transformation is to a greater or lesser extent constrained by publication. If the individual is too concerned about the judgements that may take place there, he is unlikely to take the risks involved for Transformation to be successful. In learning situations, assessors need to be aware of and sensitive to the inhibiting potential of Publication; the way they are judging and the effects of their judgements.

Conventionalisation describes the fourth operation in which the personal innovation is taken up into the conventions and accepted body of knowledge of the social order (discipline) in which it has been publicised. Argument has an important part in achieving these transitions both in the individual making of meaning and in the communication of meaning in rhetorically effective public forms.

Learning – as a process of individuation and independent thinking within changing social contexts – can be thought of as a number (potentially endless) of such cycles as Harré's model describes. The model pictures the dependence of individual utterances for meaning both on what has gone before and on the conditions of reception and in this way it is dialogic. The individual takes on what is said to him, adjusts his view and then utters it. And 'what is said to him' is itself dialogic: the 'hero' rather than the 'subject'.

But not all models of learning fit easily with the four operations I've described. Compare, for instance, as George Macdonald Ross (1994) has recently done, the Platonic and the Socratic views of education. Ross writes that in Plato's academy (from where we get the word 'academic') there was an emphasis on the learning and comprehension of a body of truths, which were objective, obtainable and separable from the language that expressed them:

> Although it is right to question pre-philosophical assumptions and inadequate concepts, there comes a point where questioning has to stop. Once the pupil has acquired a correct understanding of a concept or truth, it would undermine the educative process to encourage them to treat it as merely provisional, or revisable if looked at from an alternative point of view. The purpose is to provide the pupil with a firm bedrock of objective knowledge, as a basis for the understanding of more advanced and abstract truths. (p. 17)

The 'point where questioning has to stop' falls just short of Transformation, so that knowledge is reified rather than revised. According to Ross this model of learning is elitist, open only to initiates. Significantly, in Plato's academy learning began to be a literate activity (concerned, that is, with written texts rather than speech).

In contrast, Socratic learning is speech based and emphasises the process or activity of thinking. Thinking is not so much straightforward and unitary as manifested in dialogue which facilitates the capacity for reflection. As Ross notes, under questioning: 'instead of proceeding smoothly under its own momentum, the flow of thought is turned back on itself' (p. 12) This moment of reflection, though facilitated by social dialogue, relies upon contact with the private/individual.

In actual teaching and learning situations there are often tensions (perhaps positive ones) between the Platonic and Socratic and certainly, as I go on to suggest (see 'Exploring Ground Rules'), there are differences in the way different groups within institutions may view and publicise what count as the starting and end points of learning. The model of learning employed, and consequently the relative importance attached to each of the stages in Harré's model, varies from discipline to discipline and according to the level at which learning is taking place. In Biology, for instance, certainly at A level and for much of the degree course, learning remains largely within the second quadrant of the model: Appropriation. The Biology tutor's experiment with debates on ethical matters was a response in part to a perceived need to move his students beyond this stage. An additional factor for him was that what is public and collective in Biology is at present in a state of such continual revolution (the explosion in genetics etc.) that Appropriation of 'knowledge' was increasingly not sufficient: his students would need other skills if they were to keep pace.

Fine Art would, from the subjects included in my observations, be at the other end of the scale from Biology, at least as that subject is conventionally taught. Here the student's experience reaches right round the circle though Transformation (the creative act) into Publication and Conventionalisation: the degree show, where some students' work is offered for sale and where critics and buyers are on the look out for flourishing talent. On rare occasions, this may occur in other subjects too, where, for instance, a final year degree research project in Biology or Chemistry may achieve sufficiently new and validated results to be published and conventionalised. This would be highly unlikely to happen in a subject like Philosophy, yet a great deal of the work done there might be described as occuring in the third quadrant. Students argue constantly, always developing their own positions, rarely simply recording the views of others, yet to go beyond publication into the public/collective sphere is not easy – perhaps because they are always developing positions not consolidating them.

Acquiring institutional discourses and frameworks by managing transitions from Appropriation, to Transformation and from Transformation to Publication is, as I've suggested, problematic. The disciplinary identity of an individual is forged not on a *tabula rasa*, but upon an existing personal identity. The operation of Appropriation and, more so,

Transformation might then be seen as acts of displacement, supplanting one social mode of knowing and doing with another which may be incommensurate with it. The transition, then, is not smooth or continuous, but carries with it the potential for violence and disorientation. This was the case with both Denise learning to express her disagreement academically and with the Philosophy student who was learning to pose the question 'What is love?' in an appropriate way. The disorientation may be particularly acute where, as I've noted before, primary and secondary Discourses have little in common, or conversely, where, the Discourses are in competition to offer interpretations of what is common. Chapter 4 contains examples from Sociology where this kind of conflict is evident. Something similar can also be noted in the chapter on Fine Art[12].

Harré's model can be used as a template against which disciplinary tasks can be placed in order to assess the types of learning they elicit. The 'apprenticeship' pattern it suggests can be critiqued, however, by another provided by the psychologist George Kelly (1955). Kelly used a notion of 'loosened and tightened constructs' (ways of believing and operating) and contended that in a 'Creativity Cycle' the individual begins with 'loosened constructions' and ends with 'tightened and validated construction' (p. 528-30). Activity starts with proliferation and experimentation and these are then followed by selection and testing. At first sight the learning process Harré describes is turned on its head, since it starts with the individual and thus places the individual in a different relation to society. Yet experimentation and proliferation are made possible by collective choice; the role of the artist, as an instance, is socially sanctioned.

What Kelly's notion suggests is the way that emphasis on one or another part of Harré's model can be shifted according to social and institutional preferences. Where individual creativity is highly valued, Transformative processes come to the fore, with Publication perhaps performing the work of validation and testing. Working in this way is a risky business; there is much more 'feeling around in the dark' than work concentrated on Appropriation. The results, however, may be thought worth the risk, both in terms of what is subsequently Published and of the experience that has been undergone. The alternative, Kelly suggests, is learning which starts with 'tightened constructions', concentrated heavily, initially at least, on Appropriation. On this kind of learning Kelly comments:

> A person who always uses tight constructions may be productive – that is, he may turn out a lot of things – but he can not be creative; he cannot produce anything which has not already been blueprinted. (529)

Kelly seems to be suggesting here something of that 'trained incapacity' referred to earlier. His construal of creative/uncreative (as differing priorites within Harré's model) makes it possible to ask questions about the objectives of learning in different disciplines. Is the objective creativity or blueprinting? Is it difference or sameness? Can too much emphasis on one preclude opportunities for the other?

In general the objective of academic disciplines is enculturation into existing modes and models of behaviour. But paradoxically (or perhaps, if one follows the elitist idea,

---

12. Publication can be a site of conflict here too. What the institutionalised discipline recognises as worthy of Conventionalisation may not be commensurate with contexts beyond the institution. The chapter contains an example of this, where the degree class given to a student by the school seems incompatible with the praise and attention he receives from other quarters. For the student there is a need to balance his feelings of resentment towards the institution with the validation he receives elsewhere.

tendentiously) the 'academic' style of learning seems to militate against – or at least slow down – this enculturation. The student pursues this goal, but only when she becomes a postgraduate student or beyond is she 'qualified' to make a really original contribution. For the student, Publication and Conventionalisation rarely take place in any truly public sense before the doctoral level. The forms in which students publicise themselves up to (and perhaps including) tend to be peculiar to the transitionary apprenticeship stage of studenthood and for the purposes of assessment. These forms, as I've suggested, are often concerned with the display of knowledge and of existing arguments as much as with innovation. The innovations students can make are correspondingly small and there are, as a result, obvious constraints on the definition of argument as dealing with difference and novelty.

Return to Argument

I want to end this rather wide-ranging discussion by thinking again of the kind of **mode** (way of doing or being) argument is. I think of this as a question about argument as an attitude or stance towards the world. Kress's distinction between argument and narrative which is centred around difference (within cultures, ideologies, institutions, texts) seems to set up an opposition, but in fact as Helen's speech, as well as the example of the Cambridge History Project criteria illustrates, the functions of argument can serve narrative and vice versa. Narrative can provide a means of closing argument and argument a way of arriving at or disrupting narrative. Equally narrative can be used argumentatively, say, to question assumptions or provide a test case.

Since it captures distinct yet also interrelated activities, the narrative/argument distinction provides a useful starting point for further characterisation. An argumentative **stance** is one which resists the closing down of controversy or debate; which keeps open the possibility of change; which seeks further questions to raise and new angles to take. What H.W. Johnstone (1978) says about philosophy sums this up – the link with dialogue is clear:

> Philosophical discussion is, in effect, a collaborative effort to maintain the conditions under which disagreement is possible. (p. 19)

In contrast, a narrative stance avoids the questioning of and possible disruption of, say, information that has already been given; it is satisfied and conserves rather than changes. Ricoeur (1970) describes two modes of interpretation: the negative mode of interpretation is characterised by 'a willingness to suspect' and 'a vow of rigour' – this is the argumentative mode; the positive mode is characterised by a 'willingness to listen' and 'a vow of obedience' (p. 27) – this is the narrative mode.

The characterisation of argument as negative can be linked to the sense of its openendedness. As Billig (1991) puts it:

> ...there is always another side to the question and another argumentative counter-move which can be made [...] When an object or event is categorized, it is labelled and considered as similar to other objects or events so labelled. [...] However, each act of categorization is contestable by a cognitive countermove. One might concentrate upon the unique features of the object or event and claim that these features of the object or event are not essentially similar to those of other objects or events. The claim might be made that these differences are the crucial element (p. 47-8)

Thus similarity and difference are results of categorising processes and are open always to re-categorisation.

Different ways of thinking, reading, writing, speaking can now be characterised as argument or narrative. Texts – both those which students write and those which they read, see or hear – are produced by the practices and discourses that are brought to bear on them. There can be narrative and argument in the same text, but the text will be different (will have different meanings) if read as narrative than if it is read as argument or, indeed if it is read *narratively* (obediently) rather than *argumentatively* (suspiciously).[13] Lotman (1988) makes this point when he distinguishes between the 'univocal' and 'dialogic' aspects of a text; that is, the dual functioning of a text 'to convey meanings adequately, and to generate new meanings'(p. 34). The first function concerns the straightforward transmission of information by a text, whilst for the second the text becomes a 'thinking device' and a 'generator'. Different types of text operate with one or other of these functions to a greater or lesser extent (they are, to use Barthes' terminology, more or less readerly or writerly), but the functions are also chosen by the stance brought to bear on the text.[14]

Underlying the narrative/argument distinction are differing attitudes to knowledge and to learning: in the first, Appropriation is emphasised whilst in the second the Transformation of what has been appropriated becomes a primary aim. Different stances are encouraged at different stages of learning and by different members of disciplinary communities. How students operate and what stance they see as legitimate may not correspond with what their teachers think they should be doing nor with the stance their teachers themselves – as 'experts' – take. In the chapter 'Exploring Ground Rules' I'll look more closely at the 'narrative' stance or 'novice' status of one group in relation to the 'argument' stance and 'expert' status of another.

But for now, I'll add the distinction to a list of binaries, which seem to me to have emerged from the discussion so far:

narrative	argument
monologue	dialogue
univocal	multivocal
conservation	change
obedience	suspicion
safety	risk
replication	growth
appropriation	transformation
sameness	difference
novice	expert

The list is far from definitive or fixed; the pairs can be recombined and expanded upon. Not do they strictly represent opposites as the complex relation between narrative and argument suggests.

---

13. Narrative and argumentative readings don't have to be mutually exclusive. Examining the narrative construction of a text, for instance, can be a way of understanding it as argument. Elements in the construction of narrative such as juxtaposition, contrast, reversal, montage can be argumentative in that they are manifestations of difference and change. They suggest that meaning is not only situated within each narrative unit, but can also be constituted *in between*, in the difference.

14. The kinds of texts produced by different stances are illustrated throughout this report, particularly in the chapters on writing.

Models of Argument

The complexity is brought out by finally looking at three possible models of argument. One is **adversarial**: points of view pitted against each other (the metaphor associated with this view is war). Another is of **negotiation** and **consensus**: argument as the process of arriving at a mutually acceptable point of view (a narrative perhaps on which everyone can agree). The difference between these two might be thought of as the difference between debate and discussion. The third model, which has, I think, emerged in the course of this exploration, takes elements from both of these but sees argument as a **rupturing** process, characterised by its openness, the continual **slippage** of meaning, the search for counterpositions, positions of difference and disagreement. It's a model in which paradoxically, forward movement, progress comes about through negation and suspicion. This model is appealing but also problematic. It might describe the essay that never gets written, the action that is never taken. Nonetheless without it, the previous two models are impoverished, and also, both in their own way, repressive, abuses of power – the first through combat; the second through a more subtle effacing of difference and therefore, for some groups, of identity. The recognition of the coercive potential of the consensual model has led, for example, to its rejection by feminists, in favour of a conception of argument which lets the *individual* speak (see, for instance, *College Composition and Communication* Vol. 43 No. 3). Models of argument which lead to outcomes and resolutions raise the question: resolution in whose favour? Such a question serves as a reminder that people engage in argument and in dialogue for *purposes*: to carry through an agenda; to win others round to such an agenda whilst simultaneously giving them the impression they are involved in the process (a cynical view of democracy and of education); conversely, to feel as though one is participating; to display; and, more optimistically perhaps, to have one's agenda changed; to learn; to create new meanings.

Questions about the functions of argument, its forms and position in learning and discourses continue to be raised throughout this report. I hope now they can begin to take a more substantial form through the presentation of a case-study from the research, in the following chapter on Fine Art.

3. Forms and Functions of Argument in a Fine Art Degree Course

Public and Private

One of the main periods of observation in this research was spent in a university school of Art and Design, concentrating largely on the work of a small number of third year Fine Art students in both the theoretical and practical components of the course. I include this case study here as a way of anchoring some aspects of argument raised in the preceding chapter and, in particular, of exploring some of the issues surrounding the Harré model and the relation between public and private areas of experience.

The Fine Art degree makes a useful focus for comparison with other disciplines in this regard, because it is characterised more demonstrably than in other subjects by tensions – both creative and contentious – such as between institutional and individual expectations and experiences. The student of Fine Art finds her personal and individual resources drawn upon to a far greater extent – it seemed to me – than in other subjects where there are patterns to follow, clearly defined tasks and outcomes which are more or less predictable. In Fine Art, whilst the individual is a student she is also to some extent an artist, and is encouraged by the model of learning employed to think of herself in this way as individual and independent. The students are expected very early on in the course to follow their own ideas, to make things and to be confident about themselves. In contrast to other Art Schools they are not required to experience working in a range of media, though they do come into contact with tutors and students working in other areas and can also move between them themselves. Tutors are concerned to provide students with the necessary equipment to carry out and develop their ideas, in terms both of 'doing' skills and verbal/conceptual resources with which to talk and think about what they and others are doing. But achieving a balance between giving the students autonomy and asking them to be, amongst other things, what one tutor described as 'modest towards their predecessors' is not always easy. Nor is this way of working always easy for the students: a first year expressed to me his sense of frustration at the way the school compelled him to 'loosen up' and 'be free'. For him, freedom meant being empowered through an emphasis on skills, but since his definition did not comply with that of the institution, he was not in a fact free to follow it.

Orientation

These conflicts are very closely tied to the relations between the public and private spheres as depicted in Harré's model. The first year student felt unable to engage in transformative processes without sufficient concentration on Appropriation, whilst the school's position seems to coincide with the riskier idea of exploration and experimentation within the private and individual realm (Transformation) as a central activity. Despite the different emphases, however, the relation between the social and individual is crucial to both. Novelty comes about through orientation to the given.

The best work brings together a strong individual impact and also a sense that it gestures towards, resonates with other art forms and movements: there is a sense, that is, that it has traversed the circle between the social and personal (perhaps not strictly in the direction the Harré's model suggests) and that in arriving again in the public domain (to be experienced by others besides the maker) it somehow carries resonances from both those spheres. It seems to me that this is the kind of tension the sculpture tutor was exploring in a thesis she'd written on *The Intelligible Practice of Sculpture*: the art process as a kind of dialogue in the Bakhtinian sense, where what is 'half someone else's' becomes 'one's own', populated with one's own intention. She writes about the relations between idiosyncratic and shared discourses and shows how the private is central to the process of art making and yet situated within a community of practice both from and against which it derives its identity:

> The extra period of time [post-graduate study] I was able to devote to sculpture gave me time to reconsider the enormity of committing myself to such a specialised activity and also come face to face more and more deeply with the business of making objects of contemplation. The main characteristic of this kind of study was the opportunity to discuss one's work at intervals with a variety of experienced practitioners. In this way one was learning various ways of talking about what one was looking at, what one had done, and also learning what the difference between one's own experience as the maker and the way the specialist observer seemed to be experiencing the same thing. The difference was the crux of the matter because on it hung one's identity as an artist, from that which was one's own particular experience grew the material of the next pieces of work. Idiosyncrasy was it. This idiosyncrasy was sheltered by those specialists who could recognise it in relation to their own.

What the writer says here captures the delicate balance by which idiosyncrasy (novelty) is achieved through sharing. The balance is a delicate one: on the one hand encouraging in students a strong sense of ownership ('This is what I think' 'This is what I want to do'), which will drive their work forward and motivate their experimentation; and on the other, retaining their receptiveness to challenge, questioning and the new ideas which will keep their work from being impoverished or naive.

The emphasis on the individual can also work against the requirement of the course that it meet academic standards and create a tricky divide between practice and theory; knowledge rooted in the particular and in the physical processes of making opposed to and divorced from explicit, abstract, theoretical knowledge, elicited in critical spoken and written discourse. This divorce may be as much a result of perception and attitude, than of necessity. One of the theory tutors explained how the apparent incommensurability can be resolved by understanding what the epistemology of art is. She was insisting upon her student grounding what he was saying about an artist in his third year theory essay in the detail of what the art work consisted of: colour, texture, form. Although the function of this was in part to clarify the work for the reader, it was more importantly an epistemological basis against which other discourses would be tested. The concrete, then, precedes the abstract and generalisations are tied back to particularities. This account accords with the ways other tutors described what made good art. In one case a student had positioned two round cats flaps in a window of the building and this was deemed to be highly effective in terms of the ideas and conceptual connections it generated. The student did not, however, receive a first class degree. The reason for this was expressed as a question of whether, after engaging with the ideas, it was possible to go back to the work's physical presence and see that that had something about it too; that its presence had changed in a tangible way the space that it was in. The answer in this case was that it had not.

For the theory tutor, grounding theoretical discussion in what the art work physically is allows a personal connection with the art to be established and valued and this is important since in their practical art work, students enter into such intense relations, that unless they can grasp a personal connection in their theory work their enthusiasm for it rapidly drains[1].

Yet the relation can remain tense, construed as opposition as much as dialogue and circularity. The student who professed an inability to 'intellectualise' and commented that if you *do* virtually nothing but are able to intellectualise through talk then you can do well, was expressing a resistant attitude as much as a fact. Her paradoxical positioning within the institution – both defined by and against it – is a kind of caricature but also characteristic. On the one hand an anti-intellectualism is part of enculturation into 'being an artist', whilst on the other the institutional context and the goal of an Honours degree demands academic rigour, which conventionally is manifested in language, most usually written language. Such conflicts are acutely felt because the work in Fine Art involves extremes of commitment, both personal creative engagement and wide abstractions and contexts. In handling both *extremes* the discipline is distinguished from most academic subjects, but it also shows up tensions which are present, though less obvious, elsewhere.

Already some manifestations of argument in Fine Art have begun to emerge at both institutional and individual levels as open-ended interaction and clash between the given and the made, between oneself and others and between alternative forms of knowing. Argument can also be thought of here as thinking, a way of moving on, as persuasive, as providing evidence and rationale (i.e. as more than statement). Argument in this context is generally not thought of as a formal academic process, governed by adherence to certain pre-given forms and involving clarity and explicitness of explication. Students I spoke to described the need for explicitness and clarity as the greatest difference between writing the theory essay and making art. Although making art may be a process of moving towards a position, the position itself is elusive or exceeded in some way by the actual physicality of the art work.

Private

In the making process the individual is engaged with media to create an object which has for her 'significant form'. This process might be characterised as argument in so far as it involves:

a) the 'dialogic' interaction of artist and material in a search for form (for example Roy, working with stone, first following the stone and then adapting to the emerging form that he perceives). As in spoken dialogue every 'utterance' is shaped by the response made to it, so that meaning is made in the interaction of different entities. The material makes demands on the artist, just as he does on it. The meaning is less the subject of the interaction than its

---

[1] This approach to knowledge and discourse stands in contrast to that in, say, Sociology where theory and methodology shape what is known and at the same time can undercut each other without necessary recourse to any first hand situation.

'hero', as Bakhtin would term it: it is also changeable and can exert an influence on the other participants.

b) in addition to closely involved engagement with form, the artist evaluates the progress of her work, articulating explicit meanings, making connections with personal autobiography (as an artist and more widely), predicting directions and outcomes and critically evaluating these. The starting point for such evaluations seems very often to be based in an initial sense of liking or disliking. (The status of like and dislike in the critical discourse around the work is not clear.)

These kinds of relation to the work are often shared with a tutor and other trusted individuals like the students who share spaces nearby, or who share similar experiences in life. It appears for some students important that the art work should bear some relation to personal belief and experience. Often too this relation is not explicit in, or prior to, making, but is recognised after reflection or through the suggestiveness of another's comments.

c) it emerges from the above two instances that the artist's evaluation of her work can have a reflexive dimension to it in which doing and reflection are mutually informing. The sculpture tutor's study was not concerned with art products – what can seem to people 'messy, ugly, self indulgent and meaningless' – but rather the importance of understanding what is involved in process and practice. In her thesis she linked this to the notion of the 'reflective practitioner' (Donald Schön), where 'reflection-in-action' or 'knowing-in-practice' can be 'the key to a responsive and adaptable exercise of knowledge'. What Schön sees as important to work in the public professions, Anna saw also as relevant to the art process. She investigated her own work on a piece of sculpture in order to understand the kinds of processes in which she is engaged. Although she thought of the work as 'a system of self interaction where the object is an aspect of oneself', she also found that explicit reflection on the making and 'problem solving' (which was necessary for her research) in itself enlivened those processes. She found that 'the very process of making a tape of one's self working puts one's attention so acutely onto the process that one has the opportunity to come to terms deeper and deeper with how one's ideas develop spontaneously'. The tape makes 'objective the self-reflexive quality of creative activity'.

Public

The art work that I am talking of here is produced within the context of study for a degree in Fine Art. This context requires that the work meet certain criteria which are used formatively in the students' progress through the year and are publicly exercised in what is known as a 'cross-section crit'. This takes place for all students about once a term and consists of a group of around five students and generally two tutors. The students – a mixture of first, second and third years – come from different specialist areas (painting, sculpture, print making and so on) – hence the term 'cross-section'. The group visits the work space of each of the students and a discussion arises about the work that is found there.

The rationale behind this practice is that there is a relation between perceptual and conceptual forms of engagement and that the articulation and sharing of perceptions, ideas, resonances and connections in spoken language will inform and enrich the processes of making which both precede and follow the occasion. A link is then forged between the creative and the analytical, as though language is the key to reflexivity. In the Course Handbook for third year students it is expressed as this aim:

To encourage a developed critical awareness whereby the creative potential of interpreting issues in ways which are analytic and interrogative is recognised and acted upon.

In the crit situation, however, some students experience very strongly a conflict between their private meanings and those which are publicly demanded – the assessable criteria are not necessarily identical with those used by the student in the making-process. The student who finds herself able only to explain her work on a personal level and unable to 'intellectualise' in the formal context of the crit, feels that, as a result, the work is 'hammered' and she herself hurt. In this case the disciplinary expectation that she 'appropriate' and 'transform' the public and collective discourse into a private and individual one is quite clearly experienced as a kind of violence, a pushing under of what already exists in the private/individual area.

Even students who find the crit a far less gruelling experience than this example suggests, are conscious of giving a selective (and protective) account of their work in order to meet the criteria of the public critical discourse. They talk about strategies for deflecting talk away from vulnerable areas as if putting up barriers to what is 'really' going on. Their negotiation is crudely described as between private and public modes of engagement. The public mode is one which involves an academic discourse – critical, theoretical, contextual. It is about situating the art work within these realms, giving it an evidential status.

Surviving a crit then can be a highly rhetorical achievement. In order for me, as an outsider, to understand something of what is involved, several students agreed to talk first with me about their work (more closely approximating the private accounts described above) and then for me to take part – largely passively – in their cross-section crits.

Example 1

Carol's work is to a great extent concerned with numbers; she is interested in their universal role in systems of communication and also the personal and idiosyncratic connotations they may have. She places numbers in sequences which have encoded meanings, which are, however, accessible only to herself. For example, one piece consists of nine traditional telephones arranged in a square, with different number sequences in each of the dials, the inner circle coloured one of three bright colours. The choice of colour is also important to Carol; she likes the combination of the simple form of the telephone and the kitsch connotations of the colours. In other work with bingo cards she is exploring similar combinations. For Carol the work is very personal; she talks of what she likes about it, what amuses her. She did not object – and in fact was interested – when her tutor commented that none of the number sequences on the telephones contained a 9, but she had not noticed or intended this herself. The work she believes should stand on its own. It does not require an accompanying statement (such as she is encouraged to practice writing in anticipation of the real world demands of galleries, exhibitions, catalogues) but should be revealing enough in its own terms. She likes her work to be simple and doesn't want it to have a deep, hidden message.

In many ways, though, I found that as a viewer the work resisted this simplicity and Carol's desire that it be taken at face value. *For me*, the 'deep, hidden message' was in the desire to interpret which the work seemed to provoke. By using universal sequences and systems to have purely personal meanings, the telephones, themselves a symbol of communicative possibility frustrate taken-for-granted expectations and say something about the arbitrariness of language. The telephones are dysfunctional, empty icons, in several ways: they are empty shells, not connected, except as a formal configuration and even if they were connected, a user wouldn't know how to dial; the universal expectation of order in number systems being disrupted. The work seemed to me playful in that it allowed this kind of meta-discourse to take place. Yet this was not how Carol saw her work or particularly desired her work to be seen. As a bottom-line Carol believes that anything can be art that is made as art and is looked at as art – the circular logic of which is resistant to challenge or to a clearer definition of the parameters of art in her particular view.[2]

In the cross-section crit this resistance made itself felt when the tutor began to question the work, suggest alternative directions and offer interpretations. He noticed, for instance, that the brown and grey scratch panels on the telephones appeared not to be arranged randomly but as a pattern, suggesting an overall coherence. No, said Carol, they could be arranged in any way. The tutor accepted this, but seemed to searching for evidence of thought processes and experimentation. Carol had produced two prints of telephones with rectangular dialling panels in vibrant colours. Whereas when Carol described these, she talked about playing around with colour, the tutor talked at a more analytical level. He noted that the prints contained a tension between the telephone shape which had perspective and the number panel which did not. He suggested that she should experiment with the effect of taking away the number panel – showing in effect the processes of arrival. Carol resented this as unnecessary; she had worked on the images on a computer and chosen to develop the most pleasing effect. She rejected, too, the suggestion that in the final degree show the pieces would be presented as if linked. Her concern was with the things in themselves – a 'real-life' status for her work perhaps. This disjunction between the academic and real is experienced particularly in the third year where, as the Handbook states:

> In the studio units of the third level students will be working towards a standard of work commensurate with contemporary artistic practice.

But this status is nevertheless not achieved or accorded until the Degree Show and here academic outcomes (degree classes) result from standardised criteria which may not be directly comparable with those exercised in the varied contexts of 'real life'.

The tutor, then, is still concerned with the way Carol is *becoming* an artist. His interest in process is likely to be geared towards the purposes of course assessment: if you can see through evidence of process (e.g. the telephone shape and number panel separately, then together) that a tension between perspective and flatness is being enacted, then, as an assessor, you can feel justified in (and reward) your perception of the finished piece. There seemed, however, to be more to the tutor's comments than this: he wanted also to see whether she was exploring possibilities, rather than being derivative (the work is perhaps fairly typical of much late twentieth century art). Carol mentioned some work with the technical diagrams she'd found inside the phones; when she'd enlarged them the straight lines became wobbly. The tutor picked up on this and wondered whether this might be explored with a medium other than glossy paints: charcoal chips, for example. In a sense this practical suggestion

---

[2] Carol's tutor described her as in some ways quite typical: her work was more sophisticated than the language she had to describe it. Instead of wanting to tackle the difficult meanings of her work and to discover, perhaps, the pleasure of being unable to capture it succinctly in language, she resisted the uncertainty of this, by closing it off with a categorical statement: 'It just is art'. The resistance to ambiguity of students at this age has been pointed out to me several times during this project.

was a way of asking Carol to interrogate her use of colour and smoothness; to define and refine what it is she does by attempting to do something other. Carol's response was that this would be a waste of time since she knew already what she wanted to do. Her defence was heated and passionate. In the end, the tutor said, it comes down to honesty, whether you are following a formula or doing art. 'I am being honest!' Carol retorted.

The exchange was a curious one since it undercut both the objects themselves and the public discourse which surrounded them, going right to the core of Carol's identity and integrity as an artist. I can think of no other undergraduate degree where discussion would be so deeply tied to the individual's fundamental purposes and sense of self.[3] On the one hand, it seems, the individual 'artist' invests her work with an energy and commitment which means it has for her the status of art; on the other she needs to have an eye on the sceptical public and provide evidence of appropriate and critical processes. This seems to me a fundamental distinction between statement and argument. A statement is free-floating and can be taken over, judged, used, interpreted in many different ways. Thus I can create from Carol's telephones a commentary on language and communication; the tutor can enjoy in the prints a tension between flatness and depth. Carol rejects any jurisdiction over the meanings we make and in addition she rejects any demand to offer public meanings of her own – in fact she has encoded her own meanings so obscurely as to make them entirely private. Argument however is a way of justifying a statement and to a certain extent at least, anchoring its meaning. It is concerned with point of view and persuasion. The paradox of the tutor's recourse to 'honesty' is that he will not accept it as a statement, but needs to be persuaded. He also wants her to resist closure, to continue exploring: this is part of his role as a teacher, to continue the learning process. By finalising her position so adamantly Carol undercuts this role, signals her rejection of it.

The tutor as assessor as well as teacher also needs evidence. Within the academic context outcomes are not judged as free standing but as saying something about the student who has produced them. Though an essay, say, may be judged as a 2:1, in the end it is the student who goes away with a certain class of degree. The essay is evidence of a certain intellectual level or status; it demonstrates critical thought processes, as well as itself representing an object. Carol's statement 'I like it' does not sufficiently frame her object as part of a discourse.

The above account portrays the crit as having only two speaking participants. This is not quite the case; other students, particularly those who have reached the third year do participate, though in my limited experience they take a less critical and more supportive role, offering advice taken from their own experience. As in any interactive situation there are no hard and fast rules of behaviour and much will depend on the dynamic generated amongst a particular combination of people. In most crits, though not the one described above, two tutors are present and this helps to mitigate the weight placed on any one voice of authority, since they rarely occupy similar positions in relation to the work. Whilst this may increase the likelihood that students will be accorded a listening rather than speaking role in the criticism of any work other than their own, there is also potential here for the tutors to model argument and thus to liberate argumentative discourse more widely.

---

[3] See , however, the chapter on transitions into disciplinary discourses (chapter 4).

Example 2

A second example better illustrates the kinds of critical processes possible in a crit. This session was recorded and although the quality of the tape is poor and the crucial element – the art work – is missing, it is possible to recapture something of what went on. The student, Sam, a third year, is articulate and interested in concepts and issues. As he presents it, these have to a great extent informed his work and because they are publicly available concepts and issues they facilitate the public discourse.[4] The talk is full of analogous connections between the work and the 'world'. The work talked about here is two large paintings, both in pale blue and white which are made up of individually painted squares, which in combination reveal, in the first painting, sections of limbs as if from a figure painting, and in the second a man in a white background. This second painting is unfinished.

Sam introduces the paintings, referring to an interest in fragmentation and mass media; discussion develops about how computers can be used to break images up into squares. These are ideas which resurface throughout the discussion, which then can be seen to be returning again and again to the points of reference Sam himself has chosen to state. At this stage he puts it like this:

> Sam: The fragmentation idea is very much dealing with mass media techniques, in the sense that, I don't know and maybe more in these paintings at the moment – say, look at one individual square as a piece of information, sort of like here (pointing); when you look at it as a whole the space is disrupted more; it's harder to try and understand all the information put together. It's very selective [...] squares are blanked out. It's like censorship or giving an image and making it difficult to see as a whole.

Sam's final comment makes it possible to see what the perceptual effects of the painting are in terms of a cognitive concept, which in turn has wide political and social connotations.[5] This analogous or metaphoric movement allows both digression from and return to the work itself, as a process of testing the complementarity of the work and the discourse.

One of the tutors, Roy, returns to what appears a basic question: 'Is it meant to be something that is quite pleasing to look at?' Sam thinks that no, they are more brutal and cruel, adding that he is not attempting figure painting, but is 'deconstructing the image of a figure'. This particular term now triggers a generalised comment from Roy, who (to paraphrase, I hope, correctly) criticises deconstruction firstly as a self-defeating exercise, since it requires the support of the thing being deconstructed in order to succeed, and secondly that since you have to deal with things that are there, deconstruction is always reliant on something else for progress. Sam argues back to these points, saying:

> Sam: You've got to accept that things are there, haven't you? Really? I mean you're maybe reaffirming your position, if you're affirming anything. You're constantly in that problem or maybe the problem is your occupation as an artist. You have to think of ways of getting round it.

---

[4] There are significant parallels here with the talk which occurs in third year Sociology and which is discussed in chapter 4.

[5] It is interesting to notice here that Sam uses nominalisations (e.g. 'censorship') which create ideas as things and allow them to be understood in relation to each other. (see Halliday and Martin 1993).

Roy pursues his point by suggesting the danger of adopting a model and perfecting it, forgetting that it is equally open to question. And Sam responds:

> Sam: Oh totally! I mean the method, this method is not the end of the deconstruction of images. I don't think it's going to stand up for long – a year or so. After that it's got to sort of fold. You can't as you say, deconstruction comes out of purely process, which in itself is open to deconstruction or a process which is open to deconstruction, so that the point where, as you say, it becomes a fetish as opposed to a creative process – a critical creative process as opposed to a fetishistic way of treating the image.

There are a number of interesting things about Sam's responses here. First, he is in a position where it is natural for him to reply to the comment of the tutor. This seems to be because he has a commitment in actual practice, the evidence of which is the reason for the discussion. Sam is not defending deconstruction in an abstract sense, but is defending his own deconstructive activities. It is also interesting that the talk is not here about the object, but about the method and intent; this becomes another area into which the discourse can branch.[6] It was there in Carol's crit too, where it resulted in the resort to honesty. Sam's distinction between the fetishistic and the critically creative would perhaps be a way of characterising what the tutor was after in that debate. Carol's belief that the art work stands for itself does not allow for such consideration. Whereas Sam seems to situate his practices as a phase of experimentation which will be superseded (meaning, presumably, too that the objects will be superseded) – an apperceptive, publicly self-conscious stance – Carol is more concerned that the work is perceived – at least this is her public stance.

Another striking thing about Sam's comments is the way he attributes ideas to Roy ('as you say') which Roy did not articulate in that form.[7] Sam seems to have grasped the underlying ideas and transformed into new, slightly more abstract and succinct points. This easy communication, where one idea is swiftly rearticulated in a developed form, suggests that the speakers have shared disciplinary and conceptual resources and is apparent throughout the discussion. Words, phrases and names have for the speakers common resonances and contexts.

The discussion again takes a new starting point where the other tutor, Mark, enquires whether the paintings are finished and at what point he knows they are finished. The question is not an easy one because it addresses the relation between the painter's aims and desires and the point where the work becomes an object in its own right. In answer, Sam first mentions a comment by William de Kooning about the point where the painting is stronger than the ideas you had. What this comment actually might mean is not focussed upon, though I suspect the sceptical laughter and murmurings that follow it may indicate the kind of shared institutional judgement as was hinted at above. Going beyond de Kooning's comment, which Mark jokingly describes as 'Not bad for a fifties modernist', Sam is able to offer a tentative account of the relationship between his aims and processes and the object:

---

[6] It's interesting to consider whether method and intent are discussed in other disciplines and whether questions are ever asked about where the student now is in terms of disciplinary study. These issues are looked at in chapter 6.

[7] This is actually an unusual behaviour for a student/teacher exchange. Much more usually, it is the teacher who reformulates what the student has said so that it fits more comfortably with disciplinary discourse or the teacher's agenda. The teacher is usually, that is to say, ahead of the game.

Sam: Depends, when I stop painting or stop responding to it. The painting carries on. Whether, I mean, I physically stand in front of it swinging paint [...] or am still recriticising it. I'm not sure when I'll stop. I think it just gets to a point when again it becomes a fetish. You start becoming too immaculate. It's like doing this figure painting (*the second painting*). I'm not trying to do a super-realist figure, so spending, trying to get him more realistic than that or trying to get it a bit more like a person is not the point. Because I'm not trying to achieve that ...

This discourse of aims and intentions has the effect of justifying the object within the given terms of its production. Spelling out the criteria (that it is not super-realistic, for example) enables judgement, not of the painting, but of the painter's enterprise. The two are not actually separable, however, since each informs the other. The status of the art work within a 'real world' situation would not be dependent on such evidence of thought and reflection as is elicited here; the work would largely stand alone. But the argument would run that without such thought and reflection the work would not have the qualities (integrity? honesty? critical insight?) to give it the status of art.

To continue with the progress of the discussion – it moves back to de Kooning and abstract expressionism, the work contextualised within a wider artistic movement. Sam appears very aware of the way his work could be situated.

A first year in the group brings the talk back to the paintings themselves, asking about the use of colour: blue and white. This opens up a lengthy and fascinating area of discussion, further illuminating the kinds of justificatory thought processes valued in this public discourse. Sam first replies to the question by reference to his earlier prolific use of colour, causing him now to experiment with what happens in a picture when it is not there. He adds wryly that he is reflecting the colourless surroundings of Hull. Pressed to specify 'Why blue?' he talks about the night-time light which filters into his bedroom and then 'digresses' to a radio programme he'd heard which was about the great rarity and expense of the blue pigment, so that its use required special permission from the church. What now happens is that Roy has a sort of insight about the paintings:

Roy: There is that kind of stuff of spirituality and simultaneously you're taking the piss, which I thinks quite interesting, that. So you're actually doing both at once and in that you've succeeded, really. Using something that's got all that wide resonance, all that, whilst doing something that like doesn't matter, you know.

The talk itself within the context of looking at the paintings seems to have generated a meaning for Roy. Interestingly he seems to attribute intention to the painter rather than refer directly to an effect of the painting – yet this intention is not the one that Sam has articulated. Roy goes on to comment that Sam's actual justifications for his use of colour are 'pretty limp' – his own discovered reasons (to do with his own perceptual and intellectual engagement) seem more exciting. Sam, he suggests, needs to be more convincing. Is a convincing reason one which suggests something about the work (the way it subverts the spiritual connotations of blue) rather than one which is mundanely autobiographical, practical or fortuitous? Might Sam now adopt Roy's insight as his own? Does it add a dimension to the work which he might want to own? What is perhaps being instanced here are what the assessment criteria describe as 'the possibilities for the construction of multiple meanings in a work' and then 'the excessive nature of the work'. In a final assessment of the work would it matter that Sam had not himself grasped at the multiple meanings so long as the tutor was able to do so?

Sam continues to give his reasons on a rather pragmatic level, pursued by Roy, who wants to see his decisions justified and interrogated on the critical, ideational level he was thinking on earlier. The discussion of colour moves them into another discursive phase where common definitions are explored and tested against the work:

Roy: You mean it's illusionistic?

Sam: Well, no, I don't think it's illusionistic, because there's those squares and you can't work out what it is. Well, it might be formally illusionistic, in that you look at it and think that's how it works. At the same time if you just walk in and look at it, your eye's moving around the space trying to find this idea of truth real space in there. So it is illusionistic [...] in a formal sense, so you can look at it and think these are squares masked off in the painting, that's what's creating it.

Roy: Yeah, well, that's what I like – you know I'm not saying [...] First off, illusionistic means so when you're doing figurative you can see that's a person, okay, then you can see how it's been formed (*gives other examples from the paintings around*) but the illusion is of the person not the squares (*in the picture*), whereas if you're talking about *blue* bringing about coldness, then that is illusionistic technique, which is a mystifying technique, because people get a cold feeling from it without realising they get a cold feeling from it.

Sam: Oh, right, yeah.

Sam sees what Roy is getting at and by going on to talk about how we react to mass-media images, without realising how we are being manipulated, he makes an analogy with his original ideas. The discussion continues to range over formal issues and future directions for the work, gradually moving towards closure. It seemed, as I have noted, to be facilitated by shared conceptual perspectives, a similar fluency with ideas and vocabulary, so that the argument is both possible and contained. What happens though where this rapport is less well achieved?

Example 3

The student in this example has, after two years working with other materials, returned to stone-carving, which was his trade before he took up Art. His earlier work in metal and plaster seemed when I spoke to him to have been quite fully developed in both a private and public sense. Some of the work had been chosen for the New Contemporaries exhibition and thus had acquired a status in a public world, a significant step away from the student environment. In an important sense this public context also bestows an individuality on the maker, who, out of the institution, is invited to offer an accompanying statement to the work. What Richard wrote seems to span the divide between private and public in much the same way as the work itself. The words here fulfil a very different role to those expected in a 'crit'; at the same time, however, they paradoxically exhibit a protection of self:

I don't want to talk about meanings. I can't (it's personal, a secret). I could let you see what you want and say 'Yes it can be about that'. But then I would feel offended, because you hadn't seen what I want you to. I take things personally. I would be frustrated that I didn't tell you what it means in the first place. And I'd simmer. But that would be **my fault**. I wouldn't tell you how I felt because that may offend you, and **you might react**, and I don't want to run that risk.

So you leave thinking what you feel about my work is correct and I have confirmed your thoughts. But I'm still here simmering. I've left it too late. My opportunity is missed, but **I can't get angry** because it's my fault and **ANGER WOULD BE UNREASONABLE.**

The next person comes along and the same thing is **repeated**. This time my stomach knots, the next time my shoulders tighten. By the end of the day I want to bawl **MY WORK IS ABOUT REPRESSION**. But I can't (it's personal, a secret).

In the private sense (as I am using it here) Richard's work was developed, since in the course of reflection he had been able to work out what the work meant for him personally. Whilst making the objects he had been confused as to meaning, though at the same time, clearly aware that the work was not meaningless. Consciousness that his creative work was an expression of something to do with his own inner state came about through an urgent need to examine the actions, motivations and emotions which constituted his daily life. These two facets, the making and the wider personal exploration were mutually informing but not consciously or simultaneously so; they became explicit only after publication. The personal significance of the work to Richard's autobiography doesn't restrict or pin down the resonances that it may have when perceived within other contexts and by other people. Richard himself in the 'crit' refers to a certain cheekiness that the work has, acknowledging a dimension and perceptual possibility which has no part in the peculiarly personal meaning. It is the maker – not the work – who has to negotiate these contextualised meanings and handle both attachment and detachment. It is this sense which, on one level, the statement accompanying Richard's work expresses.

In the crit I went to, Richard deliberately did not display this earlier work, wanting rather to concentrate on the departure he had made by returning to stone. The session was a difficult, and I felt, unsatisfactory one in a number of ways. First it was concerned with work in its early stages and second with a method of working which did not easily lend itself to the sort of abstract discussion possible with Sam. Richard introduced the group to what he was doing like this:

> Richard: I've no idea where it came from or why (*laughter*) [...] What it was, um, I sort of looked at the Michelangelo tradition, where you take a piece of stone and you talk about sort of captive figures and, you know, releasing whatever it is in the piece of stone and I sat around with a piece of stone and couldn't see a bloody thing. So ('Not surprised!' *laughter*) I just started carving and sort of as a result of direct carving, where the um, you sort of take a lump of stone and then just the action of the chisel on the stone, you know, informed me as I'm carrying on so, er, this one was just a rough shape and I was carving away and it seemed like a sort of torso shape. It was starting to form so I followed that torso. Or there was (*showing*) well, it was virtually that shape so I was opening it up and trying to give it that movement [...] There's all sorts of different things happening and it was just a case of carving and letting it happen.

This is how the tutor now responds what Richard has said:

> Roy: So, in one sense, it's a process of improvisation. So you then start thinking in terms of improvisation, of where within that area there are a certain number of things which you know you could do. [yeah] So there are things which you don't know and you discover as you are doing it [yuh] and there are things which go wrong. [...] So as maybe a methodology which could also be a philosophical approach which could also be to do with how it's perceived by the viewer. If during that process of making you then think you know what you're doing, then it starts becoming something, then does that go against the principle of improvisation? And revealing (?) then make the process and the thoughts with that process?

> Richard: It does, yes. It's difficult to be rigorous down one way or the other. (*pause*) It's disturbing.

42

The narrative description of process which Richard offers is quickly interpreted by Roy at an abstract, theoretical level, which is at the same time a challenge for Richard to take on the terms (the categories and nominalisations typical of academic discourse) and justify himself within them. Richard accepts the interpretation but doesn't develop or critique it. His concern with the process is in experiential form rather than formulated from a distance where, for instance, it is possible to talk of principles of operation and consistency of purpose. He talks about his activity as a 'defining process' in which there is a conflict between following the material and giving way to the skills of stone-masonry, which he is rediscovering. On subject-matter he is still unclear, but as he says twice he is excited by this unpredictability: 'I'm trying to solve what ultimately I should be doing'. Roy asks 'So what informs your decision making when you are actually doing it?', but Richard cannot give a clear answer; he pauses, 'just like anything really ... it's difficult.'

Given the indeterminacy of Richard's position, where does the discussion go now? What other discursive spaces can be filled? Largely it is taken up with discussion of other artists working in the medium, which the tutor, Mark, finds conservative, tending to take itself too seriously. He compares this with the 'more playful' work Richard has done before. In terms of the autobiographical account of the work this comment has a certain irony, though Mark is dealing with his own perception here. Richard picks this up, saying:

> Richard: For me, these are playful objects, you know. It's maybe a case of actually presenting them like that. I sort of feel that that had to be like that (*pointing*), since there's so much going on in so many places.

Again there is the mismatch between personal feeling and public effect, which is negotiated again and again in the discussion, but which does not rest long enough with the actual maker in order to fully open up his sense of the things he has made. The discussion felt to me unanchored as a result, tangential to the objects and the maker, and having frequent recourse to a rather more ready-made repertoire of reference and opinion. So there was a common discourse, but it was not employed dynamically to make new and particular meaning in regard to the work. Attempts were made to explore architectural and archaeological associations in the work and to think of ways in which the conservatism of the form might be explored, but again I felt that these developments were not initiated by Richard nor given time in which he might develop them.

Whilst Richard felt that this could be explained by the fact that sculpture as a form is undertheorised, making a shared critical discourse harder to take part in, I sensed that this might nevertheless have been compensated for by a different 'teaching' technique – slower questioning, more time spent trying to understand the work through the experiences of the artist or thinking about (perceiving) what had in fact been achieved in the work, what it was (first order or 'aesthetic' response). In effect this would be a way of establishing the common understandings which made Sam's crit so dynamic. Whether the public situation allows for this more intimate exploration is doubtful, yet, equally, without it, a basis for rigorous related critical thinking also appears to be absent.

Richard's notion of the undertheorisation of sculpture (resulting in a generalised idea of the conservatism of stone and figurative work?) is in effect a comment on the predominant discourse of the institution which then operates criteria for evaluation and predetermines or makes predictable the aspects of a work which are talked about. The tutors, though their positions are naturally not identical with one another, lead and perpetuate this discourse.

Differentiation

As the third year went by Richard's sense of his own difference from the dominant discourses and ethos of the school developed. He felt himself to be a kind of dissident caught in the Art/Craft divide, not fully understood by either camp and the hurdle of the degree (which included writing a long essay to fulfil the theory component) made him feel resentful. The subtle ways in which work in the Art school could be validated, such as through the tutor's ability to talk about the work and give encouragement had not been present for him he felt. He had maintained his confidence through the external demands for his work (an exhibition, public work) and through a special rapport with another student. The school was unable to offer this support since what it advocated and understood was conceptual and theoretical art, and this had brought with it a de-emphasising of skills and work with material. For Richard, who defines himself very much as a maker, materiality and understanding which comes through looking and doing are central. For him the artist can never fully talk about his work, because the engagement with it is so holistic – visually, physically, mentally, emotionally – though in fact in the presence of the work he does use a very expressive form of talk in which his gestures augment words.

Richard's sense of marginality within the discipline was not confined simply to him. In a sense it is a condition of having completed the three years' course. As students progress through the Fine Art course they become aware of the ways in which their work is situated in relation to their individual tutors and the overarching institutional structure they collectively represent. For the student, encouraged to be individual and independent, the objective can become one of resistance to the institution; they overreach it, define themselves in a negative relation to it – and in a sense, this expression of their own novelty is a positive outcome of the course, though equally a painful one. It was notable how in the last meeting of all the third year students before their degree show and the assessment of their work, one of the tutors suggested that the students should not disparage the experience they had had, since it was that experience that had enabled them to think things through to the point at which they could criticise. His comment was at the same time a recognition that this disparagement would occur.

On the same occasion, it seemed to me significant that the Head of Department read out from the assessment guidelines and half sent them up. He was laying bare the dependency of the department on the system of academic accountability and assessment and acknowledging a mismatch with what the students had been doing for three years. Again the schism is between the encouragement by the school that the student be free, experimental and draw on personal resources rather than apprenticeship learning, and the necessary part played by external and public evaluative criteria which assert what it is to be 'free' and 'experimental'.

This assertion is not absolute however, because the art works produced resist objective and uniform appraisal. This is acknowledged in a necessary caveat to final degree show judgement in the Course Handbook:

> Works of art are not objective phenomena but socially determined symbolic forms. They are constituted through collective agreement based on acts of individual perception and thought operating upon circumscribed material, frequently in specific or designated environments. In the reception of art, perception of the work cannot be separated from its construction by the thoughts and desire of the perceiver, and this will necessarily differ

from one individual to another. Each person may construct a work of art and its concomitant range of meanings in a different way, to a greater or lesser extent. Similarly criteria for judgement will not be uniform.

The work the students produce can also require tutors to re-examine their criteria and the parameters of the subject. Yet how different does work have to be before it challenges criteria or before its difference is recognised as requiring a different discursive approach? When I spoke to Sam in the months before the degree show, he expressed frustration that at this stage the tutors from whom he had learnt now seemed unable to learn from him, to see what he was getting at in his work. He was resisting their advice that the degree show should contain mature, well-finished, professional work, wanting rather to push the experimental boundaries of his work still further. In part this recklessness was a response to negative comments by the external examiner earlier in the year – Sam would rather finish his three years trying to make what he wanted to say stronger – making the examiner's job harder – than buckle to the pressures of conformity. Thus the Degree Show would be double-edged: marking the end of academic study, the point of public assessment and validation, but also a more personal opportunity to make a statement about the significance of the three years. Here is the conflict between process and product and between individual transformative processes and collective Conventionalisation. The trajectory of an individual's development in art making stretches beyond the arbitrary cut-off point, but this moment of publication must nonetheless be faced: it is both phoney and real.

The announcement of degree results captures for many students the (necessary) duplicity of which they are part. It is especially hard perhaps to receive a 2:2, which is a good result as it places you within the majority, but which is also for the same reason a particularly difficult result to accept. When Richard received this class of degree it encapsulated for him the misunderstanding in which his work had been held. But the reasons which tutors expressed – that work had been included in the show indiscriminately, suggesting that he did not yet know what was good and what not, and that the work did not convey that crucial element of 'orientation' – don't betray that sense. The question remains whether the work 'really' failed to show authority and connection with tradition or whether there was a blind spot in the way the institution looked at it. The divide was perhaps at this stage unbridgeable: assessment violating the relationship between the individual and the institution. But the institution was not the only touchstone against which the art could be measured; its judgement not, as in most other disciplines, the only judgement of the work possible. Set within the larger contexts in which Richard's art continues to be appreciated and commissioned, the Conventionalisation offered by the academic degree will probably in time be superseded.

For more on Fine Art see also the section on research-based writing in chapter 12.

4. Making Transitions into Disciplinary Discourse

In this chapter I want to address some of the transitions by which students take on disciplinary discourse; in particular the way such transitions are effected through speech. I use examples from sixth form and undergraduate Sociology as the basis of a two-fold comparison: on the one hand the kind of speech that the learning situation makes possible (pedagogical factor) and on the other the kind of speech resulting from the participants' position in relation to the disciplinary discourse (enculturation factor). These two factors are difficult to prize apart in the examples themselves, but they are worth stating separately here in view of the fact that pedagogical decisions affect the kinds of speech used by students at all levels.

Transitions occur between one way of being in the world and another. The distinction I want to work with here is between common sense and disciplinary discourses. In the first example of spoken argument – from a sixth form class – the conflict between these two discourses gives rise to argument. To use Toulmin's (1958) terminology this is an inter- rather than intra-field conflict. The possibility for this arises in part from the type of speech situation this is – a group of three students working on a task set by the teacher whose intervention is otherwise minimal. None of the students has power over the others and this allows conflict to be voiced. With another configuration of speakers it may not have been heard or may, at least have taken a less vociferous form.

The example comes from a Sociology class on health and related issues. The students have been introduced to a theory put forward by Ivan Illich which contends that medicine and its institutions can have a detrimental effect upon health and well-being. This theory is called Iatrogenesis. The topic of health and Illich's theory involve the personal experiences and values of the students in the wider consideration of society and social issues. The conflict between common sense values and Illich's sociological theory drives the small group discussion.

The students were asked to do three things:

1) to think of examples of Iatrogenesis

2) to list supporting arguments for the concept in more general terms than offered by the examples

3) to list counter-arguments to Illich's theory.

The task given to the group has a simple argumentative structure and sequence following a conventional adversarial model. It guides the students from the concrete to the abstract, asking them to build a case first for one side then the other. The students are assumed to be able to work equally effectively on both sides of the issue, taking a disinterested, neutral role. In the discussion this 'macro' structure of scrutiny 'for and against' is largely adhered to, but the talk itself has a dynamic which is charged by the students' individual agendas.

The extract below is typical of the whole discussion. It occurs as the group are moving on to discuss counter arguments to Illich. The girl who speaks first (Susan) is strongly opposed to Illich's views, whilst the boy (Andrew) is more dispassionate and wants to complete the task set. The other girl (Lynda) who speaks just once has an enigmatic role. She seems committed neither way, but, when she does speak it seems to clinch a point.

Susan: All right, things like heart disease and stuff and - you need treatment. You can't just get over it, sat at home in bed. Like AIDS and stuff.

Andrew: There again you get over it anyway – I mean if you've got ...

Susan: No you're not. You're not ...

Andrew: If you've got a bad heart, you're not going to ...

Susan: What about leukaemia, chemotherapy and all that?

Andrew: You still die though don't you? It don't usually ...

Susan: Yeah, but you want to live longer, you want to live as long as you can ...

Andrew: ...cure you. Eh, you're living longer, but you're in like pain. It's costing more money as well isn't it?

Susan: Rubbish. No sorry Andrew I don't agree.

Andrew: Why?

Susan: Because I wouldn't want to die and I don't think you would and if it comes to the choice where you'd have to (breath) got a chance o' living, would you treat me? You'd have it. You would have it! (*very emphatic; crescendo*)

Andrew: Depends on – how you were living. Depends how you were living.

Susan: You would have it. (*softer*)

Andrew: If you were living w' no hair and in total pain all the time, then what's the point?

Lynda: When you're going to die anyway.

Susan: Yeah! (*shouts*). But I'm on about heart disease and stuff. If you have a heart attack and you get taken to hospital, you want the ...

Andrew: Yeah but. Yeah, yeah, all right (*conciliatory*)

Susan: ...treatment to get over it.

Andrew: Yeah, but you see, you're going back to the symptoms aren't you? They're only looking at the symptoms aren't they? Doctors, they're not looking at the causes, so once you've got it yeah, fair enough, you need the doctors, but ... it's getting it in the first place.

Susan: Yeah – but you've ...that's the argument (*tapping paper*)

Andrew: You're eating fatty foods and that, just thinking, Oh, if I do get it...

Susan: (*exasperated*) Don't you want hospitals or sommat?

47

For Susan the real-life situation overrides the academic argument.[1] She values life above everything, whilst Andrew is able dispassionately to draw a distinction between the quality of life and life at whatever cost (and, indeed, actual cost). Whilst Andrew talks in terms of 'it depends...' and uses abstract and classificatory language, Susan is arguing from absolute conviction. This is automatically a conviction about the priorities of people in general and her point takes the form of a personal attack on Andrew. Where Lynda joins in with 'When you're going to die anyway', the emotion escalates. She lacks support from both companions and is unable to defend herself.

In this emotional turmoil how does reasoning progress? It is not by a clear or 'reasoned' path and yet insights do occur and are formulated. In the second extract from this discussion, Andrew formulates the idea he resorts to above that doctors treat symptoms rather than causes. The extract occurs shortly prior to the one above:

Teacher: Well, just to start you off then. I mean he would argue that if I said to you 'Do you look after your health', you'd sort o'say 'Oh yes, well I'm reasonably careful. I don't smoke too much and I don't eat too many beefburgers and so forth, but o'course if I do get ill then yes I go to the doctors. I look after my health like that'. The very existence, the fact that there's doctors and hospitals here, perhaps that's a sort of safety net that makes us take ...

Andrew: It's an excuse for being ...

Teacher:.   Right

Andrew: ...to put off smoking. If you're going to get ill, you're going to get help

Teacher: Now just pursue that idea just a little bit more, because that's the sort of approach.

Andrew: So it's a, it's an excuse...

Susan: ...for taking risks

Andrew: Yeah, so you've got the back up of knowing you're going to get treated

Lynda: You go to the doctor (flippant). You go to the doctor (joking about general practitioners for a bit)

Andrew: Right, is that it? Is that all?

Susan: And he thinks they're a load of rubbish because ...

Andrew: Yeah, but he was saying that ...

Susan: (over the top of him) 'Cos they do treatment, they do treatment that,

Lynda: They don't look for the causes (sounds flippant)

Susan: No no no no. They do treatment. What they don't. No. (tapping with pen)

Andrew: No that's a point that ... No it's a point that. That 'cos most hospitals and doctors only do treat the symptoms don't they. They're not actually ... treating the causes.

Susan: (loud) Don't place enough emphasis on the causes. (writing down)

Lynda: Don't treat the causes.

---

[1] I would speculate about a possible gender difference here, in which Susan finds it less easy to unconcerned about the implications of the sociological theory on her everyday values than Andrew who is able to make the separation without feeling – apparently – any personal repercussions. See Gilligan (1982) for a study of the different ways in which men and women develop.

Andrew: Yeah they're just doing the symptoms.

               (*pause*)

Lynda: (*soft*) Pretty obvious really.

Andrew: So it's an excuse for, like, the government not intervening in causes of ill health, in't it.

Susan: Oh it's not the government.

The teacher helps the students to tackle the second task – arguments supporting Illich – by creating a hypothetical concrete situation. His intervention bridges the gap between the abstract ideas of Illich and their particular manifestation. He begins to generalise from his role-play by referring to 'a sort of safety net'. Andrew picks this up and reformulates it into a general reasoning statement 'If you're going to get ill, you're going to get help'.

Having focussed the students in this way the teacher leaves them. The statement they arrived at is uncontested, but the conversation begins to degenerate, Andrew reacting defensively to Susan's dismissive tone. When Lynda casually slips in the comment 'They don't look for the causes', Susan doesn't seem to hear her, pursuing instead her own thought. Andrew, however, seizes upon what she says as if it crystallises something for him. He expands the idea, building onto untreated causes the idea of treated symptom. Susan concedes the point by writing it down, but doesn't share the enthusiasm; her writing is a way of closing the discussion. Lynda can't see what all the fuss is about, but Andrew is quite excited. He takes the idea a great leap further, suddenly seeing a connection with the government: the idea of medicine as an 'excuse' is taken beyond an individual level and applied at a political one. If people are happy that medical services treat the symptoms only, government need not concern itself with causes. The two preceding points form this third one where both the 'excuse' and the 'causes' take on new significances and applications. Andrew has reached a level of abstraction from which individual institutions and practices can be seen as part of a larger overreaching pattern of relationships. It is not clear whether his insight comes from co-operation with the group or whether it has an intuitive impulse behind it. Certainly it is not methodically reached. But the moves he makes are characteristic of abstract, academic and in fact much written argument, moving away from the particular to create the world as a series of relations between concepts or nominalisations as things.[2]

Susan, predictably by now, does not receive Andrew's idea well; the idea of government investment in Iatrogenesis simply makes that theory seem even more far fetched. Yet later in the class plenary session, Andrew suggests it again this time to the teacher (the gatekeeper of the discipline) and it is accepted as a good point. What Andrew senses is an unacceptable opinion within this particular small group context, he hazards will be legitimate in the more 'disciplinary' space of class discussion.

Susan is operating with what Clifford Geertz (1993) has described as the system of common sense. Within this system, he says, the basis of meaning is taken for granted, not articulated; it operates on the 'unspoken premise'. The clash between the commonsensical and disciplinary is at once apparent if one thinks of Sociology precisely as articulating and

---

[2] Halliday and Martin (e.g. 1993) would characterise the change from concrete to abstract in the language used as a difference between spoken and written, but this is clearly problematic. Nonetheless the differences are instrumental in describing the kinds of language use which appear in our tradition at least to go hand in hand with 'higher order thinking' and certainly with much academic discourse.

scrutinising 'unspoken premises', such as for instance that we neglect our health because we believe in the ability of the health service to put us back together again.

There is an 'air of "of courseness", a sense of "it figures"' (p. 85) about common sense. This is the case with Susan's argument: she does not express it at any level above the particular, does not articulate it as a value or principle (such as perhaps life over death), which, if held, would justify any attempt at treatment and cure. If she had done, it is interesting to reflect that the status of her point would be likely to have changed from common sense to 'sociological' and to have become useful rather than obstructive in compiling the list of counter-arguments. To disagree with Illich is an acceptable part of disciplinary thinking, but criticism must be greater than can be supplied by particular instances unconnected to wider patterns.

The common sense as a system, according to Geertz, has been underanalysed because it 'has been rather commonsensical: what anyone with common sense knows'(p. 77). This circularity means that analysis and related activities such as the making of hypothetical, inductive connections and categories, the methodical and rigorous scrutiny of evidence and arguments have no part in the commonsensical. Geertz writes:

> The world is what the wide-awake uncomplicated person takes it to be. Sobriety, not subtlety, realism, not imagination, are the keys to wisdom; the really important facts of life lie scattered openly along its surface, not cunningly secreted in its depths. (p. 89)

Common sense feeling is for the 'vast multifariousness of life in the world' (p. 91). It accepts that there are inconsistencies and contradictions in life but doesn't recognise them or seek to resolve or exploit them through analysis and theory: it is immethodical. Common sense is, as a kind of consequence of this, also a conservative system. To quote Geertz again: things 'are depicted as inherent in the situation, intrinsic aspects of reality, the way things go.' (p. 85) When Susan challenges, dares almost, Andrew to disagree – 'Don't you want hospitals or sommat?' – she's using a kind of bandwagon, *ad populum* argument, which seeks to suppress protest and dissent by the obviousness of its cause. It is clear that common sense performs ideological functions creating and preserving a monopoly over what is natural and proper. Its strength then lies precisely in its premises being 'unspoken'.

In this respect common sense can be seen to be in conflict with academic disciplinary discourses, which operate by processes of suspicion and rigour, systematically exploiting weaknesses in existing theories and accounts in order to create from them new theories and accounts, which are in turn superseded. Disciplinary discourse can also offer new ways of looking at the world which break with the hegemony of common sense. This potential may be particularly strong in a subject such as Sociology:

Mary: For me, Sociology, I did a little bit of it last year and I felt that all my life I must have been living in a kind of box really, because I suddenly had my eyes opened to things. I found that fascinating and I wanted to learn more. All the sort of misconceptions I'd had about things in society, you know. I'd always felt a failure myself at school because I'd left at sixteen and I felt that I'd failed the system and I suddenly felt gosh, you know, there's a possibility here that maybe the system failed me, you know and it was really interesting to explore things like that and it opened up a whole new world for me to explore things like that.

          [...]

Mary: I think for me it was to stop seeing myself as a wife, a mother and to start seeing myself as an individual, as more than just these two or these very few roles that I was playing, as somewhere you know inside that I was with this individual whose life had been shaped by factors outside and I mean at the point that I think I started thinking sociologically, I started to see myself as more than just, as a person...

SM: That you've got a possibility. That you weren't identical to your roles, sort of thing?

Mary: That's right, yes.

SM: So that if at a level that you're not identical to your roles there's a possibility that you might be able to take on another role?

Mary: Yes.

SM: Like become a student.

Mary: But it also made me question the roles that I was already playing. As a mother and how I brought my sons up differently to my daughter, the kind of role I played to my husband and even my parents. So ...and when you start questioning things like that you do, you do sort of see yourself as an individual, you know it suddenly starts to have a new meaning.

SM: Quite unsettling.

Mary: Yes it was at first. All of a sudden you start coming across to people around you as different, you know, having all these opinions that you never had before and questioning things and ... I suppose people around you get this impression that you've gone radical or something.

Pat: Yes, I mean I really did change. Things I thought I felt ever so strongly about, I was really shifting quite a lot.

These mature first year Sociology students see their disciplinary study very much in terms of personal liberation from the common sense assumptions which they now see as having constrained them. Though the movement into disciplinary discourses requires a movement away from what we think of as personal conviction and belief it can also come to constitute that belief. Harré's model of personal identity pictures this process of change and assimilation, but, as I suggested in my discussion of it (chapters 2 and 3), the processes can involve tensions and conflicts. There are hints of these in what Mary and Pat say. For the average students, however, who have come straight from school the switch to seeing the familiar as strange is less remarked than for these two women. One of the challenges in disciplinary education is, it seems to me, to ensure that all students both experience and recognise this kind of shift: the experience of conflict is not to be avoided, despite its risks (see chapters 6 and 7).

Gee (1989) comments:

Primary Discourses [common sense Discourses] are initial and contain only themselves. They can be embedded in later discourses and critiqued, but they can never serve as a meta-language in terms of which a critique of secondary Discourses can be carried out. [...] "Liberation" ("power") [...] resides in acquiring at least one more discourse in terms of which our own primary Discourse can be analysed and critiqued. (p. 10)

However, if taking on disciplinary perspectives can be liberating, it can equally be seen as enculturation into new orthodoxy. In the second and third year undergraduate teaching of Sociology I'm going on to look at here the suspicion and rigour of the discipline become more apparent, but so too does the extent to which its discourse is itself conservative and totalising; it frames what can be said and excludes or seeks to subsume other discourses and by implication, other possibilities for the development of personal identity. Critiques such as those by Street (1984) and by various feminist writers link conventional academic practices (in which are included language use and forms) to the dominant discourse of the powerful – and male. These discourses, then, exclude, whilst claiming to be universal and objective. To get beyond both the inclusivity of common sense and the colonising claims of specialised disciplinary knowledge, argument must be conceived of as something other than the defence of a point of view or the operation of a certain legitimated method. It has, as I suggested at the end of theoretical discussion, to become something more like a process of slippage and rupture disrupting dichotomies of form/content and fact/opinion which tend to protect ideologies from whole-scale scrutiny.[3]

What has emerged so far from the analysis of the sixth form students arguing is a rather polarised picture in which argument is, on the one hand, cool, rational, disciplinary, concerned with establishing positions through processes of reasoning, and on the other heated, passionate, commonsensical and defensive. If one thinks of the way Kress (1989) defined argument as a way of dealing with difference which contrasts with narrative[4], then a rather more complex and interconnected picture emerges. 'Narrative', he said, 'is a form whose fundamental characteristic is to produce closure; argument is the form whose fundamental characteristic is to produce difference and hence openness.'(p. 12)

In the discussion between Andrew and Susan both these ways of handling difference are present, though they are not manifested as separate textual forms. Andrew scrutinises the material and tests it, exploring the possibilities for construing the world differently (which is what the disciplinary discourse offers him). Susan is trying to conserve and reproduce established belief and value. Yet they are both arguing and Susan far more passionately than Andrew. Rather than being a mode on its own, narrative is a conserving function of argument here. The narratives Susan tells are also notably *hypothetical* rather than *actual* and thus move closer to argumentative functions in that they suggest possible rather than existing worlds.

Speaking, Writing and Reading

The greater interplay between narrative and argument may be linked to the fact that the argument takes place here in speech rather than writing (Kress' distinction was based on text-types). The to-and-fro structure of speech gives it argumentative qualities notwithstanding its overall tendency towards consensus or dissent. What one speaker says is always in the differentiating context of what another speaker says. In writing, structuring narratives dialogically so as to produce argument is far less easy (see chapters 11 and 12). In addition writing – at least in its conventional academic forms – admits of less diversity in discourse than speech does and again excludes the dialogic. Where voices interact in speech whether with narrative or argumentative purposes, academic writing, in privileging consistency of style and register, can silence the distinctive voice altogether. The commonsensical has greater scope in spoken discourse (Geertz suggests that multifariousness is one of common sense's defining qualities), and, in our system at least, its status is

---

[3] In chapter 9, I look at the way text-type and institution are connected.
[4] See chapter 2.

subordinate to that of writing which is the index of disciplinary specific achievement. The differences between common sense and the disciplinary thus have parallels with the differences between the spoken and written.

In my experience writing is often used in educational contexts, not for the generation of argument, the progression of critical thought, but for its conservation. The problem is, however, that writing may not actually conserve what has been argued (in, say, class discussion), but rather what has been assimilated or known; its conserves, that is to say, other narratives. The writing of students is frequently divorced from their speaking. Written forms require the sequential ordering of material – problem, complication, resolution – whilst speech constantly uses otherness in order to progress; it is circular and multiple rather than ordered and unitary.[5]

Let me give an example of the lack of connection between what occurs in speech and what is conserved in writing, again from the A level Sociology class. The class was discussing two Marxist theorists, Doyal and Pennel, who contend that capitalism has detrimental effects on health. The students worked in small groups to come up with counterarguments to Doyal and Pennel. In the group I watched they took the example of the Chernobyl disaster and tussled with the significance of it occurring not in a capitalist, but in a communist country. There was clearly a critical point to be made, but they were unable to articulate it. In the class plenary session, however, the teacher used the proffered example to make the point that Doyal and Pennel had confused industrialisation with capitalism. When the teacher said this a collective 'Ah!' was heard from the class and there was large scale scribbling down of the point. Having the example articulated at a higher level of abstraction seemed to be greatly satisfying. The teacher was playing an important role here in providing what Vygotsky (1978, p.86) called a 'zone of proximal development', a kind of hand-up to the students which takes them to a level beyond that which they could reach on their own.

The point of this anecdote, however, is that nowhere in the essays I subsequently read did this criticism of Doyal and Pennel's argument appear. Here is an example from one student's essay:

> They go on to argue that capitalism doesn't only destroy its workforce's health, but also the health of the outer workforce, via pollution such as radiation damages to the community and pollution from factories, like Sellafield, Chernobyl and Capper Pass, as these tend to be situated in working class areas.

The Chernobyl example has been co-opted in support of Doyal and Pennel's argument, suppressing its critical potential. Why should this be? It is as if the risk – to the ordering and reproduction of the material – that might be involved in using the concrete example as a basis for criticism, is avoided in favour of a safer option. The paragraph appears at least to strike the right tone for an impersonal academic essay and therefore to be rhetorically satisfying. It achieves coherence offering a general statement supported by a list of examples: a nice balance of proposition and illustration – except that the examples themselves undermine the proposition.

---

[5] Links between the two forms are rarely directly made in the teaching I have observed. Yet it is my feeling that the learning of argument would benefit from greater interplay (see, for instance, chapter 12).

Whilst spoken discussion allows for hesitation, tentativeness, emotion, the testing of new ideas against those already held and the mixing of discourses, none of these things is permissible, or perceived to be permissible in the written form. The tendency for students to reproduce given material and ideas with which they feel entirely familiar, rather than to question, criticise or test is a reflection of the *function* of writing within the context as a whole – this function is frequently to close and therefore to conserve and consolidate.

The tendency to narrative in writing also reflects understanding, which has remained at a concrete descriptive level (the level at which students most often seem to be invited to contribute in class). Below I suggest an exercise by which students can perform a similar operation to that demonstrated by the teacher in the above example when he clinched the point about Chernobyl. This exercise suggests a direct and focussed way in which transitions into disciplinary discourse might be made through written language. Writing exercises are in my experience rarely used in teaching, as though they are a distraction from the real enterprise, yet in this case what is aimed for is, I think, central to understanding what that enterprise might be. In a sense the exercise models the 'zone of proximal development' referred to above.

Suggestion for making transitions through writing

Below is an extract from the writing of a first year Sociology student on in which she reflects on her experiences of taking on the 'role' of student. The writing was set to move the students from their personal experience towards sociological explanations. This goal is only marginally realised in the writing. In thinking about what it lacked 'sociologically' I began to use it as 'raw data' a basis from which to engage in some hypothetical sociological thinking. Taking one text, trying to 'spell out' what it is saying and in the process taking it further is what the exercise consists in. It is neither quite 'translation' nor 'paraphrase', though it may involve attempting to rewrite in other words. The meaning of the original does not, however, need to be preserved if the working suggests expansion and development. The changes that take place between the two texts can become the focus for discussion and reflection; also for comparison of different reworkings. The exercise can obviously be used with any text, especially one which is descriptive or theoretically underdeveloped – students' writing often contains suitable examples.

This is the extract:

> *Certain aspects of behaviour were spelled out quite literally – how to not appear as a freshman. For example, freshmen women tend to want to carry purses — college students just don't do that. Also, only freshmen would be seen wearing high school jackets, sweatshirts or other paraphernalia — within a few weeks these signs were completely gone as the new students adapted to their new environment.*

> *I remember not knowing the procedure for getting course syllabi and buying books. By observing and asking, I acted as if I knew what I was doing, but I was merely going through the motions. In subsequent semesters, I did indeed know exactly what I had to do. This is when I became the student. (Kate)*

And these, my reflections upon it:

Kate's writing is largely descriptive, though she registers the change from conscious adoption of the role to living the role. What does writing like this need in order to become sociological? Is it a degree of abstraction higher; a systematic way of characterising the observations; an interpretation of rules which are implicit, so that what is now description becomes illustration? Would a sentence such as 'The student conforms to certain dress codes which are picked up within the first few weeks of term' be sufficient? This is a general statement which introduces sociological categories. It might be improved by an indication that groups achieve identity also by being different from others: so 'The student conforms to certain dress codes which are picked up within the first few weeks of term and which differentiate him or her from other roles.' This seems to me to be a level of description which is sociological. I could strengthen my comment by introducing some a parallel examples to show that I am talking more widely about role adoption. From here, it might be possible to formulate a hypothesis.

Becoming a college student involves putting aside certain other identities and the outward appearance that signals them. Specifically the student puts aside both the signs of belonging to an earlier group (high school) and the signs of impending adulthood (purses?). These rejections suggest an identity which has side-stepped conventional paths of development. To make this hypothesis I looked at the particular illustrations as evidence from which to infer and then with which to support a broader statement. I had to ask myself why the purses and the high school jackets were unacceptable, rather than simply to register that they were. Do I want to differentiate student role adoption from other kinds of role adoption? My emerging theory may not be right, but if the process is an acceptable one then it might be used more widely as an exercise in moving students from descriptive narrative forms towards 'higher order' thinking and argument.[6]

Argument, or the exploitation of difference, is almost invariably the goal of academic disciplines at some level. It is a major criterion in distinguishing the A candidate from the C candidate at A level and a first from a second class degree (in many though not all disciplines). The examination system therefore distinguishes those who use material progressively from those who simply conserve it. Beyond this there are additional factors which determine the success of arguments; textual and strategic conventions which discriminate between types of argument and the value that is placed on them in the disciplinary context.

The narrative/argument distinction concerns not just speaking and writing but also reading practices. Reading is important to mention because in many disciplines, and certainly in sociology, learning is based around texts: students need to learn not just to write but to be literate. It is the fuller sense of *literacy* rather than the discrete skills of reading, writing, speaking which is the measure of insider status within a discipline.

As has already been pointed out narrative and argument are not just characteristics of texts, but are also ways of *reading* texts. A text will be different (will have different meanings) if it is read as narrative than if it is read as argument or indeed if it is read narratively rather than argumentatively. In my observations of first year Sociology students it was clear that this difference existed between the way the tutor and the students read texts. Whilst the tutor read for the way sociology was being used to explicate material, for the type of sociological method, for what the text in effect says about the discipline or the version of the discipline it represents, the students read the text for what it told them about the real world. Here is a further manifestation of common sense practice: the important features of a text are what it says, what information it imparts; it is taken at face value. In certain parts of Sociology it is easy to read in this way, since Sociology is about the everyday, linked to personal experience. Crucially, however, it does not deal with these in an everyday fashion.

---

[6] An account of a similar exercise is included at length in the Interim Report (Mitchell 1992b, p. 68-74).

When the tutor began the term with a research article on the norms of Romantic love among teenage girls, he thought that this would make an easier start than a more theoretical piece, but he overlooked the difficulties that the very familiarity of the subject matter would cause in trying to think sociologically about it. The content was disappointing to several of the students, because it was not clearly theoretical. They tended to read the text for its *descriptive* content and found that *what* it said was obvious and commonsensical. This perception seemed to act as a barrier to any discussion of the research methodology that had been employed in the study.

Related to this was the students' lack of familiarity with the type of text they were reading and this may have been the greater factor. They had no reading strategies which would allow them to see how the text was constructed as an argument and were confused as to what to take notes on. With hindsight it might have been easier for the students to have started with a theoretical piece from a text book. This is not to say, however, that the personal is not an appropriate starting point for enquiry, but rather a recognition that the form the reading takes may be as significant a factor in understanding as the content.

Suggestion: analysing for argument

One way in which students' reading strategies can be developed is through the use of questions which direct them to the way meaning is constructed textually. The first year students tried this with a text by Durkheim and questions which directed them to look at the way the argument of the text was put together and then to summarise the argument. The questions were not easily answered but they did provide a distinct focus for discussion and thence to address other texts. The difficulty they encountered suggests that the exercise would most beneficially be engaged in with the guidance of the tutor. Ways in which students might start to think about how texts are constructed as argument are given in chapter 11, 'The Imposition of Structure'.

According to the tutor some students never get to the level of understanding Sociology as a way of working rather than the talking which we can all do about society and experience. For these students the content of a text remains descriptive; a report on how the world is. For the sociologist, by contrast, the content is how the world is interpreted and/or verified: the sociological method or the way the text is sociologically significant has a substantial quality to it. The difference is that whilst the students who operate in this way keep on learning about society and Sociology, they never actually reach a stage where they are *doing* Sociology.

Yet whilst the tendency is that, at the beginning of their disciplinary careers, students will read and write narratively, as their repertoire of 'legitimated' positions from which to criticise and develop difference grows, so will the possibilities for exploiting difference and engaging in argument:

> Vera: I find that more and more in my courses, I use one set of things in another course. Remember we were using [Tutor x's] stuff that week. Mind you, that was from first year, but you've got that sort of confidence to pull in the other view points where you wouldn't have in first year, and more tentatively in second year and in third year I think you feel you've gone through it long enough to know that these other views are valid and you can pull them in to back up your argument. In fact they could be a good challenge to the existing one. Though you tend to be challenging other students rather than the teacher, I think. I don't think it's very often the teacher gets heavily challenged. Now and again…

This third year student recognises the process of enculturation that has taken place in the course of three years' study, but acknowledges also her continuing status as apprentice to the discourse of Sociology rather than as fully-fledged sociologist. In addition the institutional framing preserves the authority of the teacher. The segregation of argument so that it occurs between students but not between students and teacher is to some extent evident in the following extracts from a second and third year course on the Sociology of Murder. These indicate, however, that in the discursive context the teacher's position is also opened to change.

The tutor of the Sociology of Murder course commented that here again common sense narrative reading was a problem arising in part from the subject matter of the course. In courses which were more abstractly or theoretically based, he said, the tendency to read for story was far more easily overcome – the gap between primary and secondary discourses is more readily apparent. Yet it is worth noting that the tutor constructed a common sense viewpoint from which to begin the Murder course. He characterised this view as one which said that murderers are mad and bad; that their crime is not related to other violent crimes, but in a class of its own. The common sense view was *constructed* because by this stage the likelihood of the students supplying it was reduced: for them the sociological had become sufficiently commonsensical. But the common sense viewpoint was a useful position of otherness for establishing the disciplinary discourse as different.

Modelling the Discourse

The course constituted, in effect, the (re-)enactment of the process of authorial newness in that it followed the line of the tutor's thinking in producing his original research (PhD.) on the subject. Week by week texts were critiqued by the tutor and students in such a way that they followed the tutor's novelty-oriented thinking. The tutor reckoned that in the end the students would largely end up taking his position:

> I'm aware that nowhere does it exist in the literature, there's not a view that exactly mirrors my own [...] It's very much constructed to get them to analyse what they see or may come to understand as taken-for-granted reasons. In doing that, I like to think that I'm dragging them after me, but I like to kind of structure things so that they come to it step by step. [...] You implicitly structure the thing as a stage by stage thing. They'll make connections which I see [...] hopefully I like to it sequentially so at least they're making small logical progressions, which hopefully kind of move them in the broad direction of where I've been thinking.

The students were not learning to be novel for themselves, but were learning the process by which novelty might be produced. Though the medium for these explorations was speech, the overall structure of the seminars showed the process to be highly textual and systematically critical and in this way it corresponded to the strategies the students would need to employ in writing. The diagram below pictures the course and reveals the significance of founding the process in common sense; it represents a broad position from which to diverge. (Chapter 11 contains several other ways of representing arguments diagramatically which help to inform this one).

In the seminar from which the extract below is taken, a text by Wolfgang on criminal homicide and the subculture of violence was used. As it was the second seminar on the course, the teacher saw its function also as 'opening up the field', getting students to think beyond the

Common sense   Week One

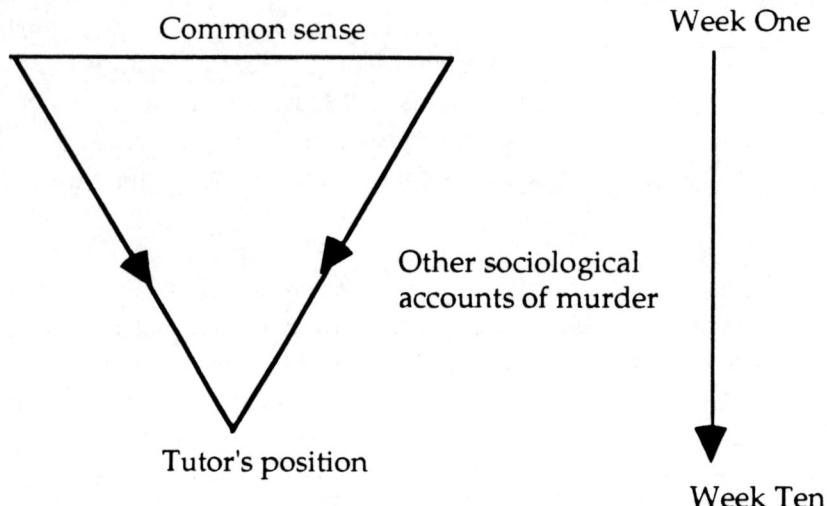

Other sociological
accounts of murder

Tutor's position

Week Ten

text and to challenge assumptions more generally. Wolfgang, he said, was 'a tool for getting somewhere else'. The diagram above indicates this liminal function of the text.

Here the group is discussing the association of violence with masculinity: if masculinity is a strong factor in violent crime, how then does it manifest itself amongst the different social classes?

Tutor: … So in a sense then you could actually try and broaden Wolfgang's argument out to say that well okay it may occur within these communities, but really the engagement with violence — the engagement *in* violence is partially conditioned not simply by subcultural values, but by kind of broader constructs of kind of masculinity and femininity, yeah? In other words the engagement can be if you like a status thing, can't it? Yes? It can be like a positive affirmation of masculinity — that's what I'm getting at. And that's why you often get this kind of asymmetrical treatment of kind of genders within homicide, in that, a man who commits murder, shall we say, is seen as engaging in violence which is a kind of subcomponent of aggression which in itself is a subcomponent of masculinity. Yeah? So in a sense the male engagement in violence – and by extension, homicide – is actually a kind of a confirmation or an affirmation of masculinity, yeah? So in other words a man committing murder could be seen to be over conforming to those kinds of constructions of masculinity, the masculine stereotypes. A woman who commits murder – and we'll see this later in the course – is more likely to be understood in terms of a radical departure from conventional ideas of femininity – the woman as nurturer and so forth.

        (*pause*)

Liz: Do you think then that premeditated murder by a man shows that, cos' I would think that says he's not very masculine. When it's premeditated it seems quite a – it's a sort of weaker thing to do. But doing an act of violence and for it then to result in murder.

Tutor: Yeah, that's right. I mean there's two points there. I think, Wolfgang argues that most of these murders are the result of violence which has fatal consequences which is not the premeditated kind. He then talks about what he terms middle class homicides, which as he would have it, is the classic kind of premeditated act – or undertaking of malice aforethought and has all the components of the classic British murder, if you like, or the classic murder. I'm, I'm I'm not sure (*pause*) whether you can see as you say the premeditated murder in terms of that same kind of affirmation.

Alison: You'd have to accept the gender stereotyping first if you wanted to discuss that.

Liz: What do you mean?

Alison: Well, you'd have to accept the generalisation that women are – that men are more aggressive before you could decide whether a man was weaker if he premeditated it. (*long pause*)

Liz: Accept it and believe it or accept it, just because that's the way society thinks do you mean? 'Cos, I don't really understand that – accept that that's the way society thinks.

Alison: If you're going to say is a man weaker if he premeditates a murder... (*pause*).

Liz: Uhm, when I say weaker I didn't really mean weak, I mean just not proving his masculinity, put it that way. As society sees masculinity – as being aggressive – I don't think it's an aggressive action if it's premeditated. Just not necessarily involving a run-up of violence – it could be a ... [...]

Vera: Premeditated means that person has got the advantage over the victim, so it could be perceived as being (?) and taking unnecessary advantage.

Liz: Uhm.

Bill: Surely it's just more calculated that that sort of aggression, it's not to say, if someone premeditates something that they're sitting there consciously thinking 'Oh I'm not aggressive enough to do it this way, maybe it's just fear of being caught – it's their value system that's making them behave that way, as opposed to behaving more aggressively.

Vera: Couldn't it be that you still have an advantage over your victim, whereas if you have two confronting opponents they both know where they stand?

Liz: I don't think someone who premeditated, decided to murder someone would enter into a confrontation with them because they could easily end up the victim and they'd planned it so there's no chance of that, so they're demonstrating their masculinity through aggression.

Alison: But in most of these murders the murderer would appear to have an advantage anyway – if they're done by young virile twenty to thirty year olds on sixty five year olds.

Liz: But often they murder each other. It's just luck who's a victim and who's, who does it. That's what he said, didn't he? That it was like just dependent?

Tutor: Yeah, I mean often – and this is born out in other studies as well....

There is a quite different dynamic here than in the sixth form small group discussion. The students are much more analytical, testing ideas through hypothetical constructions and in a largely dispassionate way. The pace and tone of the talk is much lower key than in the previous example and the students who speak appear to be collaborating in testing common definitions.

The teacher does most of the talking – there's an expectation that he will lead the thinking and that he is in control of the stimulus text, both in terms of knowing its content and of knowing how to criticise it, locate its weaknesses. Yet the students do not leave this up to him entirely; they actively test their own understandings. There is a long period here where the teacher is quiet and the talk becomes more exploratory as the students quibble over a definition of masculinity. The problematising of this category is interesting in terms of the development of the overall disciplinary argument. Alison's challenge to the generalised association of masculinity and violence arrests the development of the overall critique, which the teacher has control of and which relies upon the accepted stability of a term. Whilst her challenge is a deconstructive move in a process of construction, the tendency of the other student, Liz, is to accept the term as a generalised and generally accepted meaning. This stereotypical understanding appears important to constructing the discourse. And in this case it may be significant that the teacher doesn't respond to Alison's challenge. To do so would risk his developing thesis and the overall structure of the seminar. Having in a sense already arrived he does not need to explore, to test definitions as some of the students do. Despite this, his agenda – *as a teacher* – not only marks the parameters of what can be said, but also contains space within it for exploratory discussion. The process is both disciplinary and pedagogical. The testing the students do suggests that they are still in a state of transition. They are being academic but not quite sociological, since they still need to check whether they understand one another, whether they speak the same language.

The teacher's overall tendency in the seminar is to move away from agreement with the text; this is his primary motivation, his agenda moving him always to difference. The students' objective, as I've suggested, has a slightly different orientation and they operate, I think, on a different scale of argumentation. In the following extract towards the end of the seminar the teacher introduces new information that one fifth of murder victims had originally intervened to stop the violence. He invites the students to consider how this fits in with Wolfgang's subculture of violence thesis, 'where violence is almost…a linear process entered into by two parties who have some kind of consensus'. His own tendency is to suggest that this new evidence undermines Wolfgang (notice how he reformulates his view as a question):

Tutor: I think, if you take the bare bones of Wolfgang's argument it seems to be that people inhabit this subculture and there is this kind of localised consensus that this recourse to violence is a socially valid means of acting, yeah? Now presumably the people on the sidelines who then engage with these kind of consensual violent parties, they're actually, are they acting in accordance with a kind of counternorm of violence, are they departing from those kind of localised norms aren't they? Do you see what I mean?

Liz: But are they using violence to stop the violence?

Tutor: Uhm?

Liz: I mean how do they stop the violence? By just saying 'Excuse me, could you stop?' or do they go in with their fists and …

Tutor: Well, I mean, I don't know.

Liz: 'cos if they went in with their fists then they're also descending into violence as well no matter why. Doesn't really matter does it, they're still …?

Tutor: Yeah that's right, but I mean in having I mean I suppose this argument leads you down to psychological motives, but in intervening in the fight in the first place, y'know to try and with the idea that this is a bad thing and I have to try and stop it even if I have to use violence myself, it's still, it's not acting in accordance with what Wolfgang implies — is that there's this kind of localised consensus towards violence.

Anna: Maybe it is, maybe it's like um er I can't remember where I read it, I was reading about violence amongst teenagers, and this was teenage girls in um you know like borstals. There is a certain level where the violence is allowed to go to and maybe that also applies in this case where some kind of physical aggression is allowed but murder is obviously beyond it, and if the intervener thinks the violence is going too far, then he's justified by the rules of the culture in actually limiting it.

Tutor: (*thoughtful*) Mmm Uhm

Liz: Could it be though that you've not necessarily got any proof that the person went in to stop the violence, but they may disagree with why – the sort of cause of the violence, but they may be in full agreement with the actual violence, they may not mind the violence – it's just that they might not think it's valid for that particular case.

Tutor: Yeah, that's a good point.

The students, rather than accept the criticism of Wolfgang, employ tentative hypothetical explanations, which would support him. Their attitude could be described as a hermeneutic one, assuming the text's coherence, by finding hypotheses that fit its evidence. The tutor's scepticism, his first impulse to disconfirm the text's claims to knowledge ally him to a scientific stance (see Donald 1992). To say that the students are primarily obedient whilst the tutor is suspicious (to return to terms introduced earlier) is, however, to overlook the subtlety of the students' thinking in their contributions. If they do not seek a position of radical difference from Wolfgang, they are nonetheless thinking in terms of difference, but at a closer level, questioning the gradations of violence and motivation within the act itself, and introducing new factors and definitional boundaries. Whereas the teacher was content to take the intervention in violence at face value, these students want to know more about what is involved. In important ways, then, they are aligned with neither the teacher nor Wolfgang, but take these as starting points from which to open hypothetical enquiry. Theirs is a fluid position, which is what the teacher had hoped for. More fluid than his position in fact, since in many ways he has already arrived. Though the seminar is a collaborative occasion, the roles are not shared. The teacher's objective is to open the field to his students but also to open a space in which to promote his own thesis or theoretical position. The students in a less advanced state aim to comprehend the authoritative text and to extend it both working within and against its parameters. If this tension is there as I perceive it, it seems to be a productive one. Challenged on the one hand to reject Wolfgang and reluctant on the other to do so, the students come up with subtle interpretations and extensions of him which are new.

The teacher acts in some sense as a model for the students as they come to belong. Since he is actively rather than purely instrumentally engaged – in a process of discovery, rather than reiteration, the dialogue with others the dialogue with others can also lead him to new discovery. In the instance below, the teacher begins in an authoritative mode, formulating the ideas at a neat conceptual level and separating them into discrete, even opposed theories or interpretations. He presents to his students with a degree of clarity, which they themselves have not achieved. In doing so, however, he allows them to spot weaknesses or gaps and to demand further explanation. At this point the thought processes are new for the teacher also as he rises to the challenge:

Tutor: ... In other words that they're not kind of – as you say, looking at it from a kind of mainstream perspective, they are engaging in homicidal violence, they are engaging in deviant behaviour, but from the view of explaining violence from the inside, from within that particular culture, as Wolfgang would have it, then you're talking about people, who in engaging in that violence are actually conforming to a different set of norms and expectations. So, in a sense, they're almost kind of over conforming rather than undersocialised. Oversocialised rather than undersocialised, but it's the particular type of socialisation that you're talking about.

Liz: So if that's his argument, how does that fit in with middle class murders then?

Alison: A different type of murder aren't they? Different motivations.

Tutor: Different motivations, but I think you could still argue that the middle class murder – given that we've said it's instrumental, it's undertaken for some kind of gain, um...

Alison: So that fits in with the middle class rules and values

Tutor: ... the middle – I don't know, intuitively, I don't know this – let's say in a working class subculture, the currency is often, let's say, the ability to engage in enforced violence. The status within the middle class is often based upon perhaps a different set of criteria. If it's undertaken, if you say that murder is often undertaken for gain, then it could be financial – whatever, or undertaken instrumentally and in that sense it could be conforming or in this case over conforming to those middle class values of financial success.

The theory the tutor develops is that which Alison has given in a less developed form. Resorting as he says to intuition, there is a sense that he is formulating the argument for himself, giving it a form consistent with his earlier points. So his thinking aloud has both a private and a public function; public in that he must complete the theory for the group as a whole. The teacher's 'active' thinking role occurs increasingly towards the end of the seminar where the more frequent speakers in the class make more sustained contributions as a result of their increasing grasp:

Liz: It doesn't fit in with as well with the working class one, because the working class are actually conforming or whatever to violence which is in the subculture, but it's not just personal gain that the middle class conform with, but it's actually doing violence as well as that, so it's a sort of a step removed from their culture's value, so they're actually adding something to it which isn't part of the value structure.

Tutor: (*Throughout above making Uhm sounds which lead her to continue her point until she's grasped it.*) Uhm, that's right, yes. In other words with the working class, um (*pause*) violence is almost a kind of an end in itself, whereas with the middle class as you say, it's one step removed, it simply becomes a means to a further end, which is this kind of value displacement as it were. Yeah, that's quite right.

As the talk progresses the group's attention is no longer directly focussed on Wolfgang's text, but through their broadening out they return to him. In this last extract, the teacher makes this return, but in a way which seems to surprise him:

Bill : I think the idea that it's undersocialised, to me that indicates a naiveté, to me that's someone who goes in and premeditates a murder would not to me be naive as to the consequences of their actions or their motivations.

Tutor : (*soft*) No that's right.

Bill : It's just a definition of momentary acts.

Tutor : That's right. I think, I mean the social control model doesn't work with the premeditated types of homicide. As you say, it's um (*pause, thinking*) social – I mean, they're not, if you like, ignorant of the rules or whatever, so it's, neither is it the case that the rules aren't operative in their case. I think rather it implies that the, the homicide is undertaken (*pause, hesitant*) explicitly I think for gain (*tentative conclusion here ?*). Yes, that's right (*very softly*). Then the third question. The argument then becomes why should this particular group, you know, engage, in that type of behaviour and , as I say, the explanation could be that you've got a different type of value system in operation, which, I suppose in a funny sort of way actually confirms Wolfgang's argument, because it demonstrates that you know within different types of class or within different social groups, different social maps that you can have differences in, not just in social behaviour, but in things like motive and engagement in different lifestyles. So in a funny sort of way it actually confirms what Wolfgang is saying, the fact that you can make these distinctions between social groups, between types of murder and tie that in to particular features of that group's lifestyle in a more kind of structural sense.

The formulation at which the teacher arrives here – on the group's behalf in a sense since this renewed reference to Wolfgang is one which is based on a shared discursive experience – indicates that they haven't after all moved radically from Wolfgang, but instead have ceased to reference all their discussion to him. On the other hand, they have arrived at Wolfgang with a new understanding of him. They are doing more now than summarising or comprehending; they are assimilating, restructuring, reorganising, questioning. The continuing exploration, new forays upon the text and the clusters of ideas which surround it and to which they have common recourse – these create a pool of possible questions.

The speech is generated not freely but within the discourse which both controls and makes it possible. The most evident instance of this is the way the group uses classifications such as race, class, age, and here, in particular, gender. The use of these classifications provides a progression for the seminar as a whole as the implications of applying them to homicide is considered in turn or in combination. The classifications perform a generalising, normative and stereotypical function and are workable because they arise from what is common, rather than unique. They make up the argumentative context, which is, as I suggested earlier, in some sense, conservative; it puts a limit on the proliferation of meaning. Certainly there is far less clash *between* discourses here – there is little resistance to the sociological.

It is noticeable in the seminar how little the speakers refer to their own experience as a source of knowledge – they exclude themselves from positions within the matrices they explore. So they will talk, for instance, about possible scenarios between husband and wife in a working class setting, but do not attribute their suppositions to any first or second hand experience. It is as if they are operating on a tacit assumption that they are all neutrally equal in some way, disinterested theorists who have no stake in the phenomena they are discussing.

A number of questions are raised by this. Is it a good thing that students become 'disinterested'; that the passion Susan displayed no longer has a place in learning? Is disinterestedness actually perhaps a feature of disciplinary belief: belief in reasonableness? The students' detachment results from their enculturation; the behaviour is natural to them, the discourse familiar.

Not totally determined by the discourse however. When, at the end of the term they come to look at serial killers and to consider their motivations, the sociological discourse comes, for many students into conflict with another, perhaps more deeply held one. This involves belief in individual responsibility, in psychological factors and in insanity. The teacher insists that everything is socially determined, that the actions of serial killers can be explained by social factors, that psychology is simply a subset of Sociology, which has beneficial uses, but little value in explaining how things actually are, but all this is too much for many of the students. Their sociological allegiance does not stretch that far. There is another set of beliefs and relations which perhaps pre-exists enculturation into the discipline of Sociology (and is perhaps necessary for survival in the 'real world') which says that individuals are responsible for their own actions, that to be an individual *is* in fact possible, that there is some part of an individual which is not determined by social factors, the residue of a true self. It is to this core of the individual that the students have recourse when faced with the proposition that a serial killer is an extreme manifestation of social – not psychological characteristics. The commonsensical resurfaces as a rival discourse and challenges the attempt of the sociological to subsume all difference into a single perspective.

In the following extract from an interview with one of the students, it is evident that the discipline can become at the end of three year's study a focus of belief rather than detached method. She expresses the non-equivalence of, on the one hand, following a strong line of argument and, on the other, of making a leap of faith which will allow that argument to come to fruition purely on the basis of its disciplinary directionality:

SM : Do you think that people will end up just holding his [*the tutor's*] view [*on the explanation for serial killers*]?

Liz : No, I don't. I think today we just saw that people just can't. I mean because it is quite, he can't back it up with enough evidence, because it's very much a theory and like what a lot of people said about serial killers how, I found that very difficult to understand how, the way some do it and some don't. It's very sort of tenuous the idea that right at the end... You build up to it and it's all going along very nicely, but the very last thing it's like you just have to take it on trust really. I don't think every one will agree. I think people might understand it along the way, but at the very last if you're more, think more in a psychological way – because I only tend to believe in that I know it's Sociology, I sort of believe in Sociology, it must be right probably. [...] Yeah I think in a way as well in that particular case you could even say that the reason you doubt it is because this thing about you don't want to believe that it could be part of society, so even the doubting can be sociological.

Believing in Sociology, Liz is able to interpret the failure of others to believe as a sociologically explicable phenomenon; Sociology is all encompassing.

Liz's position is likely to be interpreted as a sign of success within the discipline. But is her disinterested belief the final position in disciplinary learning? What occurs now? Should there be a further stage in which she takes an 'outsider's' view and can critique the beliefs and practices she has espoused? Such questions return us again to the operations described in Harré's model, where Appropriation precedes Transformation, where the private and individual is first passive, subject to the public/collective and then active, contributing to and changing it. I questioned an anthropologist who has adopted radical new ways of conceiving of writing and representation in his discipline as to whether he makes these challenges visible to his undergraduate students. Not having considered this possibility, he confessed that he expected them to study the central anthropological texts and to write in conventional ways. His assumption seemed to be that you have to be at the centre before you can move to a critical position at the margins. At that stage Transformation can be more than learning to use material argumentatively; it can involve subjecting those arguments and the discourse in which they are constructed themselves to scrutiny (in the way that a feminist critic like Nicole Ward Jouve (e.g. 1991) does in reappropriating the dominant discourse of academia, asserting her right to use 'I' and to talk about herself). Before reaching this point, the subordination of personal discourses to disciplinary ones may be a necessary stage; the protests of the students at the extremity of the tutor's sociological viewpoint would not after all be interpreted as a sign of having moved *beyond* the given, but as a limitation, a sign of having stayed *behind* – of not having completed their apprenticeships.

5. Forms, Functions, Roles in Spoken Argument

A number of features emerged in the previous chapter which concerned the conduct of argument through speech and I want now to explore this medium further and introduce some more examples. It is probably true that argument is most often thought of as a speech-based activity involving the interaction of non-identical points of view. Yet in educational contexts and perhaps particularly so as education becomes increasingly academic, speech is often an invisible part of disciplinary discourses: not regarded as a measure of achievement, rarely credited with the status of product. In a complementary way, writing tends not to be seen as process. I am certainly not keen to reify such a distinction: greater integration and movement between the two media would give to writing, the dialogism of speech and to speech some of the opportunity for reflection and consolidation that occurs through writing. There are suggestions in this chapter and elsewhere (see chapter 12) which suggest more flexible relations between the two media. The low status accorded to speech is not inevitable. In the Danish education system, for example, which I have been able to observe as part of this project, speech is a well accepted medium for both learning and examination. Neither is it a token adjunct to writing: learning that 'sixth form' students of History might never write a History essay came as quite a surprise to me, and forced me to acknowledge how deeply engrained the bias towards writing is in the British system.

Whilst speech largely disappears from view as a credited disciplinary activity in this system, it nonetheless (and perhaps for that very reason) performs important functions in learning. One of the most striking features to have emerged from the extracts of spoken argument in the previous chapter was the capacity of speech to contain arguments which were both intra- and inter-discoursal, both passionate and disinterested, in a way that is often not possible in conventional academic forms of writing. As a consequence of this, speech can be an important means by which the transitions involved in learning a discourse take place. It enables consensual understandings to emerge through the expression of difference and at the same time shows how argument progresses through the exploitation, rather than closing down of difference. Speech allows for meaning to be made within, at the margins of and between discourses. As such it enables transitions to take place. The combination of speech and argumentation is particularly potent and transformative:

> Liz: Yeah, because it's so distanced from where you are, like you say, about you're up in the air, you can't just be taught it and learn it, you have to be persuaded to believe it and the only way you can do that is through arguing and discussing really. You can't, if I had to look at it from sort of... I, argue my own point of view but then come to believe somebody else's. I couldn't be taught it and just believe it. I have to argue back to get my beliefs changed as it were. Put them forward and see how they were wrong or right or whatever.

The type of argument that took place in those extracts from Sociology seemed dependent on such factors as who the participants were – students alone, or students plus teacher; what the formal setting was – small group or whole class; what the status of the participants within the discipline was – the degree to which they were encultured. Such framings determined who spoke and how and what was legitimate as argument.

Argument was also put to different *purposes*: to defend a position, to consolidate and modify a position; to discover or construct a position; to socialise into a particular kind of approach. These purposes need not be discrete, but could operate in combination or merge into one another: a participant who set out one position could come, through the interaction with others, to modify that position. The talk itself was generative. Within any given situation the purposes of the participants did not need to be shared: in the Sociology of Murder course, the students argued to agree definition, to share and modify understandings, whilst the teacher absented himself from this activity and mediated instead an argument between the individual text and the sociological discourse towards an end which he already held in view. Nonetheless, this too underwent some modification.

Arguing for Consensus

In the following extracts from an argument about the definition of propaganda in relation to World War One posters, positions are both entrenched and meanings emergent.[1] The discussion is prompted by Neil's challenge to Robert's characterisation of all the posters as 'blatant propaganda':

Teacher: Any other comments about the posters themselves then?

Robert: They're obviously blatant propaganda aren't they?

Teacher: Why are they blatant propaganda?

Robert: Because the message seems so obvious.

Neil: Why's that propaganda?

Teacher: Well, propaganda in itself has taken on as a word – it's an important word really. (*Boys; 'but...' protesting mumble*)What do you understand by propaganda? It's taken on a very sinister meaning – propaganda. Particularly with regard to Goebbels in the Second World War.

The argument is conducted on two levels; roughly a public and a private one. The private debate takes place between Neil and Robert, who at times can be heard continuing exchanges whilst the teacher is opening debate to the whole class. They have their own kind of urgency. The teacher, like all teachers, has a public voice, which is authoritative and which both commands collective attention from the class and seeks to make the discussion a teacherly one; one, that is, from which they will all benefit. He is the focus for the argument's public level. In the first exchanges, he recognises the complexity and importance of the word which Robert has raised and, rather than closing the discussion down, he throws the question open. The lesson has taken an unexpected turn, a search for consensus through discussion, in which the teacher to a great extent shares the discovery process:

---

[1] A full analysis of this discussion is included in the Interim Report (Mitchell 1992b)

Robert:	The purpose of propaganda is like to either to encourage or discourage in't it? To encourage the English effort and discourage like...
Neil:	(*interrupting*) Yeah, but you can get that in peace time if you wanted like people...
Robert:	Yeah, but...
Neil:	(*raises voice to block interruption*) It's like a job advert in't it?
Robert:	It's propaganda in peace time though
Teacher:	Neil's saying there that it's just like a job advert – is that source 103? It's quite important that, (*R and N continue discussing while T talks*) is that source 103 just like a job advert, like say, be a nurse or...?
Neil:	It is.
Teacher:	Y'know I'm inclined to kind of agree with it.

Robert emphasises the importance of propaganda's purpose, its persuasive aim. For Neil this is too general; his definition includes the idea of war. He defends his narrow focus by offering an alternative definition for the contested poster: a job advert. This is very persuasive: by implication, if Robert's ideas are accepted, anything can pass as propaganda – his definition falls down for being too wide. Robert reasserts his position, but the teacher steps in, highlighting the validity of Neil's point, making it part of the public debate by opening it to the whole class.

Whilst the definition of propaganda continues to be pursued, however, the discussion moves away from Neil's view and this he finds frustrating. Robert, in contrast, is less committed to a particular point of view, more flexible and disinterested. The teacher takes from what the two boys say, but generally speaks at greater length than either of them. The task is generally exploratory, conducted in the conditional as provisional definitions are tested against the concrete instances – the posters – they have before them:

Robert:	So perhaps the fact that they produced a poster about the ploughs, cos they're worried that women won't go and do the plough 'God speed...'
Teacher:	Quite right. That's very true. All I would suggest is that you're dealing with different scales of propaganda.
Robert:	I agree because it plays on the emotions.
Teacher:	Yeah, that's what we've said all along. If propaganda is official information to make you think or act in a certain way and that's how I would define it – all three of them are propaganda. Yes, that's true. Anyway...
Neil:	There's different definitions of propaganda...
Teacher:	Well, that's right.
Neil:	Different interpretations, personal interpretations of propaganda.
Teacher:	Propaganda is a word which has taken on more meaning than its literal meaning, because now to most people it has the totally sinister overtones of a totalitarian regime, who would, for example, y'know they would on a poster depict a Jew as a hideous person who's tearing babies apart or something. That's blatant propaganda, but its still propaganda – source 103 is still propaganda (*inaudible few words*). Ah we'll probably find time to explore that later. Anyway, let's turn back to source 89.

At the end Neil advocates a relativist position, not, I suspect, because he believes it but because this is the only position which accords value to his own definition in the consensus which the teacher's closure signals has been reached. Neil's has not become a public interpretation as the teacher's has, but remains 'private'. What the discussion makes apparent is the degree to which consensus is reached by the power the teacher has to define its scope, to direct it and to impose closure. Even exploration is constrained by authority.

Authority and Roles

Certain characteristics seem to determine the teacher's role in spoken interaction and distinguish it from the role of the students. It is virtually a truism that he teacher has the licence to speak at greatest length whilst students speak more often by invitation and for shorter periods of time. Much of the contribution students make is at the level of exemplification, whilst the teacher's role involves reformulating what they have said at a higher level of abstraction, so that it fits the discourse (is made publicly available) or so that, in a related sense, it conforms to the teacher's agenda. The following, from an A level Politics class, makes an interesting example. Here the teacher had supplied the example of making a cheesecake early in the lesson as a hypothetical (and also funny) way to get the students thinking about Marxism and the production of capital. Later Robert picks this up and extends it:

Robert: Right, you get a bit of an increase in community spirit with Capitalism. Like at work and that, because instead of one person selfishly making a cheesecake on their own, like, you get three or four involved so instead of one person settling back saying 'What a lovely cheesecake I made' three or four sit round and say 'That's a nice one we made'

Teacher: So mass production actually increases participation?

Robert: Yes.

Again, below, the hypothetical example scaffolds an imaginative extension of the argument[2]:

Robert: Because, like, you get this factory production and that, those that might not be as skilled to make like a cheesecake, they might be skilled enough to weigh out the flour.

Teacher: Uhm, yeah. I see what you mean. Capitalist society, you could argue…

Michael: Increases participation.

Teacher: Well, it's not so much that, is it? It allows people of lesser skill perhaps to play a role in society, you might say; in production. That's a possible Capitalist analysis. Yeah true.

The teacher has a legitimating role in the progress of the talk and is generally in overall control of the direction and scope of discussion. Even where discussion, as in the case of the second and third year Sociology seminar, contains 'turn by turn' space for and tolerance of exploratory and tangential speech an agenda or teleology is generally discernible. In the case of the Sociology course this agenda operated for each individual seminar and over the ten week term. In the small group situation in A level Sociology, too, a structure and teleology

---

2 This use of the concrete example which is hypothetical rather than actual was also central to the Philosphical Methods undergraduate course I observed. It testifies again to the use that narrative can play in argument.

68

had been set by the teacher. However far the talk had in the meantime wandered, this structure was reasserted in the plenary session which the teacher orchestrated. In the discussion over propaganda the teacher departed from his immediate agenda to address an area which he recognised as valuable, but it was on *his* recognition that the exploration took place. Teachers need to negotiate between closed agendas (which usually implies covering a certain content) and a more open kind, in which the discourse of the subject is more widely used and in which the teacher is sensitive to the needs of the students and to the discourses they inhabit. One way of ensuring that this more open approach is permitted is, on occasions at least, to give the initiative to the students and to ask them to raise questions about and around the subject being addressed. The articulation of questions is in a sense the setting of an agenda, one which originates in the students' own position within the discourse and which can suggest directions in which their enculturation might be taken.

The degree to which an agenda is integral to the role of teacher was exemplified for me by my experience in the Danish sixth form college, where one of the teachers decided to use some ideas on argument that I had taken with me as a stimulus for an assignment of his own devising. He tried this out whilst I was in the school and could watch, comment and learn.

Setting Forth Without a Destination

The assignment was on the theme of having children: this tied in with their eventual reading of *The Millstone* by Margaret Drabble. The exercise started with pair work where B asked A 'Do you want to have children (eventually)?' The discussion amongst the students led to the teacher summarising the pros and cons of having children on the blackboard. The teacher instinctively formulated what the students said in noun forms as themes (or asked the students to do this) e.g. symbol of love, sense of responsibility, experience. What was interesting about the list was that it was very much concerned with personal, spiritual and emotional reasons for having children and this, the teacher felt, made it a difficult subject about which to develop an argument. He was reluctant to press the students on how 'good' or otherwise the reasons were. I felt that a next stage would be to attempt to categorise the reasons and to identify the kinds of perspectives from which they originated. If the perspective were changed (if, for instance, they were to take a third world perspective) would the reasons change? The teacher began to group the reasons under more general headings, such as 'normality' 'social pressure', a difficult task since several of the reasons fitted in more than one place. My feeling was that this was a good thing rather than a problem – the headings were related rather than discrete. This complexity was, however, unsettling for the teacher as the board filled up with words and boxes which seemed to have no order to them. Again the teacher had good strategies for slowing the rush of ideas down: he noted that many of the ideas had a 'selfish' motive to them and asked the students to get back into pairs to come up with some other sorts of reason. The change in dynamic between whole class and small group talk seemed an effective way of coping with the rush of ideas and material.

The generating of ideas and arguments had been a 'loosening' (see chapter 2); what was then needed were strategies for 'tightening' the material, creating some sort of form or order. It seemed to me that one way of trying to make sense of what was on the board would be to find arguments which refuted each other and to connect them. Freedom, for example, seemed a possible contradiction of motherhood, though this raised the question of how to define freedom. Definition is an important way of tightening, though as we have seen, consensus about what constitutes a definition can itself invoke argument.

At this point writing might have been an option – putting the onus to define back on the individual (and again changing the dynamic). Writing might have taken the form of completing paragraphs, such as 'The question of whether to have children can be answered completely subjectively....' or 'There are social factors which influence the choice whether to have children or not...' These tasks may have focussed the students and helped them consolidate and link the disparate ideas generated.

The second session on the issue of having children made an interesting comparison with the first. The students got into groups some to discuss the question: 'If you wish to have a child, but for some reason it proves impossible, what do you do?' and others the question: 'If you do not want a child and find yourself pregnant what do you do?' These questions take the form of hypotheses and so whilst they can be related to individual experience and belief, they produced a wider range of possible options than the earlier stimulus question: 'Do you want to have children?' The questions raised general issues such as abortion and adoption and the teacher asked for reasons for and against choosing these options in the hypothetical situations. The range of possible arguments seemed to grow and grow and it did not seem to be particularly important that they should be pinned down. Though, again, I think, at any stage focussed writing (however brief) might have done this.

In the final lesson students read poems on the theme of children and parenthood. This might also have constituted a form of tightening, since the poems represented external positions which verified, consolidated or refuted what had been generated already. In the event, however, time limitations and the extraneous reason for reading the poems meant that they could not really be done justice to. The exercise had, in a sense, become overloaded. In addition, there was a sense in which the students found it hard to grapple with the ambivalence and ambiguity expressed in several of the poems.

The sequence of exercises seemed to me very instructive and I sensed that it contained techniques and approaches which might be adopted, perhaps spontaneously on other occasions. I think it was valuable for the kinds of ordering and reordering of discussion, the attempts to get an overview of what was being said. To lead this foray into uncertainty required courage of the teacher, but there were a number of methodological moves to make (such as categorising, switching perspective, identifying opposites) which could help to transform the material. The 'game' seemed also to involve periods of widening out and periods of consolidation. These were functions which could be achieved by changing the size of groups and between speech and writing. The game did not have to produce solutions, but the process itself had to be seen to be valuable. I don't know what the students' experience of the exercises was like; they may have felt frustrated in the processes, unable to see where they were leading. It would, however, be valuable to pursue experiments in this kind of teaching and understand the dynamics, pitfalls and rewards more thoroughly.

This experience suggests both the precariousness and potential of, on occasion, working not without an agenda, but with an agenda constituted less as a process leading to an end point and more as a process utilising a variety of conceptual, organisational and discoursal tools.

Teacher as Discourse Leader

An aspect of disciplinary learning which is overlooked by exclusively 'student-centred' approaches is the crucial role the teacher plays a 'discourse leader', his purpose being to socialise his students into the discourse. In classes where the rapport between teacher and students has been built up and when the students are at a certain level in their apprenticeship, the teacher's role starts to be shared (as was the case in the Sociology of Murder course). In the following extract from an A level Politics class the students have learnt the ritual of point and counterpoint, the deferral of closure, the construction of hypothetical positions which together create a rich texture of discourse: political argument.

> **Teacher:** So Marx would say that change in society is always due to economic things - that's the key thing. Can anybody see why many people, many philosophers would say this is totally wrong, this neglects some fundamental things about human beings? What fundamental things would some people say Marx has ignored here about the reasons why society changes? And I can think of certainly one incredible factor throughout history which some people would say is vital to human development – what?
>
> **Michael:** Self-determination.
>
> **Teacher:** Well, certainly this thing about individual ideas, that maybe every so often some incredible individual comes along who changes society, you know. Such as Hitler maybe or Einstein or Jener and the discovery of smallpox.
>
> **Brian:** Or Stevenson.
>
> **Teacher:** Or Stevenson and the discovery of steam engines. Or Jesus Christ - how about him? Where does he fit into all this?
>
> **Robert:** Marx's interpretation of Jesus Christ. (*rather mumbled*)
>
> **Teacher:** Yeah well we're going to have to look at Marx's interpretation of Christianity. But if you think about it that's a problem isn't it? If you're saying that all change in society is due to economic factors, what about ideas and beliefs – that some people would say that society changes as a result of beliefs? That's the big — we'd better jot that down – that's the big problem:ideas and beliefs. That some people would say society changes because of ideas: new theories, new ideas.
>
> **Michael:** But why do we get like Communist countries and that? It's because of Marx's ideas.
>
> **Teacher:** Ah! But he would argue that those ideas are the product of the economic society which they're formed from. He's not saying that there aren't ideas, he's saying that they come out of material changes. Yeah? Whereas a non-Marxist view would be that the ideas are the things which change society in the first place. I mean certainly you know a religious response to this would be y'know that once you've got Christianity then society's going to change. That's the thing that changes society. But again we'll have to explore that in more detail later.

The authoritative position of the teacher – as both a source of knowledge and an institutional focus of attention – is important to the conduct of the discussion. The teacher had a feeling, that despite the small size of his group, he *ought* to provide opportunities for pairwork and small group discussion, yet realised too that when he did this some of the impetus to debate was lost – the public forum and the cut and thrust supplied by the teacher's command of his subject – had a defining function on the type of learning that took place. In a very definite sense it was in the public exercise of the discourse that the *real* work went on.

The case for the academic lecture is also made here. Notwithstanding that it may at times be obscure and too drawn out, what the students who attend are witnessing is the thinking (often more provisional and speculative than in a written article) of someone who is already within the discourse. They do not necessarily understand everything that is being said, but they do experience a way of saying; a literacy practice rather than a body of knowledge. What this alerts us to is that the empowerment claimed for students in small group talk or 'buzz groups' may in fact be empowerment limited to particular frames and ineligible in other situations operating different other rules of participation. Nonetheless small groups do allow students to negotiate meanings which in the public discourse are already established. They allow underlying assumptions (Berrill 1991) to be explored and in this sense can contribute to the greater effectiveness of whole class situations. It is a limitation, however, if positions such as Susan's on the health issue should be confined to the 'safe' territory of teacher-free groups; which is to say that small groups should not be used as a substitute for open relations between teacher and students, or for the students on occasion to determine the wider agenda.

Though the modelling of discourse by teachers plays a valuable role in students' enculturation into a discipline, it is nonetheless not often apparent to those students how the discourse is being used and its relevance to learning is therefore not capitalised upon. (In chapter 6 I explore the way students conceive of what they are learning; frequently as content rather than discourse). An example will perhaps serve to clarify what I mean here.

Modelling Argument in English

The example is of a first year undergraduate seminar in English where *Tess of the D'Urbervilles* is being studied. The students have previously been given a framework through which to read the text, in the form of questions and prompts about the role played by 'Nature', 'Fate' and 'Symbolic imagery and literary analogues'. In addition they were asked to address the question of whether Hardy endorsed the ideals of the Feminist Movement of the 1880s and 1890s. At this early stage, too, the students were given the essay question they would eventually respond to:

> 'These novels [*Tess* and *Jude*] seem to me to be an expressive, irrefutable criticism of society's debilitating version of womanhood' (P. Stubbs, *Women and Fiction: Feminism and the Novel, 1880-1920*). Do you agree?

Here I give a summary narrative of the second tutorial on the novel and attempt to extract from it the tutor's agenda – his argumentative strategies, the version of the discourse he is leading.

1   GENERAL : The question of Hardy's sympathy or otherwise to the Feminist cause.
Argumentative strategy: – pose question

2   PARTICULAR: What kind of person is Tess?
Argumentative strategy: choose angle of investigation and collect evidence

–   Listing of adjectives on the board – a form of collective description, elicited by the tutor and partially negotiated by him as suggestions are given. In the discussion there is a movement between a sense of what Tess really is (what the reader or the collective readership perceives her to be) and the way she is perceived by other characters in the book. Evidence is built up at a descriptive level and expanded into discursive points of view about the character. These then feed from the textual level into the wider discussion about Hardy's feminist views.

Argumentative strategy: interpret evidence and select for emphasis

3 SUMMING UP: Tutor concludes that they have managed to bring out a good deal and that some of the features seem to contradict each other which is the mark of a realist character.

> Tutor: What does all this add up to? Is it the kind of woman that a feminist would approve of?

Argumentative strategy: test evidence against terms of question. Extend scope by raising hypothetical questions.

4 ... AND ARGUMENT:

Nadine agrees that a feminist would approve of Tess, but Pete disagrees, saying that she is too passive. The tutor adds this word to the list and asks Pete to restate his view:

> Pete: I think she lets events sort of roll over her. I mean I said she cares about what other people think – that's very true, but she lets other people, other people's actions are always, they sort of repercuss on her, they always have repercussions for her life. She doesn't lead events so in the end she goes back to Alec.
>
> Tutor: She doesn't lead events. She's passive rather than proactive, she doesn't initiate events. Sorry I interrupted you.
>
> Pete: I was just going to say about Alec. She goes back to him in the end and then kills him, which isn't very nice. It may be a very feminist ideal, but I'd have thought Alec had a bit of redemption.
>
> Tutor: So, two opposing points of view. Yes, she is the kind of woman the new feminists of the 1880s and 90s would have approved of and no, she isn't she's too passive, she's too timid...

The tutor invites the students to support either side, but to use evidence for both. He brings in again extratextual material; an account of feminist beliefs and Ruskin's account of the perfect woman, raising the hypothetical questions: 'What would Tess have felt about that?', 'What would Ruskin have felt about Tess?'. These are followed by further discussion and a second summing up:

> Tutor: Well, let's leave the question open. But there are certain very strong assertive opinions in her personality, but also she is infuriatingly passive with Angel Clare isn't she? You feel he wouldn't have been quite so cruel and tortured her quite so much if she'd been just a little more assertive.

Argumentative strategy: introduce new evidence to clarify terms of the question. More hypothetical questions to test links. By introducing the author in terms of biography, beliefs and psychology hypothesising becomes possible – which must however be validated against the text. Behind all these strategies teleology creeps in. The development of the discussion seems to demand this. The more evidence is selected the stronger the case becomes for one side of the debate that was earlier left open.

5   NEW ROUTE IN: imagery. The group comes up with types of imagery: nature and religious – and find instances of these. Both tutor and students turn frequently to the text and read out parts of it.

Argumentative strategy: again the collection of evidence, this time at a close textual level, under certain categories.

Allusions to the Bible story of Adam and Eve are gathered and linked into and found to be analogous with the characters in the novel. On the example of the cows at Talbothays dairy oozing milk the tutor comments:

> That's not naturalistic description is it? (*pause*) It's stylised description. It's symbolic, it's not realistic, it's symbolic. I mean obviously he's doing it for the symbolism isn't he? He wants to evoke the idea of Canaan and the Land of Milk and Honey. What the point of all this is we haven't decided and I think we need to leave it and come back to it.

The tutor's comment on the language here plays a significant part in the development of the discipline-specific argument. Attention to symbolism and imagery is the route to a more general critical understanding of the text. The distinction between the natural and religious categories becomes crucial.

Argumentative strategy: begin to link evidence and interpretation at a more abstract level; move towards interpretation for significance.

6   NEW ROUTE IN: The tutor leads this section going back to the connection between Tess and the natural world and taking examples from the text to show where she is identified with natural scenery. He concludes:

> Which suggests to me that all these qualities that, these natural qualities that Ruskin would have liked so much – the timidity, the passivity, the sexiness, the docility – that all these are not just one particular girl, but somehow they're natural to women.

Through an examination of the text, imagery and the theme of nature, the tutor returns to the question of Hardy's feminism. He has to lead the students here in an overt way, so that the earlier claim to open debate is necessarily overridden. Instead the tutor enacts for the students a process of exegesis. There is excitement in this since it shows an interpretative pattern forming. Student participation is, however, reduced. The argument is emergent but under control of the tutor.

Argumentative strategy: use interpreted evidence to connect with extratextual material and a wider context. Extrapolate from text to views of author. Start to pin down author's intentions.

The group moves on to consider the identification of Tess with sunshine and sunbeams, a line of imagery which culminates in the Stonehenge scene. The students' knowledge of the text is quite extensive as they pick out references here. They gather textual evidence as a collective activity. About Stonehenge the tutor asks: 'What is the point of that scene?' and a student replies tentatively: 'Is it any thing to do with Nature? Because you always associate mystical and natural things don't you?' At this prompt the tutor reads from the book:

> ...One could feel that a saner religion had never prevailed under the sky. The luminary was a golden-haired, beaming, mild-eyed, God-like creature, gazing down in the vigour and intentness of youth upon an earth that was brimming with interest for him. (Chapter 14)

7   NEW IDEA
The tutor raises the tantalising question:

> But there's another god in *Tess of the D'Urbervilles* which is the exact opposite of this kind and beneficent, loving, benign sun god. (*long pause*) Who's the other god?

The students do not supply an answer to this question but once the tutor makes it clear that he is thinking of the Calvinist God who signifies a religion of guilt and atonement, they are able to find references in the text to support his observation and comments at the larger thematic and structural level. It is clear that the tutor needs to supply the students with this information before he can draw interpretations from them

Argumentative strategy: play off one interpretation against another implicit in the textual searching.

8   CONCLUSIONS
Time constraints force the tutor at this point into an extended monologue in order to complete the argumentative process and, in a sense, to declare his hand. This is an abbreviated version:

> I think we ought to draw some conclusions, and, for speed, let me just summarise some of the things that we've been talking about. On the feminist question I think that there are different points of view being expressed and I think that we'll leave it open. It seems to *me* that there are strong anti-feminist elements in *Tess* – there are some feminist elements as well – but there are some strong anti-feminist elements – her docility, her passivism – suggest to me that Hardy's ideal woman is the kind of person that Ruskin would have liked [...] and that by associating her with nature he suggests that these things are natural in a woman [*etc.....*]

> But it's not just a naturalist story about a natural woman and her hypocritical lover with his dual sexual standards, its also a book about religion (*pause*) and this is where the *Paradise Lost* theme comes in.

> The whole poem is a Theodicy (*writes this on the board and explains it*) he ends the whole poem (*sic – novel*) with not a quote, but an allusion to the end of *Paradise Lost*. *Tess of the D'Urbervilles* is partly about the loss of paradise – she loses the paradise of her love of Angel Clare, and what's it caused by? (*pause*) It's complicated because there are two reasons really why she loses – two reasons are given in the book why she loses that paradise. One is simply social attitudes and class [...] and also a victim of socio-religious attitudes [...] but then Hardy also offers us another reason. He says the President of the Immortals has been sporting with Tess all the time (*pause*) and that the whole book is really an attack on the Calvinist religion, a kind of – not a theodicy – but an anti-theodicy [...]

> How can we resolve this contradiction? On the one hand he's given us a perfectly understandable set of actual circumstances which provide all the reasons you could possibly need for the tragedy – as a tragedy of society and social convention [...] on the other hand though, you've got all these references to fate, the cruelty of fate and the President of the Immortals (*pause*) it's almost as though Hardy wants to write a philosophical novel about Fate but what he's actually written is a social novel.

The tutor draws together the threads of the discussion, setting up a contradiction and implicitly inviting the students to be critical of the novel. Is the contradiction in fact resolvable in a such a way as to leave the novel as a successfully unified whole or is it a sign of weakness in the book?

In the course of the tutorial the text has been approached from a variety of angles. No single interpretative route traverses the whole of the text; each represents a different narrative construction. It is in bringing the various strands of interpretation together that the possibilities both of wholeness and fragmentation appear – of a validated 'text upon text' or a criticised 'text against text'.[3] In either case a process of argumentation occurs where different perspectives are brought together and evaluated for their compatibility. But there are different purposes at work in each case. The aim of hermeneutic practice (text upon text) is towards unity, and it is likely that this would be the impulse of the students too, given their prior training at A level.[4] The tutor is, however, keen to offer the students the opportunity and licence to be critical of the text in a negative way, to say, 'This is an unsuccessfully executed juxtaposition or passage'.

The tutor has modelled for the students an argumentative process of reading and interpreting the text, which though in terms of content is necessarily tendentious, is methodologically neutral. The methodology of argument, that is, is itself teleological. This strength is, however, also a weakness if the students remain on the outside of the thinking process and cannot recognise or capitalise upon it. If the essays are seen as evidence of what students have learnt in terms both of substance and method, one might hope to find there a reflection and extension of the tutorial process. How far did the students grasp the argumentative processes and strategies I identified above? How far were they aware of the direction in which these processes were leading? To what extent, in other words, were they involved the situation despite the tutor controlling its agenda?

The essays the students subsequently wrote in fact show little evidence of this discussion. They contain more in way of more deference to the work of critics than to the textual strategies, the identification and juxtaposition of themes, the analysis and categorisation of imagery that the tutor had used. Partly, I think this arises from the pre-setting of the essay question, which tends to obscure any sense that the writing might emerge from discussion. In addition, the absence in the essays of ideas from the spoken discourse is due to the difficulty of following an overall direction when one is engaged in 'turn by turn' understanding. As a researcher I frequently understand more of the process of argument when I look back at my notes and try to reconstruct them than I did when I was in the midst of it. This prompts me to wonder whether such reflective activity might be profitable to students also. When appropriate, they might be asked, instead of writing an essay, to review the process they had been through communally and to write up an account of its stages in note or prose form. This task would allow them to operate above the level of exemplification which is their main role in the lesson itself and give them insight into the way an argument can be constructed. It also allows them the chance to concretise ideas by slowing down and changing the focus of the learning. If the tutor has been in the 'position of power', controlling the discourse in the tutorial, this exercise can shift the balance back to the students. In terms of argument and discourse looking at *how* one has learnt, clarifies and even counts as what one has learnt.

Introducing Alternative Discourses

Just as speech seems to facilitate moves into disciplinary discourses so it may help to make transitions of or beyond them. This was the case with the debates held in Applied Biology and discussed in chapter 2. Below I offer an example of an initiative with Financial Accounting students which aimed to make them aware of contexts in which they might in

---

3 These are Scholes' (1985) definitions of the activities of interpretation and criticism respectively. See chapter 10 on English Theory for further discussion of these in relation to argument.
4 See Mitchell 1994b

future need to exercise their expertise. It's worth noticing too that the talk that occurs in this exercise is assessed as a part of the course. This is often the case where speech is used to address vocational aspects of a course. In these contexts, speech is not naturalised, but has named qualities: the emphasis is on presentation skills or role play within simulated settings.

Simulated Board Room Scenario

The aim of this exercise was for the students to become aware of a typical scenario in which a financial accountant might find him or herself working and to understand and work with the points of view of a range of other people beside themselves. In a working commercial environment the financial accountant's assessment of a situation is likely to be only one among several. Decisions are made as a result of a complex variety of human factors. The exercise aimed to make students aware of this by requiring them to take on roles as members of a company and to develop arguments which accorded with these roles. This involved understanding particular agendas and preoccupations and using flexibility and imagination in an unfolding interactive situation. For most roles it also involved putting aside financial knowledge and reasoning and finding other effective arguments to support a position.

According to the tutor it is not uncommon for an accountant to audit a firm without knowing what it actually produces. In his view this is where disciplinary training is at its weakest. In the highly pressurised culture of accountancy, where success is determined by purely theoretical examinations, individuals can emerge with little confidence and few interpersonal skills. The role play exercise aims in some way to redress this balance, by insisting upon students' understanding of real-life factors and contexts – the impact, for instance of a financial decision (such as closure) on a community. The accountant, that is to say, needs to recognise the argument of, for instance, a shop steward that redundancies create bad feelings which have a knock on effect.

The role play exercise followed a lecture given by the tutor on Departmental Accounts which described accountancy as an 'information system' and introduced the idea that other factors might influence a department's viability within a store than pure profit. Something along these lines:

> Do we close department D?
> Yes – it is obviously losing money.
> New information – it is a novelty department, situated next to the off-licence, which entices the public into the store. [...]
> You can see that the accounting information is only part of the story.
> There may be other factors at work.

What Happened

The exercise was developed from what had originally been a case study of 'Hopeless Store PLC', where students would be required to offer a written critique of figures produced by an assistant accountant in the chief accountant's absence. The assistant accountant's figures had suggested that there was a case for closing the hardware department in the store, leaving scope for the possible expansion of the other departments – furniture and clothing. This scenario was maintained, but members of each tutorial group took on the roles of company members at a board meeting to consider what should be done. Thus tutorial groups were transformed into board meetings comprising: the Managing Director, the Accountant and Assistant Accountant, the Heads of Hardware, Clothing and Furniture, the Store Administrator, and the specially invited Shop Steward.

The meetings were generally sustained for half an hour or so, presided over by the Managing Director (MD) who welcomed guests and invited participants to report on their interests and to comment. Some meetings concluded with a vote, in one case overridden by the MD, others with the instruction that Heads of Department should draw up more detailed reports and investigate suggestions raised. One meeting resulted in mass resignations and several groups included amongst Any Other Business, items such as staff parties and the firm's proposed sponsorship of a football team. These extensions of the basic script indicated the students' imaginative involvement and above all that the exercise was fun.

At the end of the meetings the tutor offered comments on what had taken place, praising people's strategies and ideas and pointing out where they could have been strengthened or developed and where certain behaviour may have been inappropriate – e.g. the MD antagonising the shop steward. He also presented the students with a 'right answer' to the problems raised. This, of course returned them to the accountancy point of view; in the role play, however, and in a real-life scenario, the financially correct answer is not always deemed the right one. What the company or the MD decides is right until time and circumstances prove it wrong. Caught up in the roles and argumentative processes of the Board Meeting the students were actually experiencing the fact that what is 'right' depends not on figures but on point of view.

Role Play

The students were expected to adopt a high degree of verisimilitude. They needed to produce the minutes for a previous meeting at which the accounts had been first presented in the absence of the accountant, an agenda for the present meeting and to produce minutes after the event, including a date for the next meeting. These specific tasks helped to structure the improvisation itself. There was an expectation that though the exercise could and should be playful – some students prepared refreshments and planned dramatic resignations – it was also to be taken seriously. For many students the role play offered the opportunity to ventriloquise behaviours and rhetorical forms, caught somewhere between parody and earnestness.

> Store adm.: (*business-like tone*) Right well, ah, I note with interest what the assistant accountant has to say really. It's nice to see that he has learnt all his theoretical basis at university, but, um, but really. His techniques really have no relevance to this job as we see it...

It is interesting to note the repertoire of persuasive, negotiating and conciliatory language that many students have, but which is not frequently called into use in the everyday teaching and learning situation: 'We've all seen...', 'I would agree...', 'As you know....', 'Obviously...' 'At the end of the day...'. These kinds of language facilitate interaction and suggest a degree of control over what one wishes to say.

Role play is not always easy for all people. It demands a degree of confidence to project a persona; also flexibility and initiative in developing responses to challenges for which one might not be prepared. Some students like the one above clearly enjoyed the chance to be in role and used it as a licence to develop strong argumentative or authoritative positions. Others were more reticent and spoke only when invited to, sometimes sticking closely to a prepared script. I think it was clear, however, that most of the students gained something from going through the process, even if only to realise that the simulated situation was possible and could be sustained: 'I was surprised at how well we did', said one student, who had entered into a fierce debate. In many ways the success of the role play derives from the unfolding argument which itself requires a commitment. In one case the MD sought to close the meeting with a vote for or against the closure of the hardware department, but one member of the board decided to abstain. Asked to give his reasons, he objected to the vote as an oversimplification of the previous discussion:

X: Because you can't say yes or no when we don't know what we're going to do with the hardware. I want to decide what we're going to do with it first before we decide whether to close it or not.

MD: That would need to be discussed at another meeting

X: Exactly, so I can't make a decision yet.

MD: Okay, fair enough.

Again there are moments where a rather static role play – at the beginning of the board meeting – moves into a more convincing and spontaneous advocacy as the speaker responds to the interaction. In this example the Head of Furniture picks up on an earlier suggestion that garden furniture should be introduced into the space released by reducing the size of the hardware store.

HoF: If it's going to be garden furniture, right well, that's my department. I know how to sell it. we've got the expertise which they haven't.

MD: That would mean expanding your department then? Rather than anyone else's which means your profits will go up.

HoF: Yes.

MD: Which obviously you're more interested in , more bonuses for you, which means the hardware department is still going to shut.

HoF: I'm looking at it, I'm looking at it...

MD: Yuh, but you....

HoF: An overall view of the company. Do you want to be successful or not? If I can make the company more successful what's wrong with that?

MD: No I agree with what you're saying I do agree with what you're saying, but I think that whatever happens the hardware department is going to lose out here.

In this role play a situation developed in which the Head of Furniture was distrusted as 'empire building', despite his claims of concern for the overall good. The scenario allowed students the freedom to interpret their roles and also obliged them to do so, as they were challenged by others and as new ideas and suggestions arose.

These new ideas were quite extensive: arguments put forward included the effect on local feeling of redundancies, the fairness of apportioning fixed costs, the relocation of departments, cash sales versus credit agreements, diversification of merchandise, including novelty and seasonal goods, an off-licence, a taxi service, a car park, shops within shops, the need for retraining, the effect on staff morale. Of course not all of these arguments were presented within any one board meeting, but the tutor was able at the end to suggest additions and students were then able to see how they might have used or responded to them.

Evaluation

The exercise was judged a success by the tutor, who was impressed by the enthusiasm and engagement of the students. Each group was given an overall grade based on the actual board meeting and the written documentation in the form of agendas and minutes.
In my view such an exercise introduced into a series of lectures and tutorials is worthwhile:

- it encourages students to reflect upon the discipline they are learning, by requiring them to move outside it or to see it in context

- it begins to prepare them for the application of their specialised skills outside the university

- it breaks the introverted culture of the discipline (in one simple sense, because this is a *group* activity)

- it uses and practices speaking and communication skills (and values these, because the exercise is assessed)

- it makes passive knowledge dynamic and argumentative.

These learning outcomes are far broader than those which would have resulted from the case study exercise alone and I imagine that what was learnt here will be beneficial to students' later work and importantly to their sense of the activity they are engaged in. The principles of what was learned here could be applied elsewhere. Depending on course priorities, the exercise might also be extended by a period of reflecting on behaviours, strategies and suggested solutions, possibly using a video-recording of the proceedings. The role play would also almost certainly be enhanced if students were able to experience a real life scenario. And this relates to my main reservation about the exercise: that it pretends real life on the basis of little or no actual experience. The very real possibility of stereotyping a situation of which one has no first hand experience seemed, however, to diminish as the improvisations took over and the 'players' became involved in interactive arguments. Nonetheless the exercise could not be thought of as supplying the actual knowledge students would need in a real situation of this kind (see Freedman 1994); its purpose had to be to change the students' perceptions within the academic framework rather than to act as a substitute for experience outside it (see chapter 8 where the problematic nature of addressing 'real world' needs within educational contexts is explored further).

Suggestion: Questions for the Development of Argument

The aim of this exercise is to elicit not only opinion but also the grounds for opinion and to test for awareness of alternative opinions. Its secondary aim is to give teachers and students practice in asking searching neutral questions; questions, that is, in which judgement is suspended. The exercise thus gives to speech some of the time for reflection and development which is usually the preserve of the teacher and of writing. The exercise provides opportunity for discussion of the nature and structure of argument.

The first task is to choose a question related to an issue which contains within it some potential for debate. This might be: What causes unemployment? What causes famine in Africa?

The class is split into pairs; A adopts the role of questioner, whilst B gives his or her opinion. A proceeds to question with the aim of uncovering the grounds for B's opinion – or to put it another way the arguments which might substantiate it. For instance, on the question, 'Do you believe we should have a referendum on Europe?' A asks B:

- *Why do you believe that?*

- *Can you give up to three reasons for your opinion?*

- *Taking the first reason only, what evidence do you have to support it?*

- *If you were asked to prove your reason, how could you do it?*

Then, because convincing arguments generally include an acknowledgement or understanding of another's point of view, A asks B:

- *What reasons would a person whose view is different to yours give? (up to 3 reasons)*

- *What evidence could they give to support their main reason?*

- *What could they do to prove their reason is correct?*

A notes down the results of the enquiry and reports back to a plenary session.

If there is enough time the roles can be reversed at this stage. The arguments can then be summarised on the board and become the material for further discussion. There are all sorts of possibilities open at this stage. Discussion can take place either as a group or between re-paired students with different views. As could be allowed to offer a critique of what they have neutrally listened to and Bs to defend themselves or make concessions. In this way, not only is the issue seen as one which can be viewed in several ways, but the processes of argument themselves can come under review. The discussion might move to why one person's opinion is more convincingly defended than another's. If, for example, someone has used a single anecdote as evidence, is this enough? Is it enough in some contexts, but not in others? If someone is unable to think of an alternative view, how does this effect the validity of their argument etc.?

6. Exploring Ground Rules

In the course of this project it has become clear that there are often discrepancies between the way the content and practices which constitute disciplines are viewed by teachers and students, and similarly, though not necessarily identically, by experts and students (novices). The differences have strong implications for the conduct of argument, since they frequently revolve around questions of whether learning constitutes knowledge reproduced or knowledge criticised, transformed or made new; it centres, that is, on differences between narrative and argumentative stances towards the world and these in turn are conditioned by such factors as pedagogical practices, ideological assumptions and the institutional as well as individual place of the student within the learning cycle (see Harré model, chapter 2).

In addition, questions have been raised about *how* students acquire the literate practices associated with argument in their disciplines; how, in effect, the criteria for disciplinary success are taught and learnt. In the teaching I have observed the learning of argument has largely been assumed to be a natural process embedded within the pattern of apprenticeship towards enculturation. That students do find difficulty in acquiring the skills and techniques of academic argument is witnessed in numerous places throughout this report and in other studies of students at all levels (e.g. Gorman et al. 1988, Britton at al. 1975, Gubb 1987, Freedman and Pringle 1984, Berrill 1990, 1992). How to make improvements to the teaching and learning of academic literacy and argument is by no means a straightforward issue. It is the subject of debates such as that surrounding the explicit teaching of genres (see, for instance, Freedman 1993a, 1993b, Williams and Colomb 1993, Fahnestock 1993 or the contributions in Reid (ed.) 1988). These debates spring from a general movement, more advanced in the United States and Australia than in Britain, towards teaching which explicitly addresses the features of and strategies used in workplace and discipline-specific writing. In Britain and certainly in the experience of this project, the move towards explicit teaching as a way of facilitating students' disciplinary enculturation has shown itself in the introduction of Induction programmes for first year undergraduates.

In chapter 7, I shall offer accounts of my experience of two such programmes. But here I want first to consider the differences between teachers, experts and students using both the research findings of others and some examples from my own research. Then I shall turn to questions of whether such differences need to be addressed and if so, how and at what stage. These issues raise further questions: should differences be addressed purely at the level of the teachers' instrumental expectations of what students should be doing within the discipline, or can there also be a case for 'philosophical' attention to the nature of the learning and the grounds upon which knowledge and arguments are made? These questions come more fully into focus when the examples of induction have been discussed and so chapters 6 and 7 need ideally to be read together. The final chapter in this grouping, chapter

8, is a case study of an initiative in Electronic Engineering where students were asked to argue for a certain type of technical advance and against another. Since the context for this task was given as a 'real world' one, the students were in effect being asked to operate in a new genre. However, as the study shows, the 'ground rules' of this genre were not sufficiently apparent for many of the students to complete the task successfully. The case illustrates and extends the issues raised in the preceding two chapters concerning the effective communication and learning of literate practices.

Mismatches

The difference between narrative and argumentative stances towards knowledge and authority underlies Kaufer and Geisler's (1989) characterisations of 'novice' and 'expert' writers – and by extension, readers. On the one hand, the two *experts* in their study carefully situated themselves as:

> both accountable to and different from the authors of the source material. They treated the questions 'What do I believe?' and 'What can I say that is different?' as mutual constraints on the contributions they allowed themselves to entertain. Positions that our experts judged to be deeply felt, true, or credible finally meant little to them if they did not also judge them to be *different* to points made previously. [...] They knew that sources played a constructive role in their own argument, as support and elaboration for their own inquiry. Yet they also knew they played a contrastive role as well. (p. 295)

The two *novices*, on the other hand,

> ...lacked the knowledge or skill to interplay two competing impulses: the impulse to account for the information one inherits from a cultural community (represented in sources) and the impulse to move beyond these givens by breaking a consensus within them. (p. 297)

One of the students, whilst recognising that the sources disagreed with each other, selected from them the claims she found most appealing, and wrote about them in a formal academic style. She did not however demonstrate 'authorial presence or control' (p. 296). The other student mostly developed a position independent of the sources based on her personal experiences and beliefs, so that whilst she was following the impulse to be different, she failed 'to use her sources as an enabling vehicle in her plan to be different'(p. 297). She failed, that is, to realise that in the academic context, idiosyncrasy does not count as newness or originality.[1]

Much the same distinctions between experts and novices inform assessment criteria both at A level and for the undergraduate degree (see chapter 2 for the example of A level History). Assessment guidelines for staff and students produced by a university Humanities School make the following distinctions:

Third Class

Work of this kind might contain some relevant material in relation to the topic, but treated in a largely descriptive way. For example, essays falling into this category tend to be

---

[1] This situatedness is not exclusive to strictly academic contexts. The analysis of the criteria for English Language essays at A level (chapter 9) provides interesting examples of this. Similarly the case study of Fine Art (chapter 3) reveals the extent to which highly individual art work must show 'evidence' of orientation for it to be most successful.

limited to assertions of the type: 'This is what is...' 'This is what I think...' 'This is what I have done...' In other words there is little evidence of the writer reflecting upon the material, being critical, seeing that there are issues to be discussed, arguments to be made. [...]

Lower Second

A good deal of the work produced falls into this category. [...] Work in this class addresses the question, but like third class work tends towards the descriptive rather than the analytical. It will go beyond the mere assertions found in third class work, and published work will be referred to as well as lecture material. However, authorities will tend to be accepted uncritically. In some cases it may be that reference is made to too narrow a range of background texts.

Upper Second

In addition to being consistently relevant and addressing the issues directly, work in this class has some of the following features:

- analysis rather than mere description
- sense of context
- sense of argument
- reference to relevant literature
- some theoretical underpinning

First

Marks in this band are awarded to outstanding work which:

- shows an awareness of the problematic nature of issues
- is analytical and critical
- develops an argument
- evaluates evidence
- uses theoretical and other texts critically (rather than seeing them as the 'last word')

Though the issues are not framed in the same way as in Kaufer and Geisler's novelty theory, the third class degree approximates quite closely to novice behaviour, whilst the first class degree tends towards expert behaviour. There is, for instance, a distinctly more teleological import between the 'sense of argument' which characterises a 2:1 and the 'develops an argument' of the First. At the same time, however, this teleology does not obscure 'an awareness of the problematic nature of issues'. Development of a thesis is dependent on what is problematic and contradictory; also on orientation to the disciplinary context and texts[2]. (This complexity is not always recognised in the way argument is described. See chapter 9).

I have noted the different ways in which argument is described as worthy of an upper second or a first, yet how helpful or informative are these descriptors? What do they actually tell the student about how to succeed in argument? How does a 'sense of context' show itself? What determines the 'relevance' of literature? What constitutes 'evaluation'?[3] In these

---

[2] It has been suggested to me on more than one occasion in the course of this research that another form of orientation students must learn is to the particular preferences of their tutors. Particularly on courses where students have a good idea who is likely to assess their essays, it can be prudent to gear one's argument towards the prefeerence of the marker. Part of the sophistication of final year students lies in their ability to situate their individual tutors within the broader disciplinary context and then to orientate themselves accordingly.

[3] A study by Mathison (1994), for instance, revealed that, in Sociology writing, negative evaluation of evidence was more highly rated than positive.

criteria, 'context', 'argument' and 'relevant literature' are listed as separate points – a kind of checklist – rather than as parts of an integrated process. The student below expresses her sense of bewilderment at what words such as these might actually mean for the work she does (in this case the words are part of the tutor's commentary on her first essay):

> Mary: And so you blunder along blindly actually and you make a lot of mistakes and, okay so [the tutor's] comments might put light on this or that but actually you still feel that you're plodding along blindly, because you still haven't got the overall picture. It's very difficult, I often feel that I'm plodding around in the dark...

The writer of the above criteria does in fact goes on to offer typifications of how the differences between degree classes might be manifested in essays in order to raise students' awareness 'of what they are doing in each of their sentences and paragraphs, and to consider other possibilities'. In these typifications, too, sophistication is achieved through orientation to texts:

1. **I think x... I think y...**
Primitive assertions of opinion without evidence to support the contentions being made.

2. **School text book or writer X says...**
Too much reliance on a single authority. A frequent fault at an early stage of a course, and often the result of a lack of confidence. Sometimes the result of trying to avoid mere assertion of opinion described in the previous example.

3. **Writer X thinks...and writer Y thinks...**
The glimmerings of a critical sense – displays knowledge that there can be more than one view of the matter. However, these authoritative statements are simply juxtaposed.

4. **Although Writer X says x and Y says y, I think z (or I agree with X or Y because...)**
This shows more confidence in contrasting published opinions and coming to a personal view.

5. **I think x because...** (organised evidence)

6. **I think x because theory X leads me to this conclusion**
As above this may be effective or mechanical depending on how it is done.

7. **Theory X says x; I think it can be related to my subject in this way...**

8. **Theory X says x. I will modify it (or show it to be correct or incorrect) with reference to: evidence/text/context/other theories**

9. **Writer X says x, Y says y, theory Z can explain the differences in their explanations**

The scheme is an instance of the institution attempting to clarify for its students the ways in which it evaluates certain writing strategies in contrast to others (the higher numbers tend on the whole to describe writing which is more highly valued).[4] These concrete examples seem likely to be of more help than the abstract descriptions.

What are the reasons for the differences between the most successful 'expert' writing and what 'a good deal of the work' students do is like? The reasons can be cognitive; knowledge and understanding representing low level cognitive skills and application, synthesis and evaluation representing higher ones. The amount of knowledge and, therefore, the degree of orientation will also be a factor, though knowledge is not straightforwardly linked to

---

[4] The degree criteria and the typifications were given to the students who took the Induction Module on argument described in chapter 7 when their essays were returned to them.

argument (more knowledge, more argument) but depends on strategic use. In addition it is not simply that students fail to argue, but that they fail to argue in ways specific to the discipline.[5]

The differences may also result from attitudes to and expectations of learning, which then have knock-on effects on cognitive development. Donald (1992) notes how research has shown:

> ...that many college and university students develop a surface approach to learning in which they memorize without developing either the representations or methods which will allow them to retrieve, relate and use the content at a later date [...]. If students assume that learning consists of amassing specific bits of information, they will not expend the effort to relate and incorporate them into meaningful representations. (p. 413)

Donald makes a connection between the way students conceive of areas of learning and the way in which courses are typically described – in terms of the topics to be studied, rather than the strategies to be employed (p. 413). There is thus a link between the individual behaviours of students and the institutional framing.

Another study (Spivey, Mathison, Goggin and Greene 1992) looked at the way students and teachers thought of the writing they did in psychology and found that:

> Most of the students [...] believed their professors assigned writing for epistemic purposes, to help them learn the material of psychology better. By contrast, most of the professors reported that they assigned writing to help their students learn how to think and write like psychologists, to enculturate their students into psychology. (in Goggin, 1994)[6]

Taken together with Donald's observations about course descriptions an assumption might be made that although professors might think of learning as a process of enculturation, they are perhaps not successful at communicating this to their students. There seem to be contradictory messages being communicated, if they are communicated at all.

The disjunction between the students and teachers is startling in some ways, unsurprising in others. It indicates, I think, a tension in educational aims and philosophies – roughly that between the Platonic and Socratic models outlined earlier (chapter 2). One might be seen as stressing texts as 'univocal', the other as 'thinking devices' (Lotman 1988); one stressing knowledge and authority, the other discourse and process. The emphasis on one or the other also varies from discipline to discipline and according to the level of the students, but it is rarely inherent or inevitable in any situation; a result rather of construction and choice.

As I suggested in chapter 4, the tensions between different conceptions of the educational enterprise can manifest themselves in disjunctions between what occurs in class or group discussions and what is subsequently recorded in written work. Whilst speech (interactive

---

5 Within specific contexts not all arguments are equally valued. See chapter 13 for an examination of arguments which are more and less successful in Sociology.

6 It is interesting to note that despite their aim to enculturate the students, the genres the professors asked the students to write in were either not those used by expert psychologists or were not understood as such by the students who 'held a monolithic view of academic writing (i.e.academic writing is all one genre)'. It may be that as Williamson (1988) has noted the aim of writing in this context was not for the students to become professionals in the discipline, but rather for them to use its argument for personal 'liberal' purposes. What Williamson is suggesting is that not all disciplines have an internal vocation as their aim, at least before doctoral level.

speech at least) might easily be seen as a medium in which meanings are explored and made, writing frequently has the status, in our educational system, of finished product, as carrying authority and therefore in some way needing to express certainties.

Addressing what she calls 'the cultural imperatives underlying cognitive acts', McCormick (1990) looks at three stances that students often bring to – and derive from – their schooling (specifically, their writing): 'the desire for closure; a belief in objectivity; and a refusal to write about perceived contradictions'(p. 195)[7]. Each of these stances has been evident in this research. For example, Electronic Engineering students are reported by their tutor to be reluctant, once they have arrived at a numerical answer to a process of investigation, to interpret that answer further and assess its adequacy as a solution to the particular problem set. In essay writing (see, for instance, chapter 7) a frequent tendency is to list rather than to comment on discrepancies between items in the list. McCormick suggests that these behaviours are not so much the result of 'laziness' or an unwillingness to think, but rather are underpinned by ideological assumptions, behaviours learnt in other situations and, in some cases, misinterpretations of instructions from teachers.

The following extract from a discussion between a Philosophy tutor and his first year students provides an example of the mixed messages that can pass between the different players in the educational game. The exchange starts with me querying a comment that has been made earlier:

SM: Is there a stumbling block about how much evidence, or how much you've read and picked up that other people have thought? I mean I don't know much about philosophy essays, so is that a factor?

Pete: With the tutorial essays evidence of reading does come into it a lot.

Tutor: Do you think so? Have I ever said this to you?

Pete: No no no, but if you've look, if I wrote an essay and you, I wouldn't want you to think, 'Crikey, he's done no reading for that he's just done it off the top of his head' I got, you know, I always try and put something into it.

Tutor: But what if you had done it off the top of your head and it was a brilliant piece of work, what do you think I would say?

Pete: Yeah, you'd say it was good, but, you'd have thought, you wouldn't think very much of me if you'd realised and thought I'd not done any work for it. It would be more like luck, than actually working for the essay.

Tutor: Do you think that? (To Julie)

Julie: I think you need to know what you're on about.

Tutor: I mean if I ask you to write on Plato, an essay on Plato's Ideal State and you do that off the top of your head, that might be at question. If I ask you to write on the mind and the brain and you did that off the top of your head, why do you think I would penalise you for not showing that you'd read anything?

Pete: You may not penalise me , but you'd still think I hadn't done any work for it.

Tutor: Really? (laughs)

Jane: When the answer is different, maybe. I think this is the problem I have. I think that I've got to answer it within the guidelines of what the book's talking about, otherwise it starts to become irrelevant and this is the difficulty. You've got to

---

[7] These are discussed more fully in chapter 9.

read to know which direction it's going otherwise...you know you could write about mind and brain if you'd never done Philosophy. But it's got to be tackled from a standpoint from the book.

Tutor: I think there's a practical reason why it's a good idea to do the reading, but it's interesting how strongly you put it really, because I think Philosophy is one of the subjects where it is possible to actually produce brilliant work without referring to any other reading. Of course if you're a genius you can do this. Assuming that we're not all geniuses then it is a good idea to do the reading. [...]

Jane: Wouldn't you get marked more though in an exam if you referred to a philosopher or a book, if you remember it? I mean this was often taught at college, you should show evidence of what you've read.

Tutor: Not necessarily. I think this is one of the differences between essay writing here and essay writing you've done before. You don't have to throw in quotes to prove that you've got a grasp of this.

As Pete perceives it, the tutor is interested not so much in what his students are capable of producing in the way of thought or argument, but rather what they can show they have done in the way of work. Work here is seen very much in terms of the outward show of scholarliness and seems to be contrasted with some notion of thinking (perhaps conceived of as opinion) as leisurely. Though the tutor might want to shift the students away from this way of thinking about their subject, the way Jane rephrases the problem makes the distinction more subtle. She seems to be saying that attention to precedent within the subject is necessary if they are to pick up its discourse. The way an issue *has been* discussed philosophically provides clues to the way they too must talk about it philosophically. She probably has a point: writing 'off the top of your head' is not actually what the tutor wants from students whose heads are not yet filled with philosophical thought. On the other hand, it does seem important that the tutor redress the balance: he is not primarily interested in evidence that students have spent most of their week reading to produce an essay; ultimately he is concerned with the quality of thinking and argument.

Authoritative Statement or Collaborative Investigation? – How Can the Mismatches be Addressed?

In the case above, the mismatches between teacher and students perceptions are revealed through the dialogue that took place and a number of discoveries were made on both sides. This example returns me to the questions raised at the beginning of this chapter: is it valuable for such mismatches to be addressed and if so, how and when? I think there are a number of reasons favouring increased attention to the ways in which participants perceive the educational enterprise: the reduction of anxiety is one; the improvement of students' performance surely another; a third relates to the possibility of reflexivity and critique in regard to the forms, conditions and tenets of study; and a fourth, arising in some way from all of these, to the increased participation of students, the sharing of power.

A number of options – and difficulties – in achieving this kind of 'openness' and approaching these kinds of ends have emerged in the course of this project. They can be roughly divided into the following types: the 'presentational' (which involves direct, explicit and generally decontextualised teaching) and the 'environmental' (which involves the use specific criteria on concrete materials and problems) (Hillocks 1986). The environmental approach values the experiential, but also structures what the experience shall be in quite deliberate ways. It is thus distinct from an approach which sees learning as natural and to some extent inevitable (an approach which also, it seems to me, favours natural selection). In the next chapter, on Induction, two examples are given: the first attempts to be explicit in a largely presentational way, the second, through a more environmental approach. They are drawbacks in each case and some important questions are raised about the induction process.

I want here, however, to consider the context in which the tutorial discussion above arose and to explore through it some of the complex issues which crowd around this area of academic literacy learning.

What is significant about the extract above is its exploratory nature; the discussion itself seems to have brought about increased understanding, rather than any explicit instruction. The Philosophy tutor, Steve Burwood, decided to address the question of communication between teacher and students in regard to one of his discipline's central activities: the writing of essays. Essays in Philosophy form the basis of tutorial discussions, rather than their outcome. Steve was suspicious of using a checklist approach to 'essay writing' since he didn't feel this would deepen the first year students' understanding of the enterprise in any significant way. Nor did he really feel that the features and purposes of the essay could be accounted for in that way without misrepresenting the holistic way in which he would actually read or listen to and assess an essay. He therefore decided to produce an extensive discursive 'Introduction to Essay Writing', with full sections on 'Why Write Essays?', 'The Nature of the Essay', 'Preparing and Writing the Essay' and 'Assessment Criteria'. It was significant that the assessment criteria were introduced only towards the end of the booklet with the caveat that 'marking essays in Philosophy is more of an art than a science' and that 'the criteria themselves allow of a certain degree of flexibility in their application'; the idea was that students should get to these only after immersing themselves in the fuller discussion. The following paragraph is an example of the approach Steve took:

> Academic style, for example, often prefers an impersonal approach which avoids contaminating the essay with the personality of the author. You should be aware of this aspect of academic writing, but do not let it unduly worry you. Emphasis on this can be overdone. In adopting this style one is expected to put forward views as if they were not one's own, in an attempt to obtain some pseudo-objectivity; "It may be argued that…", "Later in the essay it will be shown…", "The analogy drawn earlier…" etc.. However, I would contend that one thing which distinguishes philosophers from mere disputants is a commitment to the truth of what they are arguing and a belief that *their* arguments make a difference […] Therefore it may be argued that a personal style still has a place in the context of the Philosophy Essay; "I wish to argue that…", "I do not agree…" "In my opinion…" etc.. More important than this is that academic style demands the essay must be **argumentative**: not, of course, in the sense of being quarrelsome but in the sense of supporting what you say with **reasons**. This is a requirement of ALL academic writing regardless of subject and particular situation. In my view it is acceptable if you write "I believe that Plato's Ideal State is an authoritarian nightmare", for example, but only if you go on to say why you believe this is so. By itself, your belief is worthless in the academic context: it is simply an uninteresting fact about your psychology and tells me nothing about the failings of Plato's political theory. You must therefore be prepared to back up what you say with evidence and reasoned argument. (Burwood 1994, p. 5)

Just taking this extract, there a number of things to be said. First, there is a sense in which the writer is communicating personally with his readers, rather than seeking to speak categorically for the department or discipline as a whole. Steve seemed to think this was important and he was reluctant for the booklet to be seen to represent the department's views. His attitude in this respect appears to be a recognition of the variations which exist within the disciplinary community and that satisfactory communication always involves the negotiation of specific contexts rather than standard generalised responses. This leads me to a second point about this particular paragraph: the general statement that all academic writing requires argument supported by reasons. This it seems to me is not true and where it is true is too sweeping to be useful. The students themselves know differently – and this takes me to my third point: the booklet shouldn't be seen as an end in itself, but is activated by the discussion and reflection it is allowed to generate. In discussion, Steve's general statement is modified by the experiences of the students themselves:

Jane: I think so yeah, because I want to know what I'm not doing enough of or too much of as regards writing philosophically. Because it's a totally different way of writing.

Tutor: To what?

Jane: To doing an essay that's factual, like on the N.H.S. or like something to do with the E.D.O. [Extra Departmental Option]. I've just done a Women's Studies essay on a medical problem and it's a lot different to writing philosophically.

Tutor: In what way?

Jane: You can't really put...You can put your own opinion, but evidently we, I have Sociology as part of my E.D.O. and she told us in no uncertain terms that she didn't want our opinions in it. It had to be really regurgitating material and as long as it was relevant to what we were talking about, but there wasn't much scope for your own ideas. But on saying that to write philosophically you don't always have your own ideas.[8]

Steve gave out his booklet, *Essay writing: an Introduction*, at the beginning of the second term of first year study and the discussions which were based on it took place at the end of that term, so that the students had time to read and make use of it during the term. Prior to the discussions he also asked students to write an essay which would be assessed by a fellow student rather than read aloud or marked by him. The opportunity of **peer assessing**[9] gave the discussions a concrete experiential grounding, which seemed very effective:

Pete: I think its quite useful to try and look for things in an essay and you've got to, like it makes you think about how you write more as well; it makes you look more at certain things.

Tutor: What sorts of things?

Pete: Reasoned argument and developing it from one point to the next. Mal did it quite well, where I think it made me realise how disorganised I was as I was writing, because I was just chopping and changing.

Reading an essay other than one's own goes against some deeply engrained assumptions about the individual nature of writing in educational contexts, but here it allows the reader to bring to a level of consciousness certain features and techniques of writing and from there to reflect upon his own practices as a writer. The discussion also revealed that the students wrote differently for each other than for the tutor; they made a greater effort to be clear and one student felt he had more licence to be polemical, since he knew that the reader

---

[8] Jane's final comment again picks up on her sense of disorientation within the discourse of Philosophy. What she expresses can be neatly matched against Harré's model of learning: she feels she needs to have appropriated sufficiently from what is public and collective before she can have her own opinions.

[9] See the section on dialogic forms in chapter 12 for an example of how students can engage in extensive questioning of their peers when given the opportunity to do so through writing.

of his essay shared his own views. The effect that the particular reader made on the writing was not an anticipated outcome of the peer assessment, but it catalysed the discussion in useful and enlightening ways.

Towards the end of the discussion, the tutor's view began to emerge more clearly. In the end it was one of the students, Jane who managed to pin it down:

Jane: Really writing an essay in another subject, now I think is probably easy, but with Philosophy it's being able to have the idea of the 'for and against' and 'why' that is probably the hardest part of writing. You've got to really know what you think about it before you can write and sometimes you don't even understand it.

Tutor: This 'for and against' is interesting as well isn't it? Because we in a sense, one of the things I'm looking for is you're weighing up different positions, and that's why in a sense it's not a bad thing to find yourself questioning your own opinions. And nearly all the time a method that people will use in philosophy is to test their opinion against another position. And especially you will try and find the strongest position to try and test it against. You know, this is what Descartes is doing with philosophical doubt. You know he's testing it with another one.[...] I mean it doesn't have to be specifically against an actual philosopher, it's the position that you're interested in, that's why Paul might say 'It may be argued that...' and then introduce an argument which may be contrary to his own and then try and see which one of these is the stronger. That's the important thing really.

Jane: So when you're looking at a philosophical essay and you mark it, it's not so much all the knowledge you have, it's how you've written it and how you've argued it that's important, is it?

Tutor: Yeah, precisely.

Jane: So you can have like three ideas and argue them well, and have ten and not put one good argument to it.

Tutor: Absolutely. I couldn't have said it clearer myself. That's exactly right.

In effect what has occurred here is an airing of 'ground rules'. This is the term used by Sheeran and Barnes (1991) to describe the frequently inexplicit messages that the student must recognise in order to perform successfully within disciplines, for particular occasions and for individual teachers. The invisibility of ground rules can make the educational process a guessing game and can disadvantage students who fail to pick up on what is required. Sheeran and Barnes make the point that:

> Though we use the term "rules", we do not see them as similar to the binding rules of a club, for example, but rather as a description of patterns of behaviour that can be observed, but which are open to change and reinterpretation. Thus they are a topic for collaborative investigation rather than authoritative statement. (p. 120)

This distinction seems vitally important and it links to what happened with Steve's project in philosophy. Valuable though the discursively written booklet seemed to have been to students, its full potential only began to be realised when it acted as the stimulus for the exchange of perceptions and experiences. The role that experience played in the discussions should not be overlooked; it warns against the kind of approach to explicitness which gets it over with in the first week or so of term and leaves no space for retrospective reflection in the future. In the circular model of learning and personal identity projects offered by Harré (see chapter 2) the operation of Publication where the individual moves into the public can be seen as an opportunity to review and reflect upon the *processes undergone*, before moving on to renew the cycle. The question of when to address what students perceive and what teachers expect, is, I think, answered here: periodically, as part of on-going processes of negotiation and re-negotiation. Such processes open, in addition, possibilities for change as well as blueprinting; for teachers to adapt to the needs of students as well as students to align themselves with the expectations of teachers.

Saying this does not mean that a course of study should not begin with some discussion of expectations both on the part of teachers and of students, but that these should be provisional and open to revision in the light of experience. Within limits, of course: there is always a question of power in such discussions – and the teacher's is the powerful role. But the sharing of what the powerful want is also to some degree a sharing of power. What was impressive about the discussions Steve instigated for his students was his evident capacity to be surprised and interested by what they said to him: the learning was not all on one side.

The question remains, however, as to whether Steve's approach will produce *better* essays from his students. There is considerable debate about what, if any, forms of explicit teaching can improve students acquisition of skills and this would need to be tested further. Notwithstanding the discussion, misunderstandings may still be present and, beyond this, what the students now know at a conscious level, they may yet not be able to translate into practical knowledge in writing.

Moves Towards Meta-awareness

What is beginning to emerge here, I think, is the possibility of more than an instrumental motive and outcome for the investigation of ground rules and instead, or in addition, a new dimension which might be termed a 'meta-understanding' of the processes of enculturation.

This gives us two ways of looking at argument here; firstly as a form of behaviour appropriate to or embedded within the disciplinary discourse and context; secondly as a form of reflection or of reflexivity – a position of otherness – in relation to that discipline. James Gee (1989) maintains that explicit instruction in a discourse is not possible:

> Discourses are not mastered by overt instruction (even less so than languages, and hardly anyone ever fluently acquired a second language sitting in a classroom), but by enculturation ("apprenticeship") into social practices through scaffolded and supported interaction with people who have already mastered the discourse. (p. 7)

Whilst this issue is not resolved for me, I am interested in what Gee sees an alternative approach to learning discourse – through some kind of meta-awareness. What he proposes has a distinctly political edge to it, because as he notes discourses themselves are political and exclude as well as include:

> … there happens to be an advantage to failing to master mainstream Discourses, that is, there is an advantage to being socially "maladapted". When we have really mastered anything (e.g., a Discourse) we have little or no conscious awareness of it (indeed, like dancing, Discourses wouldn't work if people were consciously aware of what they were doing whilst doing it). However, when we come across a situation where we are unable to accommodate or adapt (as many minority students do on being faced, late in the game, with having to acquire mainstream Discourses), we become consciously aware of what we are trying to do or are being called upon to do. […]

Vygotsky (1987) says that learning a foreign language "allows the child to understand his native language as a single instantiation of a linguistic system"(p. 222). And here we have a clue. Classroom instruction (in language, composition, study skills, writing, critical thinking, content-based literacy, or whatever) can lead to meta-knowledge, to seeing how the Discourses you have already got relate to those you are attempting to acquire, and how the ones you are trying to acquire relate to self and society. Meta-knowledge is liberation and power, because it leads to the ability to manipulate, to analyse, to resist while advancing. (p. 12-13)

Whilst Gee makes the case for meta-awareness or critique as a powerful tool for those disadvantaged by institutional systems, what he suggests also has strong implications for those students for whom entry into academic environments has been a 'natural' progression. It is frequently these students who have internalised such ideological assumptions as McCormick identified above and which hamper the progress of their apprenticeships.

Courses are being developed which centre on the critical study of academic practices[10] and their development often derives from a concern for students who are not typical in higher education, such as mature and overseas students. A position at the margins can offer such students possibilities for critiquing dominant discourses, and may equally allow them to value alternative ways of operating, to esteem themselves, rather than feel subsumed in an unchallenged and apparently natural rather than naturalised environment. Such positions at the margin need to be valued for and in themselves as well as for what they reveal about and make possible at the centre. But they also, I think, need to be seen as more than special cases, their possibilities *confined to* the margins. The opportunities for reflexivity and change that they hold might become part of mainstream experience: it is, after all, only a very few students who complete their apprenticeships at school and university to the point of total enculturation. It might also be considered a student's right that they have some position from which to critique their own situatedness.

There are questions here, however, about the language of meta-awareness: to what discourse does *it* belong? Some disciplines clearly lend themselves more readily to critique or reflexivity than others. When the first year Philosophy students have dutifully answered their first essay question: 'Does this table exist?', their tutor challenges them: 'Doesn't it strike you that's an odd question to ask?' It is this question which gives enculturation into Philosophy the jolt that raises it to a meta level. Liz' comment in chapter 4 that her fellow students' failure to accept the tutor's sociological theory could itself be interpreted sociologically is another instance of meta-knowledge representing a sophisticated version of the discourse itself. In English, the introduction of Literary Theory can be intended also to have precisely this effect (see chapter 10 for a discussion of the complexities of this).

These examples suggest that critical reflection need not be a tangential enterprise to disciplinary doing but can play a part in enhancing it. The question of the relation between enculturation and reflection is embedded in a discussion by Rowland Wymer (1992) about the purposes of teaching literary theory courses in English:

> When we teach literary theory, are we engaged in a philosophical project, encouraging students, in a Socratic manner, to question their most basic assumptions? Or are we offering a form of technical training designed to familiarise students with the terminology employed in academic criticism? (p. 276)

---

[10] In February 1994, for example, a workshop entitled 'Studying Academia' was held at Lancaster University, to discuss possible approaches to these issues. Roz Ivanic runs a course there using linguistics as a meta-language.

Wymer claims that these two aims are 'so different from one another to be almost mutually exclusive', yet both are versions of the discourse and in fact can be seen to be mutually dependent. It would follow from a questioning of 'basic assumptions' that students would want and need to test this questioning with alternative ways treating texts. As students do this they will need to retain their questioning attitude in order to prevent one orthodoxy replacing another. The potential for disciplinary argument comes in the interaction between these two approaches; the ability to mediate the interstices between apparently discrete wholes. This is , then, an important form of critical or meta-awareness – not, in fact, beyond or outside, what goes on in the discipline itself, but rather continually informing it and catalysing the processes of argument.

In other disciplines, however, a meta-level may only be achieved by adopting a discourse from without. The case study from Electronic Engineering (chapter 8) provides an example of where the tutor had few linguistic resources to talk about what he required of his students (at an instrumental as well as more political level) and where I was equally disadvantaged in bringing my understandings to bear. Nonetheless, it doesn't seem beyond the bounds of possibility that questions such as 'What is this subject all about?, 'What is counts as knowledge in this subject?', 'What is it that we do and why?' 'Why do we write in the ways we do?' should be asked as part of teaching and learning in any discipline. Such questions would need to recur throughout learning so that students could both use them to reflect on their experiences within the discipline and conversely could use that experience to reflect on and refine the questions.

It is not clear, as I've suggested, whether hints of philosophical reflection or meta-awareness can reap benefits for successful apprenticeship or the more instrumental aspects of disciplinary learning, but I have a sense that it may create more flexible students, who are also more able to move beyond Appropriation to use strategies by which they can transform both the discourse and themselves. The implications for argument are clear, but this is argument of a slightly different, more challenging, more political kind perhaps than may result from good studentship, conventionally conceived. Moves to address the differences between teachers and students, to open communication between them, contain, it seems to me, both potential benefit for straightforward instrumental and enculturating processes and a more radical, disruptive or liberating potential.

Let me end this chapter with a summary, before moving on to the two examples of Induction programmes:

- There are discrepancies in the way students and teachers conceive of learning and its purposes within disciplines;

- A number of approaches might be taken to address these mismatches:
    - the production of effective written guidelines
    - discussion based on shared experiences
    - use of peer assessment
    - the development of separate courses to take a critical stance on academic practices (a meta-language outside the discipline)
    - the integration of reflection about disciplinary purposes and practices into courses (a meta-language/dimension within the discipline).

7. Induction

Induction programmes are increasingly being thought of as a way of clarifying to students who are starting out on a course of study what will be expected of them and what kinds of skills and approaches they will need. Such programmes have been of interest to this project because of the opportunity they offer for significant behaviours within a discipline to be elucidated. Decisions about what to include in an induction programme (as in, say, a department handbook) can give important clues to what the department's values are and where the emphasis in learning will be placed. Such programmes may, however, also contain potential and actual misunderstandings or mixed messages and be otherwise inadequate introductions to disciplinary cultures and practices.

The very concept of induction – 'initial step in an undertaking' – is a problematic one. Who defines the initial step – the department as a whole or an individual? How does the first step direct subsequent ones? More fundamentally *how* is a first step to be defined? Is there a danger of infinite regression or can this undertaking satisfactorily be distinguished from those which have preceded it and therefore constitute a kind of new beginning?

In addition to these concerns there are all sorts of practical constraints on induction programmes which determine the kinds of communication possible between the various groups involved. Below I include two case studies of Induction programmes: the first took place in the first week of an undergraduate degree in English; the second consisted of a module on argument which I devised in conjunction with a colleague.

1. Induction Programme in Undergraduate English

In the year I undertook my observations, undergraduates who came to university to study English spent the first week in an induction programme, designed to prepare them for the new environment and its expectations. They engaged in shared tasks in their eventual tutorial groups in order both to get to know each other socially and to discuss their expectations and perceptions. The induction addressed four main areas: use of the library, lectures, tutorials and essay writing. It seemed to me that the induction constituted a kind of informal contract-making: discussion was the medium, though ultimately the terms agreed were those of the institution and its gatekeepers. Here I will concentrate on the discussion of lectures and essays (these inform other discussions in this report).

Lectures:

This introduction took the form of a sample lecture on *The Turn of The Screw*, a text which students had been encouraged to read before their arrival at the university. The lecture dealt with the text in four ways: as enigmatic, as intertextual, as ideological, and in terms of its narratology. The level of discourse was immediately different to that at sixth form. It was noticeable how the rhetoric of the lecture form presumed a certain level of shared knowledge, so that the lecturer would say, for instance 'You remember, of course, that the Gothic was poked fun at during the nineteenth century...'. The sixth form teacher cannot make any such presumption and talks to the students at the level of their individual awarenesses and largely in terms of the features of particular texts. Here by immediate contrast the lecturer both creates and assumes a shared cultural repertoire, certain taken-for-granted knowledge. In the new and unfamiliar environment the students must rise to this kind of implicit and half hidden challenge in the rhetoric of the lecturer. In another way her 'You remember, of course' is a kind of compliment, a signal that one belongs. The tutor is both modelling the discourse and inviting the students to join it, not interactively, but, in a sense by raising the stakes.

The students were asked to discuss the lecture in groups and to answer certain questions as to its main points and as to how they had discovered what these main points were. They were asked whether they reached any conclusions on good ways of listening, taking notes from, remembering and being critical of a lecture. Also what use the lecture was and how it might be made more useful. The results of the group discussions were recorded on paper and handed to the induction lecturer who fed back to the whole year the overall impressions the next day. Again this was a useful and involving tactic, which enabled her to both praise the students' responses and to enforce an idea of how lectures should generally be treated. This was done in clear and positive terms – the importance of selectivity in note-taking, of using one's own terms, of remaining open-minded and sceptical. On the other hand where a number of the students had said they would have liked page references for the quotations she had used, she expressed her resistance. She was wary, she said, of imposing her own structure on the text and for the same reason had not given a summary at the end of the lecture. In a sense this was a denial of control that she couldn't help but exercise. Whilst the students at one level recognised the possibility of multiple interpretations of the text and understood the need for scepticism, they were also concerned to pin down the evidence she had given, render it somehow secure and then presumably reproducible by themselves. The tension here between treating the interpretation as purely stimulating and treating it as some form of knowledge is understandable. The lecture is an authoritative form and the lecturer a source, the voicer of authoritative insight: hard therefore to really believe in one's own scepticism, however much one knows it to be sanctioned; to see the lecture not in fact as a source but as just another resource. Nevertheless it was significant that the lecturer should put a caveat on her knowledge and authority in this way and that her starting point for doing so was the views and comments of the students themselves. What they learnt about the lecture as a teaching medium was experientially based and to a degree collaboratively investigated.

Essay Writing:

For this part of the induction students were asked to look at two sample essays and to discuss their features in groups. The grades for the essays were given in advance so that the students' judgements had a framework in which to develop, without threat of being wrong. One of the essays would fail and the other receive a B/C grade. Whilst offering reassurance there is no intention to test or trick (the expectation that students might suspect this is itself rather telling), the advance warning also signalled that the criteria for judging essays was non-negotiable. This was a form of disciplinary training based on predetermined outcome rather than discovery. It did not address the experience or perceptions that students would certainly already hold about the writing of essays.

The comments of the students on the sample essays formed part of a whole year group plenary at which the lecturer first ran through points that she felt were relevant to the writing of a good essay. Again the session was organised so that the criteria for success were always pre-given: the students included, but also instructed.

The following is a paraphrase of what the induction lecturer said:

> Firstly an essay has an argument, that is, a thesis; it moves from point A to B to C and so on and in a certain way. An example of a hypothetical essay on Thomas Hardy's pessimism which would show an accumulation of evidence and move from 'and' 'because' structures to 'but' and 'furthermore'. A case in this essay would be argued and then qualified, whilst the central idea 'pessimism' remained the same. The title is crucial in shaping the argument and should be 'milked' for the clues and opportunities it offers. 'Essai' means a trying out of various propositions. This trying out should be done:

> Discursively; in a fluid prose, which isn't abrupt or inconsequential. It will have these characteristics because it is a *literary* essay. The sense that the essay is in itself a 'piece of writing' is particularly true of an English essay. It is a creative activity – the same can not necessarily be said for essays written in History, for example. A certain amount of rhetoric is involved in making essays pleasing objects.

> Much of the above could also be said of a letter, but the personalism expected in that form is not what is required of an essay. Impersonality is necessary, a certain level of abstraction, since this is an academic exercise.

> Finally it should be a critical essay – English students are literary *critics*. In two ways

> a) There are ideas in a novel or poem and these have to be understood. Just to explain or explicate the text is not enough.

> b) The writers that are studied are remarkable not so much for what they said – which was often rather banal 'life is short' 'time passes' – but for the way they said it. English students therefore need to be acutely aware of the language that is used. At a crude level this is 'appreciation'.

What kinds of understanding would the students have picked up from this account? Argument is signalled as important, but is described as a matter of formal organisation – as, in a sense, formulaic. The notion of 'essai' as a 'trying out' of propositions fits uneasily with this variation on the 'for and against' model and also with the requirement of the essay not to be abrupt or inconsequential. That sense of the English essay as opposed to the History essay as in some way creative is also contradictory (there is nothing creative about the model of argument she gives). It suggests a kind of mystique about writing in English; perhaps it is the appeal to the individual touch? But if so, it must be disguised, since the essay requires that the student must not name herself. When it comes to describing how students should be critical, the lecturer gets no further than the need to 'understand' and the 'crude level' of 'appreciation'. As an explanation of what the disciplinary practices are (besides writing essays) this seems quite vague and also strangely uncritical.

What is striking about the lecturer's account is the emphasis on form and formal structures. When it came to discussing the sample essays themselves this emphasis was repeated: poor spelling, punctuation, use of conventions, paragraphing. With the better essay – for which there was more to be commended rhetorically: shape, succinctness, appropriate use of short quotations – cognitive features emerged more – someone felt that the writer had dodged the question of what made good poetry, others that she had not thought through carefully what was meant by the words in the title. An instance of using an unexamined example was picked out and some 'blah' words were challenged as attempting to do the job of more careful analysis. Implicit here was the sense that quality of thought follows from effective formal and rhetorical strategies[1].

In the early days of the undergraduate course the features of the essay were reiterated several times (as they are also in the student handbook). In the tutorial group I was observing the ground was covered in much the same way, except without the help of concrete examples. Again it was possible to observe a tendentiousness in the way students were asked to suggest the essential quality of an essay, so that the group arrived 'democratically' at a consensus. Such discussions offer interesting examples of argument in themselves. The possibility of dialogue is opened up, but for strategic negotiating purposes. Everyone is guaranteed a say in the discussion, but its outcome is already determined.

In this case the tutor had prepared in advance a sheet which would be used in assessing essays, the aim of which was to make clear to students the criteria the tutor would be using in giving a grade. Amongst the criteria, cognitive features are hard to isolate and the emphasis is to a large degree rhetorical. Different aspects of the writing task are separated out so that argument is discrete from structure, knowledge, response and viewpoint. The checklist does nothing to suggest how each of these is interrelated in writing and provides no sense of how the student might go about successfully improving performance except in rather a scattered way, such as by reading more contextual material.

In some senses the time and attention given to the essay form at this early stage of the course might seem natural and sensible. The students will, with a grounding at A level, accept that the essay is the common currency of exchange between teacher and student and also that it is the principle – in most cases, the only – object of assessment. Yet there are other aspects of study that might be addressed: ways of reading, of writing impressionistically or experimentally, of generating responses and argument, of planning. These 'unseen' aspects of study are subsumed by the emphasis on the public form. The assessment sheet breaks writing into constituent parts, but focusses on these as elements of product, without consideration for process. The knock-on effect of this emphasis on writing is, as I've argued before, the corresponding lack of emphasis on and devaluing of speech. In most academic disciplines a student's ability to contribute to the production of spoken discourse is not valued in assessment terms. Here, though the institutional expectation is clear that students will write essays, there is no similar expectation signalled that students will play a significant role in any other form of discourse production. This absence communicates messages to students as eloquently, I suspect, as what is stated over and over again.

For the students I subsequently observed formal elements of essay writing were a predominant concern. They were aware of new 'scholarly' features which had not been part of writing at A level, such as the need to give footnotes for every reference and to show a reading not only of the literary text, but of critical sources as well. How these sources were used as a cognitive resource is less apparent in their texts than the way they contribute to an overall formal effect and to an impression of scholarly endeavour. Again the argument is of course likely to be that this emphasis on form is an important element of training, that what the student employs mechanically at first she will eventually come to control and adapt to more creative, original and argumentative uses. It's not a model I would want to reject as

---

[1] The links between cognitive ability and the conventional forms through which this is displayed in educational contexts are explored in chapter 9.

unsuccessful, but I would like to question its emphasis here, its conservatism (the unquestioned relation between conventional form and clever thought) and the mechanistic approach to disciplinary success it implies.

ESSAY MARKING CRITERIA

Student's name   *Key To Grades*

                                                          A outstanding
Essay Grade   B very good overall
                                                          C satisfactory
Tutor   D serious inadequacies
                                                          E inadequate
                                                          F fail

KNOWLEDGE

Text   deep, thorough, detailed ....superficial

Author   wide knowledge used in analysis ....no knowledge or not used

Genre   wide knowledge used in analysis ....no knowledge or not used

Historical   knowledge used in analysis ....no knowledge or not used
wide social context

Critical theory   used intelligently ....no knowledge or not used

ESSAY

Structure   clear, logical structure ....confused, rambling

Argument   clear development, ...list
                        answers question

Quotations   correct, well chosen ....incorrect, not documented
                        properly documented

Other sources   wide range, relevant ....few, irrelevant, not documented

Grammar, spelling, punctuation   correct ....many errors

Style   lucid and concise ....clumsy, difficult to read

PERSONAL

Response to text   independent, original ....derivative, no personal
                                                                        response

Viewpoint   clearly expressed ....no viewpoint

FURTHER COMMENTS

_____

_____

_____

Can the Emphasis Be Changed?

The English induction might be described as predominantly instrumental, in that aims to make explicit some of the features and purposes of the main forms of learning, to expose to the students some of the 'ground rules' by which their performance will be judged. In the case of the lecture, the students were alerted to the stance they should try to take, whilst the essay was brought to the fore as the formal expression of learning. What was missing was any attention to, much less discussion of, the nature of the enterprise in which the students would be engaged; there were few insights into the discourse of the subject. As I describe in chapter 10 this begins to occur with the introduction of Literary Theory as a discrete course in the second term. The concerns of the induction and of this course are presented as distinct, the first dealing with modes of study and requirements of form; the second with theoretical and epistemological issues. Yet the two are not unconnected and the emphasis on form, I would argue, is impoverished without accompanying discussion of the types of the meaning that form is used to express. To do this to best advantage it might well be worth waiting until the students have some experience behind them and can engage in informed but exploratory discussion, of the kind that occurred in philosophy.

Induction of the kind described above seems to aim at neither enculturation nor reflexivity. It gives instruction in certain formal aspects of the discourse, but does not offer the experience necessary for enculturation, nor does it invite thought about the discourse. Learning in fact is only tangentially thought of in terms of discourse at all. Induction might nevertheless be used to raise some important questions and to signal that these will be raised again in discussion later on the term or year. But this would require its purposes to be integrated more fully into the course 'proper'. It would require, that is, a rethinking of the emphasis that is generally placed on covering content; an emphasis which relegates reflection on process and learning to the margins of study. Induction programmes can epitomise this separation of content and operations, form and mode.

2. Induction in Generating Argument from Sources

The module on generating argument formed part of a university induction programme for first year Communication Processes students and I was, in this case, directly involved with both the design and teaching of the process. Starting with exercises I had previously devised for use with sixth form English Language students, Dave Kenyon of Humberside University and I put together a teaching sequence of exercises which would lead to the writing of an essay.

As is noted elsewhere in this report, students commonly have difficulty with writing argument; they use, for instance, forms of narrative and summary in their essays and reserve evaluation and the expression of opinion until the concluding paragraphs. Such evaluations and opinions as they then give often appear to be tacked on and formulaic rather than to have emerged from a process of argumentation in the body of the essay itself. Analysis of students' essays shows how organisational structures can influence the tendency of the writing towards summary or evaluation and argument (see chapter 11). Summary seems to be an important stage prior to argument as an operation by which students gain a firm understanding of the material with which they have been supplied; yet if satisfactory argument is to be produced, summaries need to be processed and reconfigured in ways which make them comparable with one another and which enable their themes to be abstracted. These steps between narrative and argument rarely seemed to be addressed in the teaching I have observed.

The exercises which formed the induction module aimed to take students through processes of summary and categorisation towards the generation of argument. The outcome of the exercise was to be an essay, which I hoped would show evidence of the generative processes undergone. The sequence of exercises was influenced by the work of Geisler and Kaufer (1989) who introduce the idea of a 'literate conversation' to describe the interaction which occurs between the activities of reading and writing. This, they say, allows the participants the opportunity for reflection – 'thinking that turns back – or 'reflects' – on itself' (p. 229). They devise a sequence of activities aimed at making such literate conversations accessible to students. There are four linked writing assignments:

- a set of Summaries of other authors' argumentative texts,
- a Synthesis of multiple authors' arguments
- an Analysis of the strengths and weaknesses of those arguments, and
- a culminating original Contribution. (p. 230)

As will emerge, there are areas here which were not fully addressed in the induction module, though there is nonetheless scope for improvement in any future revision.

The fact that the exercise was first devised for use by A level students of English Language explains the use of a popular radio programme as the source from which students would develop their arguments. The programme is Radio 4's 'Any Questions?' in which four panel members are asked their opinion on the topical question of whether the press should be regulated. The spoken sources and the topic seemed to be equally suitable for the Induction Module of the Communications Studies degree course.

What the Students Did

The students' version of the module is reproduced as an appendix at the end of this report. The students were supplied with newspaper cuttings relating to the Calcutt Report[2] when it was first published, and when they had completed the note taking exercise they received a transcript of the tape they had heard. The appendices contained a sample grid and some advice on essay writing which was geared largely to rhetorical aspects of the writing and to the reflexivity of the writer in thinking about her communicative aims. In addition they contained a questionnaire with questions relating to previous experience of writing in certain forms, definitions of argument and evaluations of the module. The module was worked on in two group sessions (two and a half hours in total), in which the tape was listened to, and activities and discussion engaged in. The discussions concerned the difficulties encountered in the various tasks and, later, the way in which the processed material could be used in generating argument. This last was not explicitly signalled in the module instructions but was felt to be necessary by the tutors involved. Between session one and two students were expected to produce a grid of the common points they had identified between the speakers. The purpose of this was to reconfigure the material towards issues and away from individual accounts. At the end of the second session students were asked to write a short essay on the topic of Press Regulation. They were not given a title or question to work with as we hoped that the orientation towards the issues provided by the preliminary exercises would be sufficient.

---

2 This was commissioned by government to provide recommendations on the regulation of the Press.

Evaluating the Exercise

Student perspective: This is gauged from the questionnaire which was included in the module, but represents only a 42% response. Briefly, 27% of the respondents thought the module overall 'very helpful' [10% of all students]. Those respondents who thought it was either helpful, or at least not actively unhelpful outnumbered the others by 4:1. 18% thought it was not particularly helpful.

58% of respondents thought the module was 'clear' and the two most successful parts seemed to be the grid making exercise [58%] and the first batch of essay writing advice [53%]. In contrast the note-making exercise was found by 60% of respondents to be unhelpful. (We wondered whether this might be in part accounted for by us giving out the transcription of the radio programme at the end of the first session, thus making the preceding activities appear pointless.)

From the written comments made by the students, it was clear that, as I have mentioned, some aspects of the group sessions were found repetitive and boring. The major problem expressed as concerned the essay writing was a sense that the area was very broad and that a question being supplied would have been useful. (See, however, my comments below which suggest the value of there being no title.)

81% of the respondents said that they would recommend the module be repeated next year.

Tutor perspective: There were four tutors teaching the module, including myself. Several points we felt needed to be taken into account in any future revision of the module:

– The time spent on summarising, whilst beneficial in the first instance, became repetitive. The tasks, that is, were not sufficiently differentiated. The most frequent comments by the students in their questionnaires were to this effect too.

– The contributions of the panel members to the programme discussion do not have the textual complexity nor level of content that these students would subsequently need in their disciplinary work. The relative simplicity of this as source material may have added to the pedestrian feel of parts of the exercise, making, for instance, the distinction between summarising and working with the grid rather unclear.

– Time spent discussing the particular difficulties of summarising from spoken sources, whilst broadly relevant to the degree (and interesting to discuss) was less directly applicable to the task of argument development.

– With the balance of the work too heavily on summary and making accounts, the other major flaw in the exercise was a failure address the transition from the categorised notes towards a structure of argument, from which the student's own position might emerge. In the event the tutors recognised this omission from the laid down material and spent less time discussing the grid and more addressing the move towards essay writing. Some introduced the idea of spider diagrams or mind maps. I asked my group to try and work each of the common points they had raised into a linked pattern so that they could make and explain connections between them. From this, causal and inferential links began to appear. The students needed then to be able to consider whether some of these might be stronger and more useful in building an argument than others. To recognise, that is, that selection is another important skill (besides summary and categorisation) in formulating arguments. Time might very usefully have been spent 'playing around' with different ways of configuring the material, using it for different ends and allowing students to identify or construct positions of their own.[3]

Despite these misgivings the tutors generally seemed to feel that the sessions were valuable, not least in raising their own awareness of ways in which argumentative tasks are presented to students.

The Positioning and Status of the Exercise

The fact that this exercise was part of an induction programme and therefore set apart from the 'real work' of the term militates against its effectiveness. It was taught by tutors who had no real expertise in the Communication Processes area and who would not see the students again. In addition it was not assessed work, being thought of rather as a diagnostic preliminary. This inevitably affected the seriousness with which it was viewed by the students. In addition, although the subject matter was relevant to the course, it was not integrated with the content of the course as such.

So there are distinct disadvantages with the induction approach. However, the alternative – in which attention to skills such as the generation of argument becomes part of the course proper – is not easy to envisage. Coverage of content is a driving force behind most courses and this one is no exception. This emphasis would need to be changed to allow time to be given to prolonged engagement with a limited body of material – what Kaufer and Geisler refer to as 'micro-worlds' – for the purpose of exploring strategic moves in argument generation. And since there is increasingly little autonomy for teachers in Higher Education the prioritising of process over knowledge would need to be built into course outlines and allocated sufficient time. Modularisation might well reduce the likelihood of such emphasis.

The Students' Essays – a Commentary on Some Noticeable Features

Some of the points identified below as problems in students' essay writing might be addressed by improvements in the teaching module. As outlined above there didn't seem to be enough attention given to the generation of individual points of view (the student's own) as a result of (or, indeed, before) the preparatory work on the views of others; nor to ways of relating different ideas together and selecting and prioritising them in relation to an overall or developing argument. These areas do seem, however, to have been addressed in some way by the tutors.

When it comes to essay writing, though, a number of other factors are involved, which are not accounted for in the preparation. Writing an essay is what Flower and Hayes (1981) have described as a 'rhetorical problem' (p. 369) which includes both the situation in which, and the audience for which, the writing is designed as well as one's own goals in writing. Along with the goals specific to the particular task in hand (in this case to develop an argument around the issue of press regulation) there are other goals which are 'well-learnt, standard ones, stored in memory' and which 'will often be so basic that they won't even be consciously considered or expressed' (p. 381). Such goals as these affect the writing of essays, heavily influencing the way the way a particular task becomes manifest in writing. (59% of the questionnaire respondents said they had in the past used essays very often and 86% of them had received their qualifications of entry within the past two years.) Flower and Hayes also note that:

---

[3] Ways of 'playing around' with material and ideas to construct argument are suggested in chapter 11.

Even when the planning process represents one's thoughts in words, that representation is unlikely to be in the elaborate syntax of written English. So the writer's task is to translate a meaning, which may be embodied in key words (what Vygotsky calls words 'saturated with sense') and organised in a complex network of relationships, into a linear piece of written English. (p. 373)

Thus although what the exercise sought to do was to improve students' ability to think argumentatively about an issue, in order to improve what were perceived to be common problems in essay writing, at the point of writing the essay itself a number of other factors come back into play. This – what Britton calls 'shaping at the point of utterance' – needs to be borne in mind when looking at the essays and assessing the success of the exercise. If the process of learning is not yet over with the completion of the 'preparatory' exercises then neither is it when the essays themselves are written.

One of the striking things about the essays is the implied lack of reflexivity on the part of the writers about the effectiveness of writing. One of the tutors commented:

> One of mine [an essay] was hand written first then typed out – with still this kind of thing [various confusions and mistakes] abounding! No answer to this. From the module I am reminded how difficult (and ultimately non-existent) they found it to talk about each other's work. To look at that objectively was hard enough; they aren't used to looking for mixed ideas because they read text-books (and trust them!) rather than read poor writing and argument.

One way in which reflection on the purpose, significance and effectiveness of writing might be enhanced is to ask students to consider the kinds of points identified below. My comments are based on a random selection of ten essays from the groups I taught. One other was also included, since it seemed to me to be particularly effective. A single sentence or paragraph often contains a variety of complex operations and so the sections given below inevitably run into each other.

1. The **lack of a specific title or question** for the essay seems to have produced a greater variety of opening paragraphs than would often be the case. The students have to frame for themselves a position from which to start. This might be historical, comparative, declamatory, balanced. The lack of a title makes greater demands on the writer rhetorically – a challenge which they often rise to very well. Although several of the students commented in their questionnaires that the lack of a title made the essay writing task difficult, my feeling is that this was not necessarily a bad thing. Time might valuably have been given in the module, however, to generating titles or questions as an extension of the work which moves categorisation towards argument.

The following examples reveal a range of rhetorical techniques and models in the students' repertoires. They are executed with varying degrees of success, but they illustrate that an important dimension of argument (not addressed by the preliminary exercises) is effective display.

PRESS REGULATION: WHERE SHOULD THE LINE BE DRAWN?

The issue of press regulation has unfortunately become an exercise in line drawing.

Many suggestions exist as to where the proverbial sand should be marked. The recent Calcutt report did not suggest so much a line over which the press shouldn't step but a legal cage in which it should be kept.

(concluding sentence of essay) The place where those in power would like the line drawn is around them: the place where a journalist will draw it is the bottom line. (007)

The metaphor used here is a little forced and inconsistent, but the student is nonetheless trying to find a – rhetorically satisfying – organising theme or image which both opens and closes the writing.

> The demand for freedom, at its most basic is the claim that every human has the right to do exactly what he wants to do, at any time, provided only that he does not infringe the equal right of every other individual to a similar freedom. When applying this definition to the Mass Media, one immediately encounters complexities, especially when the right to privacy is endangered. (006)

> Ever since the introduction of the idea that the people of a nation should have a say in the governing of their nation, for their own good, there has been the need for a body to keep them informed and up to date with matters that concern them, a body which creates the vital link between the decision makers in power and the ordinary citizens, a body of essential importance: the press. But in recent times it has become clear that the press often oversteps the mark when it comes to informing the people of what they 'need' to know. (005)

In both these examples, the structure is similar: an opening definitional or contextualising sentence, followed by a shorter problematising one, which tips the reader from narrative into argument. A more extended version of this occurs in the first example below where the choice was to present the specific details of the Calcutt Report first:

> In early January 1993, Sir David Calcutt put forward proposals recommending that invasions of privacy be classed as criminal offences. These new offences ... (paragraph 1)

> He proposed ... (paragraph 2)

> Taking the above proposals into consideration, many opinions arise with respect to regulations of the press ... (004)

> "THERE IS NO LIMIT TO WHAT MIGHT BE REPORTED. THE NUMBER OF OBSERVABLE DESCRIBABLE EVENTS IS INFINITIVE. EVERY EVENT IS A SERIES OF SMALLER EVENTS, WHICH THEN IN TURN CONSISTS OF STILL SMALLER EVENTS" (News Ltd., Brian Whitaker, 1984)

> If the above statement is true then the press, world-wide, has a very selective job to organise our news into an order of importance, interest and newsworthiness. However over the last few years there have been many accusations made to the press about their standards of investigation and the quality of their news. (002)

In this example kicks the argument off by positioning her own voice in relation to another. The approach is impressive, but the problematising sentence which ends it does not capitalise on the implications of what has gone before and the potential of the quotation to organise the essay is diminished. The use of 'however' is not logically correct (though she may sense that *rhetorically* it is, as a way of rounding off the introductory paragraph). It would have been better to continue by asking what the criteria are by which the press appears to make selections.

One recurring feature of the openings is the use of **temporal contextualising phrases**, such as 'for a number of years' or 'for a period of time'. These are imprecise, suggesting perhaps a lack of knowledge, but they do fulfil a need to situate the discussion. This is a feature of other kinds of writing too: research articles, for example, often start with an account of thinking 'in recent years' or of recent debate or controversy.

The issue of press regulation is not a new one. Through the years there have been many attempts to control the freedom of the press ... (003)

2. The **careful construction of the opening is not always sustained throughout the essay**. There is a **tendency to degenerate into a list**, which suggests an inability to select material which is relevant to the particular argument or, perhaps more precisely, an unwillingness (anxiety) to discard material which doesn't fit. In these cases it is as if all knowledge must be displayed at whatever cost to the argument. In addition this tendency seems to suggest a difficulty with keeping contradictory positions within the same frame of reference or with acknowledging the differences between two positions. Argument flourishes on the exploitation of such differences. Such **reluctance to confront contradiction** on the part of students is probably a combination of cognitive and cultural factors. It can be linked to the function of writing in educational settings as a means to display what one has learnt (this will achieve an adequate grade at A level) but it works against the equally important function to show evidence of thinking and argument. If students have difficulty in making an *informed* choice about which material to include in an essay in order to argue a position, then by putting it all in they are hedging their bets.

In the following example the writer has worked through the complex arguments and reached a conclusion that any solution would need to be equally complex. Notice though that the solution is not seen in terms of synthesis of the many factors or of prioritising some above others but only in terms of individual handling:

> That is, as the argument is so complex in its structure (each having good and bad points, strengths and weaknesses) the solution could be of a similar complexity, taking into consideration every point thus trying to deal with them individually. (004, conclusion)

Much of the listing that occurs in the essays occurs towards the end (though before the conclusion) as if the writer is unable to judge whether she has shown enough evidence of knowledge to have made her argumentative case. For example:

> [paragraph starts with the Watergate scandal] Ken Livingstone used this example in the Radio 4 programme and argued that for our press to be able to uncover such standards as this then they will require greater freedom of investigation. He also reasoned that if greater press freedom was available then the press may concentrate more on important social issues rather than less important sleazy showbusinessy issues. Mary Archer and Sheila Lawlor agreed with Ken Livingstone on this point, but yet again Robin Page had other opinions.

> In his view the press have too much freedom and should be controlled more. He thinks the press are appalling but yet matches the ever decreasing standards of this countries MP's[sic]. In this respect Page believes we have the press we deserve. One interesting thing to point out here is that Page is actually a journalist himself and is therefore criticising his own profession and colleagues. (002 paragraphs 10 and 11 out of 12).

When the writer moves into this reporting mode, she stops dealing with issues. The subject of her sentences becomes the people rather than their ideas, indicating that very little abstraction is occurring. (Incidentally, I remember suggesting the irony of Page's remarks given that he is a journalist – did I unconsciously signal this as an important point?) The lack of a strategic approach to knowledge and argument, including the ability to be selective and to exploit differences in source material was a target of the induction module, which such examples suggest it was not able to meet.

3. **Tentativity about the expression of a critical point of view**. The writers are noncommittal about interpretations and opinions. They distance themselves from them by the use of impersonal language. Here is what McCormick (1990) has described as the 'subjective/ objective paradigm' at work. This polarises opinion and fact and expresses the tension between the injunction on the one hand to be impersonal and cool in academic contexts and on the other to develop and express a position of one's own.

In the example below the two interpretations are strung together casually as alternatives. In fact they need not be mutually exclusive, but could be worked together to provide a stronger argument. Again, however, the potentially useful contradiction is evaded:

> The political bias of the press is usually obvious when reading a newspaper. This largely due to the political interests of the publication's owner. This could be considered dangerous, as the power of the press is so strong or merely an expected feature of the mass media. (006)

The tentativity is in part due to a lack of control over the language so that the rush of thought is condensed into a single imperfectly formed final sentence. Two sentences would have created the impression of a more considered reticence about making a definite interpretation one way or the other.

There is a tendency to qualify conclusory statements with 'maybe' or 'perhaps', which suggest a reluctance to express a firm commitment. In the questionnaires several of the students emphasise argument as a process of reaching a conclusion:

> 'a process used to agree or disagree with a point'
> 'two or more different views coming to a conclusion'
> 'two or more opposing or differing views on a subject. Its purpose should be to air these views and arrive at a point most valid to that subject'
> 'To consider all ideas and end up with the best by evaluating others'

Yet the essays themselves often avoid the expression of conclusions. There are a number of ways in which this discrepancy might be accounted for: that the process in which the student has been engaged was not actually thoroughly argumentative (did not help in formulating a position); that the student has not found a voice (is trapped in the subjective/objective paradigm); or that, more positively, the student is expressing a tolerance for uncertainty, a sense of the provisionality of conclusions. It may also be that the student is unable to judge the strength and effectiveness of a process of argumentation and is therefore unsure of the weight to attach to a conclusion. These possibilities might usefully be discussed with the students themselves as a way of helping them reflect on their positioning in relation to the issues with which they are dealing and the form in which they are writing.

4. **Misuse of language and structures**. Again various interpretations are possible here. Misuse of language and structures can indicate a transitionary stage where the students' ambition (their attempt to find a suitable style and vocabulary) overreaches their accuracy, or it can be evidence of mislearning or mishearing, or, of course, of carelessness. Such inaccuracies often seem to occur in phrases, such as '[they] viewed their opinions', 'being lenient about the truth'.

Sometimes the writer is engaging in a kind of poetics. The introduction which used the image of line drawing is an example of this, as is the following: '... the issue of press regulation will always be a controversial one, causing arguments all along the political and journalistic ladders'. Here the image is unconventional, but the concept it alludes to is similar to the more usual notion of a spectrum (though that metaphor has become so familiar it no longer seems like one). I think these are positive signs in a student's writing, since they suggest both an attempt to pattern ideas in language and at the same time to communicate them distinctively to a reader. There are of course dangers in moves away from the literal – failure is as likely as success – but these can be contained if students can be encouraged to reflect on their own writing.

The **overloading of sentences** so that they contain both idea(s) and example is another related problem. The essays contained numerous examples:

> It could be said that the introduction of legal bodies, which make it illegal to remain on people's property, record or take pictures of people on private property, without consent, with a view to publication, which can restrain publication of material in breach of a code of practice, inquire into certain complaints, require the printing of apologies, corrections, replies, enforce publication of its adjudications, award compensation, impose fines and award costs is a good idea. (001)

The writer of this difficult sentence needs a descriptive phrase to cover all her examples in the first sentence, such as 'engage in certain actions', and then a second sentence which simply specifies these actions. Even if she were to do this, however, she would still not be demonstrating any discrimination between the measures or commentary on them.

5. **Use of persuasive appeals**, such as 'clearly', 'obviously', 'surely'. These very often stand in for demonstration of an argument's validity and can also be contradicted by an idea developed later in the essay:

> Obviously if these proposals came to fruition they would be of benefit to the general public since they would almost certainly deter the press from violating our privacy ...

> Indeed the proposed measures could be considered detrimental to the public since there is a risk of self-censorship by the papers. (003)

Rhetorical questions are a less closed form of persuasive appeal, since being questions they are to some extent always negotiable. They can also be a way of making a distinction or articulating an argumentative position.

> Where, though, does the public's right to know end? And where does privacy begin? (004)

> If the press do not respect their role to the public, if they abuse their freedom should they not be controlled? If we do not have a sensitive press does this not actually restrict personal freedoms? (009)

The success of the rhetorical questions depends to a great extent on their position in the essay, however, and the extent to which they are used in developing thought. Here they are at the beginning and so give the impression that they will be answered. In other instances they occur throughout the text and may not be further addressed. For example:

> It is also interesting to note that the Calcutt report of two and a half years ago, of almost identical content, was not acted on or implemented by the Government; an indication of their feelings on the subject of press regulation? (010)

This curious example of the use of a question is quite commonly used. It suggests but does not directly express an opinion and in an academic essay where explicitness is important, this is a weakness. Throwing the question out removes the onus from the writer to answer it or explore its implications.

But what happens after regulation? Will the press take any notice? After all, existing libel and privacy laws seem not to create any deterrent. Is it not impossible to prevent the tabloid press from indulging in what they thrive on – muckraking? (010)

Something similar happens in the following example, which is a densely packed paragraph of separate and largely undeveloped ideas, linked however to the idea of the limits of legislation. At the end of the paragraph the writer arrives at a new idea expressed as an exclamatory statement:

Even so the legislation may be said not to be completely effective. Those most vulnerable: the less famous and less wealthy, would be at a disadvantage to act against the press if it wronged them. They, unlike the rich and famous, may not have enough money to take newspapers to court or to get good lawyers. To cope with this one listener to Radio Four suggested that legal aid should be extended. Another flaw is that although apologies would now be guaranteed, peers would not be obliged to give it the same position or space as the original article. The proposal does not take into consideration either that the press may not be solely to blame when it strays from the truth. Perhaps even more outrageous is that as Ken Livingstone points out, politicians deliberately misinform the press. Maybe there should be a legislation against this! (001)

The weakness here is a lack of control in handling the new idea, which is a good one. The essay goes on to offer examples of the political manipulation of information, but doesn't explore what might be done, nor evaluate Livingstone's ideas as a solution. The exclamation, that is, seems to stand in for further thought and discussion. It relates to the reluctance to engage in hypothetical thinking (see below).

6. The **lack of explicitness and expansion** underlies much of what I have said and is a common problem with the students' essays. How can students be helped to realise where there is a need for less cursory treatment? How can they find additional factors on which to comment?[4]

The scope of an argument can be extended by **broadening the perspective** from which the issue can be viewed, as here, for example, at the beginning of an essay:

Press regulation means the government passing sanctions which restrict, to some extent, the freedom of the press in certain areas and actions. Such regulation can range from total censorship of the press as in communist Russia to small changes forcing the press to respect privacy, personal rights and private property as suggested in the Calcutt report.

To have a completely democratic and free society, it can be argued it is necessary to have a press capable of investigative journalism, able to scrutinise the governing body of the given society and inform the public freely of its findings, whatever they may be. This argument is a strong one and carries much feeling among those who believe 'democracy' and 'freedom' should be available to all, a basic human right.

From this stance it could be argued that any censorship of the press would mean a drop in the personal freedom of any member of society, and therefore, any regulation is morally wrong, the public becoming uninformed and so unable to act. (009)

In this example the writer first contextualises the issue of press regulation, showing it to operate in varying degrees. He then develops an argument in which press regulation is related to the wider issues of freedom and democracy. By showing the press to be a constituent part of society, he is then able to make a connection between press freedom and

---

4 One effective way is to ask students to engage in peer assessment/reading which has challenge and extension as its express aim. See chapter 12 for an example of this.

individual freedom. This is an example of widening the context in order to expose new connections and new possibilities for argument and is an important strategy to make students aware of. It is used again in the following extract:

> The fact that people do buy the papers that are accused of printing lies and fabrications must also say something about our society rather than leaving the blame at the door of the press. (008)

7. Another means of expansion is to **think through practical solutions**. This involves creating hypothetical positions and can improve an argument by making it testable. The following examples are from an essay which makes consistent use of hypothetical positions from which strong policy claims are made. The writer does not evade the contradictions of the situation, but treats each point as complex. Notice the effect of using the modal verb 'should':

> But if they had evidence which was substantial to suggest that the people who are to be bugged are involved in some kind of criminal activity together and it is in the best interests of the public to be informed about it, then it should be allowed. (023 paragraph 8)

> If papers are going to attack the weak and vulnerable, then it is only fair for the person in question to have some means of comeback. There could be a reduction in the prices needed to be paid to begin libel proceedings and legal aid should be made available. (paragraph 9)

> The reduction in libel laws should allow the press to concentrate on the misdemeanours of large targets, instead of concentrating on less important goings on in ordinary citizens' private lives. This coupled with new laws regarding the intrusion on private property should help the individual. It would be difficult however, to reduce libel laws against 'big targets' whilst making them more available to the public (paragraph 11).

On the whole the writers gave little attention to possible solutions to the problems raised. This may in part be accounted for by the limitations of the essay form, in the sense that the essay is about the expression of argued opinion rather than the proffering of solutions. It was certainly not a dimension of argument that was addressed in the preparatory module. Any future revision might bear this in mind though one should be wary of trying to make the module cover too much.

The **use of hypotheses** is as I indicated above a way of extending argument, though it was rarely used in the essays I marked. There are dangers with it, similar to those involved in developing analogies or metaphorical language, but as in that case the hypothesis is a demonstration of active thinking and the manipulation of ideas and material. In Philosophy, hypotheses are an essential means of testing positions, but in other disciplines teachers may be more wary about encouraging their use. The reasons for this reluctance would be interesting to explore. An example of what seems an effective hypothetical discussion is given here:

> Anyone who has gained an influence over other people should not be protected from investigation just because they are not in public office. This non-protection from investigation should extend right from power-brokers like Maxwell to say a driving examiner who is suspected of taking bribes to pass people on their driving tests. The subjectivity of the issue now comes in. If Maxwell had been suspected of sleeping with prostitutes would he be fairer game for investigation, because the morals of someone who has had his huge public influence are of public interest, than a driving instructor who was suspected of the same thing? Officially the driving examiner holds a more responsible position in society but realistically Maxwell had far more influence and it is therefore more in the public's interest to know about Maxwell than our hypothetical driving examiner.

Summary of Suggested Improvements to the Module

- the use of more complicated, probably written sources, either as extracts or a limited number of articles. This would highlight the purpose of the grid as a means of bringing the sources into contact with each other.

- experiment more with ways of configuring the material into argument, through the use of diagrams and patterns. This can be both an individual and collective exercise, with the emphasis on creative patternings.

- other bridging exercises could be based on the notion of argument as a form of language use. These would involve analysis and 'translation'. Here the student is asked to abstract the argument from a piece of writing (either a source or something the student has written). Where the argument is unclear or only partially expressed the student then moves into the task of trying to clarify it by putting it into her own words. As she does so she adds to the original and transforms it into her own meaning. This process involves very careful consideration of language and an awareness that translation also involves interpretation. At the end of the exercise the student can compare her version with that of others (an example of this approach is given below).

- this is part of the goal to allow students to find positions in relation to the issue which they want to adopt.

- direct discussion to the nature, purposes, forms of argument itself. This might include consideration of the student's own writing and experience (though the positioning of the module in induction might not facilitate this). The observations I have made above on the students' essays are probably familiar to many teachers. But as one of the tutors suggested – 'Who is used to reading poorly put argument apart from us?' – they may not be familiar to students, at least not at a level of explicitness and reflection.

- the exercises need not culminate with the writing of an essay. Instead, to remove the emphasis from producing a final form, students might brainstorm a number of essay-type questions in pairs in order to show that the same material can be configured in different ways.

- again, instead of writing an essay ask the students to collect a selection of sources on another topic area and work on it to develop argument in the ways suggested and in other ways they develop for themselves. The aim here would be to enhance the students' sense of the transferability of the techniques they have used.

Conclusions

The module, though flawed in several ways, provided a good basis on which to raise awareness of the importance of argument – as distinct from, say, essay writing – in the academic course. However if such an environmental approach is to be capitalised upon, all members of staff need to be aware of its aims and methods and to integrate these into their teaching. The induction merely scratches the surface of learning and its status amongst students is low. The opportunity to stand aside from the content of a course and to reflect on processes and, importantly, on one's own writing needs to be part of the student's on-going learning. Only in this way, it seems to me, can techniques be learnt as meaningful and integrated with content, and both the individual's experience and the institutions requirements be brought into a thoroughly productive relation.

8. Tacit and Explicit Knowledge: a Problem of Genre in a 'Real World' Simulation

The case with which this chapter deals – an exercise in 'argument' for MSc students – serves to exemplify issues raised in earlier chapters: the misinterpretation of messages passed between teachers and students; the difficulty for experts in making their tacit and practical knowledge explicit and usable; the dependency of successful argument upon a proper and subtle understanding of context (highlighted here by the 'real world' orientation of the task); the consequent interdependency of substance, form, context and motive in the effective production of genre – what Miller (1984) calls 'social action'.

An Innovation

The work described here resulted from the idea of a tutor in Electronic Engineering who was teaching a Master of Science course in Radio Systems Engineering. The course, which was being offered for the first time, attracted students (all male) from a variety of backgrounds; some had recently completed an undergraduate degree in Electronic Engineering and wished to specialise; some had worked in the field and wanted to update their knowledge or retrain; some were from overseas and needed, in addition to following the course content, to develop their language skills.

I was involved in the work as a result of a request I had made to university teachers to be allowed access to any work they were doing which involved their students in argument. The request was also an offer to collaborate in thinking through any innovation they might make. In this instance I was both observer and joint experimenter, though I was limited in this latter role by my lack of familiarity with the complex technical subject and, as it turned out, by the means by which and contexts in which it is communicated. I was, that is to say, very much an outsider. In this sense the case illustrates the problems of intervening in a discourse community which does not share a meta-language with which to discuss its practices. Some of what follows is written in a personal narrative mode and this is because my own position in the innovation is itself revealing and pertinent to the issues of communication and explicitness I am exploring in this and previous chapters.

The tutor's innovation developed from his sense that the course needed to give students access, not only to technical and theoretical expertise, but also to the wider vocational skills needed in work. He felt that to ask students to work within a framework in which other factors besides technical ones were important would be one way of addressing 'real world' constraints. The need to argue was central to this and was in fact highly relevant to the radio communications systems being studied. At present – put simply – two systems for mobile telephones are being developed, one in Europe (TDMA) and the other in the USA

(CDMA). The dilemma is that the two systems are incompatible, the technologies developing away from, rather than in tandem with each other. Clearly there is great scope here – and, in fact, a technical and commercial imperative – to argue the merits of each system. The arguments are complex technical, practical and economic ones. Since many of the MSc students would go on to look for work in this field, it was important for them to know how to find their way through these arguments – and also how to use the arguments competitively to advocate one system or the other. These two aims, as it turns out, are quite distinct. The students were placed in small groups in support of one or other of the systems and asked to research the area, before giving an oral presentation and writing a report advocating that system. In this chapter I'm considering the written reports only.

Tacit Knowledge

It was really only when I reviewed the process the students underwent that I began to recognise the pitfalls the assignment contained. My understanding of these pitfalls was significantly different from that of the tutor. They derived in part from my own ignorance of the 'reality' of the 'real life' situation the students were presented with. The tutor, on the other hand, was surprised at some of the work the students produced, because it did not match up to his expectations. These expectations were connected with form as much as substance and with a sense of the 'social action' that the combination of these would perform: that is, the tutor was operating with a distinct expectation of genre.

The important point is, however, that the tutor's expectation was tacit. I had no clear access to it until I had read the reports, read his comments and assessments and engaged in discussion with him as to what precisely had been so surprising. Until we had shared the students' work, that is, we had little to go on. The delayed emergence of his criteria may have resulted in part from my own failure early on to ask the sorts of questions that might have made his knowledge more explicit. Nonetheless it was clear that the tutor had little 'discursive consciousness' (Giddens, 1984) of what he required the students to do; he could not talk about his discourse within anything like the fluency that he could talk in it (what Giddens would call his 'practical consciousness'). The gap in understanding between us was bridged only by sharing examples – a kind of objective correlative for what we both knew, but differently.

Some distinctions need to be made to the claim that the tutor's expectation were tacit: some aspects were more tacit than others. His copious comments on the students' work refer largely to weaknesses in their arguments and to aspects of the subject they have not considered. He engages with the students on the level of technical debate, replying to their contributions and extending them. In the following comment on a student's work for example:

> The idea of the parallel sub-channels is an extension of the Kineplex system used for overcoming HF propagation delay and will naturally improve the immunity of the system to intersymbol interference. I would have liked to have seen some discussion as to the frequency allocation problem and in particular whether hand-offs are necessary in a CDMA structure. I think you tend to assume that the CDMA will be narrow(ish) band and so hand-offs will still be necessary. In a true wideband system it may only be necessary to simply pass the spreading code to effect a hand off to a neighbouring transmitter.

Nothing in the tutor's comments, however, gives away his expectations about form and presentation, though these are, in fact, frequently disappointed. It is as if he has no remit, authority or words to address these aspects: this is not apparently where his expertise lies. The 'omissions' in the commentary are a reminder that some areas of learning are more susceptible to explicitness than others and that concentration on some areas leaves others uncovered. Miller's conception of genre as uniting substance, form, context and motive may be an important way of righting imbalance.

In contrast to the tutor's reading of the students' work, mine was focused much more explicitly on form and rhetorical features – by default, since I was only vaguely aware of the details of what was being argued. In order to know which of the forms was successful and which less so, I had to gain access to what the tutor was taking for granted in his own practice, but had no words to describe when it was missing from the practice of his students. What I saw in a piece of work as immediately of interest was as surprising to him as what he saw was difficult or opaque for me.

What Was Required

The assignment was framed as a kind of role-play:

> You are part of the research and development team, investigating multiple access techniques .... The company for which you all work has invested vast sums in research into Time Division Multiple Access (TDMA) techniques for the proposed network.

> In response to a European initiative, your company has been asked to outline its recommendations for the multiple access techniques required for such a mobile network. An acquaintance at the European Telecommunications Standards Institute (ETSI) has secretly told you that the only scheme, other than TDMA, which is being considered is Code Division Multiple Access (CDMA). It is therefore essential that the European recommendation finds in favour of TDMA techniques so that your company can exploit the expensive research it has already undertaken.

Whilst this description may sound a little melodramatic, the tutor was drawing upon his own experience in tendering competitively for grants and this was in fact an accurate (if incomplete) representation of the way in which systems are researched and financed. This is how the brief goes on:

> You have been asked by your research director to produce a written report (10-20 pages), outlining the two opposing techniques. In particular concentrating on the benefits of the TDMA protocols when compared with CDMA. These reports can be universal in nature or can highlight specific characteristics of TDMA which offer definite advantages over the opposing CDMA schemes. Furthermore your group will be required to give an oral presentation of their findings in front of an invited audience. Both the written and oral presentation will be examined, not only for technical content, but also for the development of a reasoned argument.

This description was also – in retrospect – incomplete and the incompleteness turned out to be not incidental, but crucial. What was unsaid determined the extent to which the students recognised the reality of this scenario and the degree to which they were equipped to deal with it, as much as what was said or easily implied. For instance, what could be understood was that there is a need for persuasive argument, but what was not said was how to produce persuasive argument. What happened as a result of this was that several of the students equated strength of motive (need) with blatancy of appeal. This was, as it turned out, a highly indecorous response to the situation.[1]

The phrase 'the development of a reasoned argument' evoked too general a notion of argument to be helpful. The most immediate meaning of 'argument' is a vernacular one, played out most usually in oral forms, so that where the term is used unguardedly in an apparently general sense it seems to be understood as a blatant activity, as overtly persuasive or as overtly geared towards winning, establishing one's own position. Our use of the term argument in this context seemed to mislead students who were unaware of the particular social, rhetorical and, in this case, economic, contexts it was to be exercised in. Moreover, it did not seem to have been necessarily any more transparent to native speakers than to non-native ones. 'Argument' was an inadequate description in the same way that telling students that an essay should have a 'well-structured argument' leaves them none the wiser as to how to generate or structure an argument.

A Real Life Example

The difficulties students got into in interpreting the assignment in terms of genre – form, substance, context and motive – are looked at below, but first it may be worth taking a look at a 'real life' example of what the tutor was after. It was only after discussing our surprise at what the students had produced and after my questioning him whether the scenario the students had been given wasn't in fact just play acting, that he produced examples of what he meant. To him, it was clear that the scenario he offered was true to life.

The main example is in two parts: a letter from the DTI (Department of Trade and Industry) inviting proposals for the 'Space Diversity Research Project' and the 'preliminary research proposal' prepared by the university department as a response. The DTI letter includes a specification for the project, set out as follows:

1.0 Objectives (– *this clarifies the project's aims and areas to which consideration should be given, including costs*)

2.0 Benefits (– *the use to which the results could be put*)

2.1 Background (– *a brief look at the problems that have been identified*)

3.0 Statement of work (– *what the preliminary part and final phase would be*)

3.1 Output from project (– *a final report*)

4.0 Project monitoring (– *project will last about 8 weeks and be divided into 3 main phases*)

5.0 Delivery (– *what the final report should include*)

6.0 Payment

The specification appears offers a framework; just sufficient hints about the area of investigation and a series of headings to be used by the proposers, but a far greater degree of explicitness in regard to form than the students were given. (The proposal which the university put forward does not adhere to these exactly, but the overall organisation is similar.) The cover letter reiterates the areas in the specification:

---

[1] See Bazerman (1988):

  Understanding the genre one is working in is understanding decorum in the most fundamental sense – what stance and attitude is appropriate given the world one is engaged in at that moment. (p. 320)

115

Your proposal on how you would fulfil the specification to the Department's satisfaction should include in reasonable detail, the following:-

a   the method to be employed;

b   estimated cost including an analysis of man days, costs and expenses. VAT should always be shown separately;

c   timetable for the work;

d   names, qualifications and relevant experience of those who would be members of the team, if successful;

e   an indication of which team members would be responsible for which part(s) of the project.

You may comment on the specification if you so wish.

The letter goes on to say that proposers may be asked to a selection interview at a later date.

The proposal submitted by the university opens with a section on aims. Here it is proposed that the task will be divided into five parts; in effect the first three are a break down into greater complexity of the first phase suggested in the DTI specification. Immediately this refined classification gives the impression that the writers are thoroughly conversant with the field.

In the 'rationale' section which follows, the division of the task becomes clear through the development of an argued account of the technical history of using 'macroscopic diversity'. The rationale is the largest part of the proposal and is about 850 words long. In the first paragraphs the present proposal is placed in the context of other available options. The focus is gradually narrowed to what is being proposed – as in the following sentence from the end of the second paragraph. The bracketed number refer to footnotes containing references to the relevant literature:

> At present there several techniques for filling these holes using either repeaters or passive reflectors [6], microcell implementation [7] and finally, the subject of this proposal, macroscopic diversity [5], whereby the diversity sites are widely spaced compared with those used to combat fast fading.

Its style is impersonal, but this does not make it a neutral account; it is in fact constantly evaluative (italics added):

> Simulation studies of macroscopic diversity in mobile communications have indicated *significant* improvements [9]...

> *Unfortunately*, the overhead in terms of positional information together with the possibility of mobile movement means that such techniques are impractical ...

> However, since azimuth separation has been shown to affect macroscopic diversity performance *dramatically* [7], the necessary limit to the angular separation means that sectorisation is *not an efficient* means of macroscopic diversity ....

These qualitative judgements couched within the discussion of technical procedures and principles aid the advance of the argument which justifies the particular areas of investigation proposed. The discussion does not include detailed coverage of all previous research, but gestures towards it, as in the first sentence above, where there is a footnote. Such gesturing both acknowledges an informed readership and indicates the writers' competence in the field. In addition, it is economical on space and clarity, preventing the rationale being overcrowded with technical arguments.

In the final paragraph of the rationale the argument is consolidated. The writers signal a confidence that the investigations they propose will find positively in favour of macroscopic diversity and are therefore able to project beyond this towards future work. The process of what Swales (1990) has called 'creating a research space' (p. 141) is evident here as the writers show how what has already been found (indicated in the references) can be interpreted and taken forward with confidence and 'great promise' (again, evaluative phrases in italics):

> Having established that macroscopic diversity has *several advantages* within the mobile environment, the possible techniques for combining should be analysed. Because of the inherent analogue nature of present systems, selection combining has been widely detailed; Lee's approach *effectively uses* RSSI as the method of selecting the appropriate diversity branch. There will *clearly* have to be a compromise as to the diversity performance and interconnect capacity. The maximal ratio combiner can offer a 2dB advantage when compared with simple selection combining [6]. However the associated phasing problems [11] mean that such a scheme is *extremely difficult* to implement. Therefore, the study will examine the feasibility of incorporating various combining algorithms within the mobile environment. Specifically, it is felt that *the optimum* symbol-level combining , which can offer a performance approaching that of equal-gain combining [12,13] whilst offering 1.5-2 dB improvements over selection combining for fourth order diversity, shows *great promise* for implementation in the mobile environment.

The 'great promise' of this final sentence represents an opening up. The initial narrowing of focus at the beginning of the rationale led to the middle paragraphs which introduced the specific areas of investigation and then to the wide and unspecified promise of the future. This movement from wide to narrow to wide again, or general to particular, particular to general has been found to be common to research articles (Swales, p.134).[2]

The proposal is completed with sections on required resources, a work plan and timetable, personnel and responsibilities, deliverables, additional research group background, references and additional information. The whole runs to five sides of small type.

Mismatch Between the Real-life and Simulated Task

Although this tender was offered by the tutor as an example of what he was – in retrospect – expecting from the students, there are immediate differences with what they were asked to do. First, they were writing a report for, in the first instance, their research director rather than the European initiative. Since they were not directly answering the tender, the function of the writing may therefore have been somewhat different. Notice, for instance, the option they were given in the task specification to take either a 'universal' or 'specific' approach. If the report were aimed at informing the director about the current research and its applicability to their team's preferred technology, then it would tell him or her what could be argued, rather than in fact persuading of it. In this case one might expect knowledge to be displayed in greater detail than in the tender. In addition the students' brief asks for a report of between 10 and 20 pages, far longer than the research proposal. The proposal also, by its very nature, has a future-orientation to it, whilst the report outlines and defends existing systems.

---

[2] This 'hour glass' pattern is reproduced in chapter 11, where suggestions are made about making such structures available to students.

What can be learnt from this disjunction between the real life task and the simulated one? Is there an educational objective in asking students to write reports, in that this requires them to display knowledge and understanding which cannot be otherwise assumed?

This doesn't seem to be the case, at least not explicitly. The tutor commented that in general the students' reports contained far too much technical and mathematical material, which should instead have been included in an appendix or been simply alluded to and referenced to a particular paper. Just as in the proposal, extensive research/reading must have been undertaken but only signalled, not recounted. Similarly, it is the understanding which has been taken from it, the significance that has been attached to it and the authority it conveys that are important. The tutor was clear that these features distinguish this report quite clearly from the kind of report a student would write on a final year undergraduate project for example and from papers written in journals (the research reading).

The distinctions were not, however, made explicit to the students. Given that the display of knowledge is often an assumed purpose in writing undertaken in academic contexts, the issue of 'presupposable' and 'non-presupposable' knowledge was perhaps of crucially important to bring to the fore. At the same time, however, it is probably one of the most difficult aspects of disciplinary learning to specify with any clarity (see Giltrow and Valiquette, 1994). And as these authors point out the indeterminate status of the student – 'novice or neo-insider or recent outsider' – complicates any attempt to specify what they should and should not presuppose their reader knows. The reader is always also the teacher and, given that, display is always more or less acceptable: the pedagogical factor creeps into the 'authentic' task.

The Students' Writing

Having considered the expectations of the tutor and some of the confusions potential within the task the students were given, we need to look now at what they actually produced. I want to start with the most successful of the reports, which received an A grade.

The numerous subdivisions in Rodney's report convey a strong impression of control, of the material having been selected and categorised. The argument itself, however is emergent, rather than categorical from the outset.

The introduction to the report does not indicate a tendency in the report to highlight one system or another. The task is, in fact, to support TDMA, but the greater emphasis in the opening paragraph and in the body of the report is actually on CDMA:

> This report compares the features of Time Division Multiple Access (TDMA) signal multiplexing techniques against Code Division Multiple Access (CDMA) in a cellular mobile radio environment. In the absence of working details of a practical CDMA system, considerations have been given to the features of such a system that would be required to make it work in practice, and from this assessment, an estimate of CDMA call capacity has been made.

Since CDMA is the newer, less well tested system, the emphasis on it here may be a deliberate tactic: thorough consideration which nevertheless results in rejection inspires more confidence in the decision than an out of hand dismissal. The slant of the report is towards a kind of experimental engagement with the issues. He aims to set up a hypothetical situation by considering the necessary practical features and to estimate the usefulness of the system from that. The introduction promises a movement towards considered and tested judgement, rather than the demonstration of a foregone conclusion: it is future – rather than retrospectively – oriented. In this way it resembles the real life proposal.

The remainder of the introduction sets out a background to the new technologies which have given rise to both CDMA and TDMA, placing them initially therefore within the same historical and developmental framework. In other words he establishes a position of commonality before beginning to differentiate. This again is similar to the real life proposal. When he has given an overview of the systems currently available, he begins the task of differentiation by setting out terms under 'System Specification' – 'what consideration will be given to'. He makes two subdivisions here: 'Essential system requirements' and 'Desirable features'. This discriminating methodical approach suggests again that the eventual recommendation of the report will be a result of analysis objectively undertaken against clear criteria.

Within the minutely organised structure of the report the language is similarly discursive to that of the proposal above, for example:

> Multipath problems can be eliminated in a single carrier FM TDMA system by channel equalisation, which has been demonstrated to work satisfactorily within the GSM system. When using small cells in order to increase system capacity, propagation times are relatively short compared to the data rate, and significant multipath components do not develop. It is therefore not necessary to equalise single carrier FM TDMA signals in small cells removing the expense of the equaliser.

Again, the language is not neutral but consistently evaluative: systems do not simply 'work', but work 'satisfactorily'. By making these nuances the writer suggests a more sophisticated understanding of the field; he exercises judgement about sufficiency and quality; he weighs things up rather than simply pronounces them to be true or false.[3]

Another feature of this report is a section towards the end summarising the 'Assumptions' upon which the analysis of CDMA was based; such things as the radius of each cell, the number of channels in use. These show the limitations as well as the scope of the analysis. They fulfil the promise of hypothetical experimentation raised in the introduction. Failure to do this was a problem in several of the other reports where the students based their judgements of CDMA on its specific application in US contexts, making an evaluation of its use in Europe difficult to make. An adequate comparison of the two systems needed to be based on the same conditions for use.

In his analysis of the two systems this writer includes a section on hardware costs. Unlike some of the other writers who referred broadly to economic factors, he is specific (as it is a requirement of the real life tendering process to be).

Where has this writer learnt these requirements which were not stated in the task he was given? As he states in his questionnaire:

> I have had to write many similar reports in the past usually involving more time and producing a final result to a higher standard, in a working environment. This has frequently involved very close co-operation with colleagues.

---

[3] This is a similar effect to that achieved by the extensive use of hypothetical 'if....then....' constructions used in another of the tutor's proposals – the writer is able to think not only what *is* but what *might* be in a given situation. Rodney also makes use of hypothetical situations: 'Consider this...'

He had learnt through experience and, it seems, through collaboration. The impression is that he has learnt through being a member of a discourse community, one of the defining features of which is the existence of certain shared genres (Swales p. 26). He is successful because he is able to interpret the task correctly; what is required is as obvious to him as it is to the tutor.

This is not, however, the case for several of the other students. Whilst certain features of the writing seem to be fairly constant, such as the presentation and explication of one system and then the other, followed by a conclusion on the basis of a point by point comparison, there is nevertheless a good deal of variety in way the task – particularly the argumentative requirement – has been interpreted and in the kinds of technical material used.

In this example Amin outlines his argument strategy in the opening summary and returns to in the conclusion:

> [Summary] In view of the vast amount of money invested by our company in research into TDMA for the proposed network I shall endeavour to concentrate on benefits of the TDMA protocols when compared with CDMA so as to convince the company to carry on with their research into TDMA instead of funding a brand new CDMA protocol research .....
> ... My arguments in favour of TDMA will be overwhelming enough to convince the company to stick with TDMA.
>
> [Conclusion] It is not always on technical reasons for the adoption of techniques, we have to weigh all the options and make a balanced judgement which is economically sound at the end of our decisions.

The model used appears to be closer to an oral one than one commonly used in scientific writing. It makes use of the personal pronoun and blatantly promotes the value of its argument. The scale of the argument is also too large; phrases such as 'technical reasons' and 'economically sound' state rather than demonstrate; they describe publicly what the report should be enacting at the level of the specialised discourse community.

Within these opening and closing frames the development of the argument is actually inconsistent. The section which describes CDMA, for instance, is entirely positive, no more so than in its concluding statement:

> With all these inherent advantages, CDMA appears to be the logical choice henceforth for all of the next generation digital mobile radio networks.

In order to convince of the value of TDMA after such a positive endorsement of its rival, the writer has recourse to economic considerations. The section on TDMA ends:

> As I shall reinforce, TDMA protocols have been proven to work especially in the Europe-wide coverage of the GSM system. Because of this very important reason it will be economic suicide if my company embarks on CDMA techniques which is mainly North American based and still to be tested even as this report is being compiled.

It may be the case that economic considerations are paramount in retaining TDMA, but does it do to show these flying in the face of the technical advantages clearly displayed as belonging to the rival system. This assertion is a good example of the naked way in which the argumentative task has been interpreted. The diction here is also inappropriate as occasionally in other places too:

> But wait for it, additional code sequences degrades the code quality. What you gain from one you lose in the other.

The context for the writing seems to have added an element of melodrama, which undermines the authority of the report. The statement of intention and proof stands in for the actual demonstration of the case. The way that economic and financial reality relate to technical aspects, for example, is more complex than is assumed here and needs to be more pragmatically handled.

Amin comments in an accompanying questionnaire 'Stepping up my argumentative prowess was the most difficult task in this report'.

> As a scientist and an engineer we deal in factual reports and analysis of our findings. Therefore, this writing is similar in that case. But different in the sense that I have to convince a body of experts by the addition of economic and financial reality of not adopting my proposals.

Although this commentary suggests he has understood the *purpose of* the writing, the rhetorical situation and strategies are not understood. Knowing the purpose is clearly not sufficient to be able to carry it out; the other factors in genre are also crucial.

Other students also frame their reports in the 'real world' context they have been given:

> [Introduction] As part of a research and development team that has undertaken extensive research into CDMA, I feel that I am in an ideal position to outline the properties of CDMA that will make it the obvious choice for the third generation of personal communication networks.

> [Discussion and conclusions] For the reasons stated I am sure that a CDMA system is the obvious choice and I cannot think of a single reason why one would choose a TDMA system. I hope that this report is useful in your final decisions and that you come to the only sensible conclusion. (*Stuart*)

What is interesting here is that although the student has recognised a need to signal his suitability to comment, he has not used an appropriate form of doing so. In actual reports of this nature the credentials of the writer are signalled towards the end as a short, impersonal statement of relevant responsibilities and achievements to date. Authority is thus conveyed indirectly and in an objective form.

Another way of framing the writing task was the non-committal approach:

> [Introduction] Both systems have advantages and suffer disadvantages and these are also presented so that the reader can draw their own conclusion as to which is superior.

> [Conclusion] This report has presented a basic overview of the TDMA and CDMA systems. The reader has been introduced to the fundamental operation of each technique and their properties discussed. It appears that TDMA is superior to CDMA. However CDMA does offer a challenge to current systems and certainly to future comms. systems. (*Derek*)

However comprehensive the discussions contained within this report, it fails to fulfil the task requirements – sitting on the fence is not an option (as it certainly can be in the essay for instance). Again the difference is between the relatively more epistemic purposes of writing in educational contexts and the categorically action oriented purpose of writing in workplace contexts. The tutor related (though not apparently to the students) how, in some earlier work experience, he had whittled a choice down to two for his employers, who told him that until he had actually made a decision he hadn't completed the task (see also Freedman 1994).

Other students move towards confident impersonal discourse, but still fall short of satisfactorily interpreting the very particular argument strategies that are needed:

> [Abstract] With the proliferation of mobile communications in Europe and the rest of the world, the need for standardisation is obvious. To achieve standardisation, any competing techniques must be independently evaluated and the superior technology chosen as the standard. The inferior technique must then be avoided to maintain compatibility. (*Fred*)

This introduction (labelled as the 'abstract') appears to form a satisfactory opening for the report, yet the grounds for argument which it sets out are highly simplified and are not in fact carried through. The writer's task is to argue for the older system TDMA and he has as a result recourse to economic grounds. The straightforward notion of a 'superior technology' has very little use in the actual situation; the technology is superior, in any case, not in an absolute sense, but in context. The introduction has therefore preempted the practicalities of the situation. In his conclusion he concedes to this:

> [Conclusion] The advantages of using Time Division Multiple Access instead of Code Division Multiple Access have been clearly stated. Although many advocators of the spread spectrum system quote figures for capacity that are many times that of TDMA, the reality of the situation is that very little extra capacity is available when dealing with **real** systems. CDMA does not offer the same flexibility, compatibility and efficiency as spectral resources as TDMA. The whole technology of spread spectrum systems is still fairly immature but may one day offer a viable alternative to the time-slotted multiple access scheme. At present, though, the victor in the battle between the two systems is clearly TDMA and its use in the third generation of personal communication networks must be assured.

The balanced approach of this conclusion makes it more difficult to assess in terms of effectiveness. It may be that too much is conceded to the other side and that support for TDMA is not therefore conclusive enough. Notice also the use of the 'argument as war' metaphor, which sits uncomfortably in the cool scientific discourse.

Thoughts on How to Improve

The aspects of the students' writing I have selected here were not, as I mentioned above, picked out by the tutor in his extensive comments to the students. Whilst he is able to engage fully with the content of the writing, he does not alert them to their rhetorical and generic errors. He received no instruction himself on how to write tenders and proposals. Such knowledge is not the topic of conversation in his field and neither does it seem – at least initially – a matter for teaching and learning. Yet having acknowledged the potential for enormous misunderstandings and lack of knowledge in these areas we now have to confront the question of how to overcome them. Do we have any choice but to engage in explicit teaching? If the tutor learnt his own trade through experience and membership of the discourse community alone, is this sufficient for these students also, or can more be done to alert them to the techniques they will shortly need in work?

At this point it may be an idea to introduce a postscript to the discussion of the real life proposal above. The university were not successful in competing for the DTI tender. As the tutor put it, there had been a problem of communication, something akin, he felt, to that which had occurred with the simulation exercise. The DTI, it transpired, were not actually concerned to push technology ahead, but wanted rather to receive ideas about the management of analogue techniques. The university, in proposing investigations into digital techniques, were pitching the argument a generation ahead. In this case, then, the future-orientation noted in the proposal was not appropriate.

What the anecdote illustrates is that operation in real life genres is as fraught with complication and potential for misinterpretation as in the simulated scenario. Some attempts to produce appropriate generic solutions will be more successful than others. In every tender there will be one winner and several losers. The implication for explicit teaching is clear: there can be no formula to guarantee success. Are there steps which we can nonetheless take?

As a result of this experience, coincidental with our discussions about the students' work, the tutor decided to use a modified version of the letter from the DTI as an for the following year's students and also to offer them examples of the genre in which they would be expected to write. The letter contained a strict stipulation on length and just one clue to the kind of research the students would be expected to engage in – a reference to a relatively obscure article. This, it was hoped, would prompt them to use the on-line searches in the library – one of the exercises residual but related academic aims. Although the tutor has not yet evaluated the students' responses to the DTI's invitation, a first glance suggested to him that the form and style at least are more convincing than in the previous exercise: 'they look far more professional'. His conviction seems to be growing that his students should learn through doing complex tasks which involve them in researching and comprehending for themselves and, then, additionally, in responding rhetorically to particular situations, to the display in effect of context-specific literacies.

It is interesting, as a final word, to note that the tutor, whilst pleased at the apparently improved generic performance of the students, nonetheless regretted that the element of arguing for and against the competing systems had been lost. This had been a valuable element of the first exercise and he would attempt to incorporate it next year with what he had learnt from the DTI exercise. The tutor's enthusiasm for argument is perhaps slightly different in nature to his interest in eliciting workplace forms. The first relates to his desire that his students understand the competing influences on scientific or technical 'right' answers; the second to his sense that his students need to be literate in the fields in which they will work. The first perhaps veers towards meta-understanding, the second to functional skills.

The difficulty in combining these aims in a single exercise is, I think, to find a language – and forms of invitation – which will elicit the first in the service of the second. As Rodney's report showed, it can be done, if the sense of argument as 'for and against' is not understood as a template for written form, but rather as a signal for overall purpose embedded within a very different structure and style of writing. It is this combination which the tutor hopes to make available to his students next year – not, I suspect, a straightforward task, but one which, through experience and experiment he is perhaps better equipped to carry through.

9. Writing Argument: Cognitive Control, Cultural Construct

Written argument has been alluded to in earlier chapters of this report: the identification of it as a problem in schooling; the dominant forms it takes; the attitudes students and teachers have towards it; the connections (or lack of connections) it has with spoken argument; the complex ways in which it is shaped by context. Here I want to continue the exploration of what writing argument means in academic settings. This has been a central concern in this project and it seems to have two pedagogical implications. The first is to help students to improve in their skills of written argument as it is required for academic success – in practice this frequently means becoming better writers of *essays*. The second implication or impulse is to look for alternative ways in which argument might be manifested in writing. In some ways this second aim might seem to undermine the first, but I don't think this is necessarily true: improvement to traditional forms can come about through change as well as consolidation.

Thought and Form

In their study of the writing abilities of students in grades 5, 8 and 12 in two modes, Freedman and Pringle (1984) used the following criteria as an instrument for evaluating written argument:

> First the whole piece of discourse must be unified by either an implicit or (more commonly) an explicitly stated single restricted thesis; that is, the whole must be so unified that each point and each illustration either directly substantiates the thesis or is a link in a chain of reasoning which supports that thesis. Secondly, the individual points and illustrations must be integrated within a hierarchic structure so that each proposition is logically linked not only to the preceding and succeeding propositions but to the central and indeed to every other proposition within the whole text. (p. 74)

This description seems to be underpinned by Vygotsky's idea of concept development in the way suggested by Applebee (1978). Applebee found a correlation between the changes in the way children told stories and the stages that Vygotsky outlined. His representation of developing story structure can also be used in relation to the structure of written arguments (see diagram below). In the final stage each of the elements or incidents in the story or argument are related both to each other and to the central unifying idea. Applebee comments:

> Each incident not only develops out of the previous one, but at the same time elaborates a new aspect of the theme or situation. Such stories seem to have a consistent forward movement and often, though not necessarily, a climax at the end (p. 65-6)

The link suggested here between textual structuration and cognitive development is apparent too in the description of argument Freedman and Pringle give. Notice the stress that is placed on unity and coherence. The thesis works to subsume and order all other ideas. It is also singular; only one line or 'chain' of argument exists in the whole. And the 'piece of discourse' is a 'whole'; it is closed and finished.

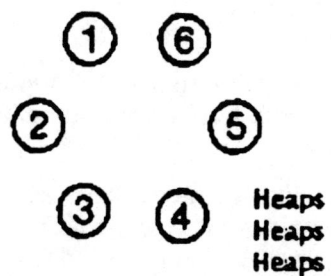

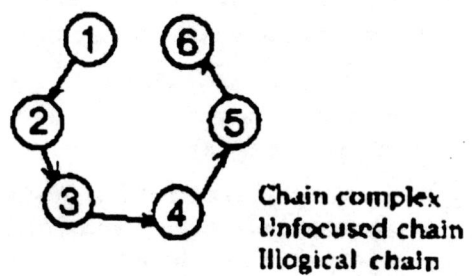

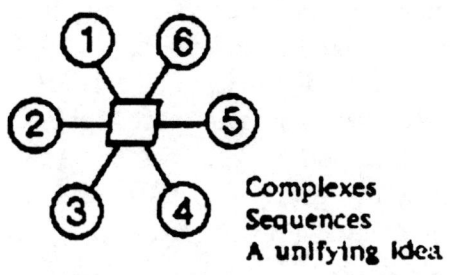

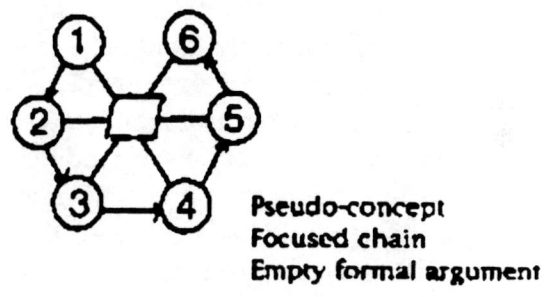

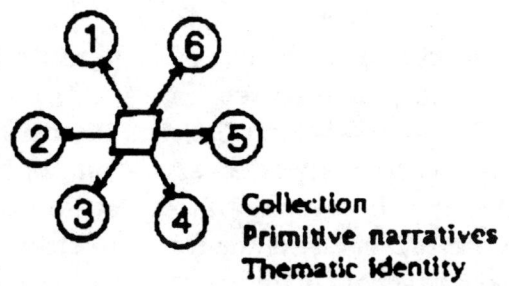

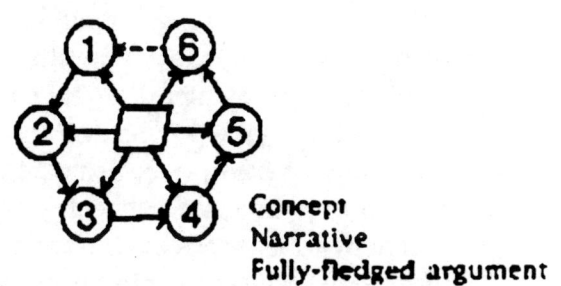

Heaps
Heaps
Heaps

Chain complex
Unfocused chain
Illogical chain

Complexes
Sequences
A unifying idea

Pseudo-concept
Focused chain
Empty formal argument

Collection
Primitive narratives
Thematic identity

Concept
Narrative
Fully-fledged argument

In this chapter I want to suggest that, whilst the successful mastery of complex form may indicate advanced cognitive development, the relationship between argument and such form is not an inevitable convergence, but rather a well established and, it might be argued, gendered one.

The instructions Freedman and Pringle gave to the students participating in their study specified no single form for the writing ('write a composition (or an essay, or an article or letter)' 1989 p.74). Nonetheless, in my experience at A level and beyond, the type of thinking they describe as argument is often conflated with particular forms.[1] Research by Berrill (1992) is a useful illustration of this. In her hierarchy of argumentative ability the

---

[1] It is also very different from what argument is like in speech.

accommodation of alternative points of view represents the highest level and this is interpreted, using models of cognitive development, as a cognitive and educational advance on egocentric forms of argument. Students' writing which does well on her scale of argumentative ability receives commentary such as the following:

> ... it is not only the inclusion of alternative points of view which demonstrates Donna's appreciation of their legitimacy: it is also the language she uses to express those points of view which demonstrates the *reasonableness* of the alternative positions. (p. 91)

Writing, on the other hand, which does less well and is considered to be egocentric and thus to represent a low stage of cognitive control, is commented on in the following ways:

> ... the short, terse style and the hammering repetition of the word 'control' renders the statements assertive. The lack of elaboration combines with this assertive tone to make the sentences didactic [...]

> [on another example] It is interesting to see writing which uses sophisticated stylistic structures of repetition and varied metre still lacking in attention to readers' other needs of explanation of terms which are highly connotative such as 'manipulation' and 'fear'. (p. 93)

It is interesting to note the positive emphasis in these comments on 'reasonableness' and the implication that language which is other than neutral is somehow bad. In addition a generalised reader is assumed, for whom it is necessary to be clear and explicit. Other studies (e.g. Giltrow and Valiquette 1994) have shown that readers' needs are highly dependent on reading; that is, on who is reading and in what situation. Berrill, I think it is clear, is reading within the essayist and academic traditions, which precisely favour reasonableness and suspect emotion (see the section below on A level English Language). The way she understands argument and cognitive development can not be set aside from the expectations she holds of form.

What strikes me strongly about her study is the possibility that the students interpreted as displaying egocentricity and, therefore, as less highly developed cognitively, may in fact simply be employing a different *form* of argumentative writing. Rather than the essay form with its requirement to be even-handed and to differentiate between the sources of ideas, they may, for example, be using polemic. In contexts other than educational ones, such as in politics or journalism, egocentric argument may be just what is required. But Berrill on the whole overlooks the constructed and contextual nature of the forms, interpreting them as representing insights into an individual's psychology, rather than their ability to learn appropriate and legitimate ways of doing things.[2]

It is as likely to be this, rather than some absolute measure of cognitive ability, that makes for successful writing of the kind described above. I am reminded of the mention made in John Swales' book *Genre Analysis* (1990) of how culture-specific, rather than universally valid, the forms we value are:

> Kaplan and Ostler (1982), in a review of the literature, conclude, despite a minority of studies to the contrary, that different languages have different preferences for certain kinds of language patterns. For instance, they argue that English expository prose has an essentially linear rhetorical pattern which consists of:

---

[2] Kuhn (1992) has noted the impact of educational experience on an individual's ability to conduct arguments in which the possibility of alternative points of view is conceded and what they might be imagined.

> ...a clearly defined topic, introduction, body which explicates all but nothing more than the stated topic, paragraphs which chain from one to the next, and a conclusion which tells the reader what has been discussed ... no digression, no matter how interesting, is permitted on the grounds that it would violate unity.
> (Kaplan and Ostler, 1982:14)

> They then contrast this pattern with the elaborate parallel structures found in Arabic prose, with the more digressive patterns of writing in Romance languages which permit 'tangential' material to be introduced in the discourse and so on. (p. 64/5)

Street (1984) has argued that our understanding of what constitutes logical and abstract thinking is tied up with a dominant mode of literacy in which explicitness and clarity are major factors as are objectivity and the singularity of meaning. These qualities have the status of ideals within our culture, become associated with cognitive capacity and are thus used as the means to discriminate between individuals in the education system. They are associated specifically with *academic* language and forms and thus are the products of particular contexts and purposes, but are often assumed (as I suggested they were in Berrill's study) to be context free and 'autonomous'. Street says of those who use the autonomous model, that they:

> ... derive doubtful generalisations, often implicitly rather than explicitly, from the specific character of 'academic language'. They assert, for example, by implication that non-academics in their own culture and members of other cultures, particularly illiterate 'primitives', cannot have the skills of 'objectivity', 'neutrality' and 'logic' which their own academic language is specifically designed to facilitate. The fact, however, that they have designed a language to fulfil these functions does not necessarily mean that these functions could not be fulfilled in other ways, nor that their language is intrinsically connected with them, nor that the language has necessarily been proven to succeed in achieving these ideals. (p. 77)[3]

Street puts his objections very strongly and I think he gives pause for thought about the dominance of certain forms within our tradition.

Let me turn for a few pages to an example which illustrates the value placed on the expression of certain types of thinking within certain forms.

A Level English Language: Argument As Balanced Discussion[4]

The example of an A level English Language examination syllabus is particularly pertinent to this discussion because of the sense in which – not being a content-based subject, such as, say, History or Sociology – the writing it elicits is seen to be the outcome of natural rather than discipline-specific developmental processes.

The course syllabus (AEB 660 English Language and Literature) states:

> Candidates should prepare themselves for the examination by their own wide reading, including daily and weekly newspapers and periodicals .... They may bring into the

---

[3] For example (p. 76), Popper who argues 'that the evolutionary emergence of "our self transcendence by means of selection and rational criticism" depends upon developments that have taken place in academic language: "It is only within a language thus enriched that critical argument and knowledge in the objective sense become possible"' (Popper, *Objective Knowledge*, 1979, p. 122).

[4] This account was written in collaboration with Mark Reid as part of a wider consideration of writing argument in English Language.

examination their own experience of many different forms of written and spoken expression, and should be encouraged to use radio, television and film in their preparation.

There are no prescribed texts or specified topics; the examination paper in Language requires simply:

A piece of writing on one of a number of subjects, which may include current movements and events, social, scientific, technical and economic topics of general interest, literary and artistic topics.

Certain types of content are, however, allied to certain modes of expression:

Some subjects will require argument or balanced discussion; other topics will provide opportunity for reflective, narrative or descriptive treatment.

In the course aims two vital qualities are yoked together: 'the development of a critical sense and of a personal response'. Since these qualities are not demonstrated in response to any particular texts or body of knowledge, they seem to derive from a vaguer qualification – that of being a well-educated, thinking and expressive individual, as a result perhaps of reading newspapers and periodicals. The sense is of the 'man of letters' who employs informed common sense and everyday philosophy: critical but not theoretical, personal but not sentimental.

The examiners' reports on student responses to particular questions suggest how these qualities are manifested in the essay form. On the 1992 paper was the question:

Religion: "the opium of the people" or "the means of salvation"? What is your view?

The examiners comment:

Whilst the best responses were wide ranging, with sustained objectivity, relevant example and often historical knowledge to support material, there were many candidates who used the opportunity only to write extensively about their own religious faith, or lack of it. The best response balanced discussion of the alternatives suggested and demonstrated a personal viewpoint which was supported by the conclusions drawn from that discussion.

The question asks for the candidate's view, but also sends out signals, via the two opposing quotations, that more is needed than this.[5] The personal viewpoint must be developed and constructed in a particular way: it must emerge from balance and objectivity rather than faith. Similarly with the question 'What 'rights' do you think animals have?', the examiners considered that:

inverted commas around 'rights' should have alerted them to the necessity to attempt a definition and put this at the heart of their discussion.

---

[5] It is worth noticing the subjects about which the students are asked to write in both Freedman and Pringle's and Berrill's studies. In the former this was the following prompt:

There are probably things happening in the world around you – at school, among your friends, at home, in the country, in the world – that you think ought to be changed.

and in Berrill's: 'Should parents be able to control the lives of their teenage children?' Both topics make an appeal to personal opinion and experience even though successful completion of the task may involve moving away from these. It is perhaps hardly surprising that the writers in Berrill's study 'seem to be strongly consumed by the apparent desire to describe to the reader 'all about' parent-teacher relationships.'(p. 83)

The question asks the candidate what she thinks while at the same time masking (by the use of inverted commas) a restricted notion of what and how she can think. Freedom of expression is, in fact, illusory.

The examiners had little patience with emotional or passionate responses:

> One does not expect (presumably) eighteen year old A level students to write, in all seriousness, about cute little bunny rabbits. Little understanding was shown about farming methods or the natural behaviour of animals: one suspects that the leaflets produced by certain action groups have had a strong influence on the thinking of some of these candidates. There were, however, a few refreshing examples of candidates who were prepared *to think for themselves*, and who had accurate information to support their arguments. (italics added)

English, it is clear, carries with it strong cultural expectations about appropriate attitudes, content and style and, to be successful, students must be alert to the signals implicit in the questions. The expectation behind the comment here is that students' knowledge should be wide-ranging and reasoned, yet the candidates were given no access to information, material or alternative views. Atkinson (1989) has traced this lack as a long standing tendency for examination boards in England when asking for opinions on controversial topics. The reason for this reluctance seems to stem again from the image of the man of letters whose habitual armchair reading is (quality) newspapers and periodicals – rather than, for instance, the information put out by activists. Clearly 'appropriate' reading is amongst the ground rules of successful essay writing. The difference between these types of reading is significant; one is about being kept passively well-informed, the other about being persuaded to action. In a similar way the essay is not a place for a display of conviction or an impulse to persuade or change; rather it is the site of disinterested interest. The essay is, in this sense, the vehicle of an ideology of consensus where differences are allowable and necessary, but where no particular viewpoints are privileged.

The 'naturalness' of students' writing about issues of general interest is, as I've begun to suggest, closely associated with the history of the essay form. Womack, (1993) traces the essay as a *literary* genre back to Montaigne and Bacon for whom it represented 'a marginal space in the system of rhetorical genres, ... a bracketed and unofficial discourse' (p. 43). Later – the early nineteenth century – the essay became conflated with another form – the 'theme' – which required a far more formal treatment of material. It was this new conflated form of the essay which then became dominant in English composition in schools. Addison and the *Spectator* were also highly influential in creating a tradition in which:

> The essay is to be analytic up to a point, but it is not to subject the text to the inhuman mechanical analysis of the professional scholar; rather it is to express the cultivated response of a man of taste. (p. 44)

Here then is the reluctance to stipulate content or method beyond what can be picked up from broadly cultured reading. The examiners of the A level course, for example, acknowledge the place of knowledge brought in from other disciplines, but make clear that writing in English should not be equivalent to it. On the question 'What do you think makes an effective advertisement?' they noted:

> There was evidence that Communication Studies students had much relevant material to bring to this answer, and many of these used their knowledge well. This did provide the occasional trap for *the unwary*, with too much emphasis placed on the marketing techniques of commercial companies at the expense of analysis of chosen examples of advertisements. (italics added)

The appeal again is to the personal, but it is unclear what kinds of analysis are presupposed here: would they be of a general literary nature, descriptive, parodying or semiotic? Should the advertisements be treated as the objects of practical criticism?

Womack's descriptions of the essay as it has evolved capture very well the ideal which appears still to underlie the comments of the examiners we have quoted:

> The non-rhetorical rhetorical genre...its judicious amateurism signifies detachment.... It is the practice of education as opposed to training; it prepares the student writer, not for the accomplishment of any particular task, but for membership of that bourgeois public sphere in which disparate private subjects interact harmoniously on the basis of a shared discourse – a universe, not of reason exactly (since that suggests an un-English rigour unresponsive to intuition, sentiment, custom) but of *reasonableness*. (p. 44)

To complement Womack's slightly parodying tone, we might bring in here another example from the 1992 examiners' report. On the question 'Is class an outdated concept in Britain?' they say:

> It was depressing to note how many candidates equated wealth and/or income with class. There were, however, some elegantly argued and well-informed responses, which ranged more widely in their supportive material and evaluated as class indicators such matters as dress, accent, leisure activities, holiday destinations, and a variety of aspects of social behaviour.

Should this comment be read as a disappointment at the lack of sociological insight displayed by the candidates or as a failure fully to understand the delicate nuances of class differentiation? Do the examiners regret perhaps that class should be reduced to anything as material as money?

The problem is of course that the apparently 'universal' form of the essay is in fact the basis for discrimination. Within the assessment and examination system, as Womack points out:

> the essay becomes the *most* functional kind of writing, even cynically so; the essayist's free disinterestedness is called for in a real context of compulsion and self-interest. (p. 46)

The successful student writer in the essayist tradition has learnt to convey socialised and civilised thought within a romantic tradition of sensitivity and expression. These ground rules are not natural, nor – necessarily if we are to use them to discriminate – equally accessible to all. Sheeran and Barnes (1991) also make this point:

> ...what older pupils write often proves to be more consciously managed than seems to be implied in the teacher's rhetoric of authentic first hand experience. Writing of this kind is skilful rather than passionate: the writer seeks for effects rather than seeking to reveal his or her soul. (p. 83/4)

To this description we might add that the writer seeks to be balanced and objective, rather than to express actual opinions. The expression of neutrality and detachment is not, however, a neutral one, but a highly value-laden learnt behaviour. Once again it is a reminder that definitions and expressions of argument are not all equally valid or powerful within contexts. Certain definitions, such as that explored here, can have an excluding effect on others, by virtue of the fact that they are espoused by dominant ideologies and institutions.

One of the ways in which these ideologies have been addressed and challenged is from a feminist perspective. Meyer (1993), for instance, considers writing which requires the development of a thesis as aggressive and oppositional (see the definition of argument as 'a connected series of statements or reasons intended to establish a position (and hence refute its opposite)'). She takes the *Norton Reader*'s definition of the "formal essay":

> "The formal essay most often presents a serious subject for a specialized audience; its author writes as an acknowledged authority whose purpose is to inform the reader; the tone of the formal essay tends to be impersonal"

and comments that it requires students to play

> a confidence game. One synonym for confident is "cocksure" and indeed, that is my point – to have confidence, the students must participate in an illusion of mastery: an illusion of "being cocksure" of themselves, their control of the language, their mastery of the literary text, and their superiority over their audience. (p. 47)

For Meyer, then, the type of argument required of a formal academic essay is a very masculine, patriarchal form of behaviour, which seeks to win over its reader, rather than accommodate her or express any trace of hesitancy, doubt or deviation in purpose.[6] Meyer's position offers an alternative way of reading Berrill's positive endorsement of writing in which there is 'accommodation of alternative point of view':

> Argument explicitly acknowledges validity of alternative point of view and incorporates that view in the structure of the argument, either through partial support and incorporation of that view or through some degree of refutation of the alternative view which recognizes the validity of the claim but which posits a stronger validity claim to the writer's view. (Berrill, p. 85)

It's possible to read this description of what Berrill calls 'meeting the needs of one's audience'(p. 82) as instead a way of subsuming the positions of one's audience in order to confidently and convincingly assert the 'stronger validity' of one's own view. (This kind of motivation underlies Kaufer and Geisler's novelty theory, see chapter 2). The writer takes a detached and impersonal stance towards the world and towards issues in the world, seeking to convince by effacing the self, but at the same time allowing no possibility for the interpellation, objection or response of any other. The result of this projection of power through writing is, in Meyer's view and my own (see next chapter), the disempowerment of the writer.

The Essay as Closure: Its Place In the Process of Learning

The practices of detached objectivity and argument as the development of a unified thesis are within the same broad tradition. The value placed on unity and coherence in argument and impersonality and clarity in style sets in play a number of apparently contradictory demands. For instance, the need to develop a position without acknowledging a place for oneself in the process; the need to be unified and yet to put both sides of the argument. Persuasion is required without passion and critical thinking is matched with certainty and singleness of purpose [7]. Processes of thinking are equated with the presentation of thought as a product. These are difficult pairings for the student to manoeuvre.

---

[6] The way Freedman and Pringle's research task was presented to their students conforms to the imperative to be convincing:

> to convince someone else (preferably someone who has the power to make changes) that what you object to is really bad and ought to be changed. (1989 p. 74)

[7] Kaufer and Geisler's research (see chapter 11) suggests that arguments progress through following 'faulty paths' as much as a straightforward main one, yet there is no scope for this strategy in the idea of 'a chain of reasoning'.

It seems to me likely that complexities such as these help to form the assumptions that students bring to writing. McCormick (1990) lists these, as I've mentioned before (chapter 6), as 'the desire for *closure*; a belief in *objectivity*; and a refusal to write about perceived *contradictions*.'(p. 195) These assumptions clearly overlap and influence one another; they suggest very much that writing is viewed as a procedure where closure is placed on ideas rather than a process by which ideas are explored and new ones developed.

This is, in fact, often the way in which essay writing is presented to students, especially if the essay is invariable to be written as the outcome of a period of study. The English tutor I mentioned in chapter 5 specified both the text to be read and the specific question to be answered on it at the same time and in advance of the tutorial discussion. It seemed to me that this arrangement would impose a distinct frame around the text, determining the way it was read and the kinds of exploration that would be possible in the essay and the discussion. After the essay was written, another reading and essay assignment would be in its place, so that no further discussion would take place, beyond, at most, a few comments passed between student and tutor at the handing-back time.

In another subject I observed an essay was to be handed in at the end of the first term of study, from a choice of questions contained in the student handbook since the beginning of term (and indeed unchanged for several years previously). The tutor marked the essays high in order to encourage his students; he knew what they didn't that this first essay had little value in assessment terms. Its function was formal and ritualistic: to initiate. In a sense the students did pick up on this. Some of them wrote their essays on topics from the list of titles which had not been covered in the weekly seminars. They drew on previous knowledge with which they felt secure, rather than risk or explore areas which were new to them. It seems ironic that whilst the students had on this occasion really nothing to lose from taking risks in their writing, their impulse was nonetheless to play safe. Except, of course, that the way writing the essay was presented, suggested not so much an interest in thinking as a testing of ability with form. These convolutions point to a clear disjunction between the learning that had taken place in the course of the term as spoken discourse and shared experience and that which was demonstrated in the writing. This disjunction uncovers a further assumption to add to McCormick's list: writing is an individual rather than collective or collaborative activity. The department signalled that writing the essay was an institutional hurdle rather than a developmental process and students apparently fell in line with this.[8]

Peter Womack (1993) writes of the different interpretations of different groups of people on an Open University course:

> The academics thought of the course as essentially consisting of the units; the part-timers [tutors] thought of it as essentially consisting of the direct teaching; and the students thought of it as essentially consisting of the assignments .... So students' writing is important, not only because it's privileged in the assessment system, but also because it naturally forms, for the students, the central action of the course. What they learn is arguably more powerfully determined by what they write than by what we teach. (p. 42)

---

[8] A further dimension is the contention put forward by Freedman and Pringle in another study (1980) that many teachers assess writing for its rhetorical rather than cognitive features and that this results in them overlooking or undervaluing the rhetorical breakdown that can be a sign of cognitive development (attempts to cope with more complex or contradictory ideas). Again this results from too close a conflation of formal ability with thinking. The result of emphasising rhetorical coherence may, Freedman and Pringle suggest, be that students are encouraged to play safe in their writing.

Womack's comment suggests both the important formative potential of writing and that students have little investment in teaching situations, in which, by implication they play a passive part. The emphasis only falls on them when it comes to essay writing (see next chapter, where students actually express this sense). At the same time, however, that passive role in speech situations may carry over into writing and account for the tendency there to summarise and narrate rather than to offer critique, evaluate or argue.

The place given to the essay in the process of learning influences the extent to which writing is seen as closure (as well as having repercussions for the way students view and participate in other areas of their learning). But changing the position of the essay within the learning pattern does not necessarily mean that students will use the form more openly. Although in undergraduate Philosophy, essays are written prior to tutorials and used as the basis for discussion, the student in the following extract very much wants his essays to be conclusive and for this reason writes a single draft:

Pete: I find if I start doing drafts I start getting off the point sometimes and doing too much and not – I'll be redoing a page and then redoing another page and then it'll cut it all to bits rather than have the whole thing altogether. Because before I do an essay I have you know, I have my views and I know what sort of conclusion I'm going to come up with. And if I start redoing it I'm going to start disagreeing with myself and changing my views and then the whole essay has to be redone

Tutor: Right. Is that a bad thing? Disagreeing with yourself?

Pete: Well in the end I'd end up keep on changing it all the time. When you've got a certain deadline, you don't have time. What I tend to do is put notes down and think about things that I agree and notice about the topic and then bring it together within two days of when it's got to be brought in. [...]

Mal: I think it can help you sometimes; it's just a matter of the subject – you can't help disagreeing with yourself, even contradicting yourself, you change your mind half way through.

Pete: Rather than rewriting the essay though I would bring it up in class.

What emerges here is the importance – given the way the essay form itself is resolutely conceived of as closed – of having the opportunity to raise with the teacher and other students doubts which have been suppressed in the essay writing process.[9]

Many of the assumptions governing writing are deeply engrained – for both teachers and students. As McCormick notes, summary of information becomes privileged over other types of responses (tentative, exploratory, questioning). She suggests that this 'results from a kind of misunderstanding between teachers and students' of the kind exposed in the extract above (see chapter 6):

Teachers want a polished, organised, coherent, and unified final draft; students often only want to write one draft, and hence to achieve closure, by refusing to engage with the text in a questioning, tentative or argumentative way. (p. 205)

Though McCormick directly attributes the desire for closure here to the students only it is clear that what the teachers want is also a form of closure and, in addition, a closed form.

---

[9] The word 'essay' is used in very many contexts in the British education system and probably connotes too much. A wider repertoire of both names and forms would, I think, certainly enhance the possibilities for argument and the expression of thought through writing (see chapter 12).

The misunderstandings which exist between teachers and students do not result their inhabiting different worlds or speaking different languages, but from the differing kinds of access they have to meaning in that world. McCormick argues:

> Students naturalize (both in the sense of adapting and as seeing as natural) the demands of the particular educational structures in which they are trained. They choose certain aspects of reading and writing for their apparent effectiveness – but effectiveness is a cultural category, defined by institutions, social structures, the every day practices of the culture. In short, effectiveness is defined by and within a particular *ideology*. (p. 198)

One way in which the assumptions (and limitations) that students bring to their writing (and other aspects of their education) might be overcome is, she argues, to teach them to become aware of the way their own behaviours are ideological.

These issues have, in part, been discussed in the earlier chapters which looked at Ground Rules and Induction Programmes. What happens in the first year English Literary Theory course (the subject of the next chapter) extends this exploration and is particularly pertinent in the light of McCormick's argument. It reveals the extent to which, although critiques of ideology are very central to the content of the course, ideology nonetheless remains hidden in terms of the practices through which the learning is manifested.

10. Writing Essays in English Literary Theory

Some Context for the Discussion

The development from A level to undergraduate level in the discipline of English is most marked when students are introduced to literary theory. This constitutes for most students a distinctly new way of operating in relation to literary texts as well as a new body of knowledge to be assimilated. In this chapter, I shall look not only at the ways in which students operate upon texts, but also at the ways in which they express these operations; the way in which they come to be known publicly.

Scholes (1985) has described three ways in which a text may be read, each of which is (in some way) constructive of further texts: 'reading' constructs 'texts within texts', 'interpretation' 'texts upon texts' and criticism 'texts against texts' (p. 24). These three terms form a basic vocabulary for this discussion, since they are presented as a developmental sequence. Some adjustments to this conceptualisation become necessary, however, as the purpose and impact of theory are considered.

Generally speaking, when students are studying for A level and when they first come to university they appear to be operating in the first two of Scholes' modes: reading and interpretation. Reading is the primary activity upon which the others are based – it is as much knowledge (of codes and conventions) as skill. Interpretation is the activity by which the reader builds or constructs a meaning from what is inexplicit in the text. The 'character study' which is a common feature of A level work would be an example of this: the reader puts together a picture of an individual character independently of the narrative sequence through which the picture emerges[1]. Making the picture whole – or the character credible – may also involve drawing upon moral codes and psychological questions of motivation and responsibility. These are generally assumed to be universal and therefore left inexplicit. Invoking the author as a unifying intentional principle is another way in which coherent interpretation may be achieved.

Interpretation is a hermeneutic activity – the rendering clear or explicit of meaning. As Scholes notes:

> ...we value and tend to privilege texts that require and reward interpretive activity. This is, in fact, one way of defining literature, and it is one reason for preferring fictional texts to thematic texts, stories to essays. (p. 22)

---

[1] See Mitchell 1994c for a case study which looks in more detail at the way texts are approached through such heuristics as character at A level and beyond.

Interpretation seems, then, in some sense, to be foundational to literary study, since it is the activity that defines and selects the texts to be studied: the content or subject matter of English.

So far the activities Scholes describes can be linked to a broad tradition of thinking about literary study. One fairly easy parallel may be drawn with the ideas that C.S. Lewis in *An Experiment in Criticism* (1992, first published 1961). Here Lewis describes two types of reader: the 'literary' and the 'unliterary'. The distinction between these two does not lie in the fact that the unliterary do not read books since they very often do; but rather it lies in the way that they read – predominantly for the story, told in as transparent a way as possible. The unliterary reader, he says, 'attends to the words too little to make anything like a full use of them' (p. 35). It follows from this that the unliterary reader tends to like 'unliterary' books. Lewis' argument is circular in this respect, though it does seem to correlate with Scholes' idea about the interpretive potential of texts: the literary reader likes literary texts because they enable him or her to respond in a literary way towards them. This kind of formulation involves a value judgement simultaneously of the reader and of the text: the text is validated as literary by the attention given to it by the literary reader and the reader likewise is identified and validated as literary by giving the text the appropriate form of attention. For Lewis this mutual relationship is what distinguishes literariness; there is no activity beyond this.

Lewis' account belongs to the humanist tradition which began with Matthew Arnold and which has a pedagogical impulse to disseminate the supreme value of literary texts in a disinterested way. In this tradition texts are understood as unique events which can be described and paraphrased, but which retain their intrinsic value. Davis and Schleifer describe the 'vantage points' which underpin this way of treating texts:

> the 'meaning' of literature independent of its reader/critic, the 'genius' of its subject/ author independent of the psychological and historical occasions for writing and utterance, the 'truth' of literature independent of the discourse that articulates it which the teacher passes on. (p. 52)

These vantage points are held moreover as self evident and natural; as unquestionable grounds on which the literary is and is valued. I would add here that though response to texts should be 'disinterested', it is nevertheless constructed as a matter of individual merit or perceptiveness. The rhetoric and belief in the individual response, the independence of the 'literary reader' remains important to the way many students conceive of their activities.

The dissemination of knowledge – and of value – in the humanist tradition, however, does not take place as straightforward transmission – the teacher instructing the students – but rather more obliquely through modes of activity – reading and interpretation, discussion and writing. There are a number of ways in which within the educational/institutional context the way a text is read is shared rather than personal. In classroom discourse, for example, particularly that which is led by the teacher, consensual readings are an easy outcome. This is the case even where acts of reading and interpretation are understood by those who engage in them as subjective and individual. The maintenance of the subjective sense within a consensual situation can be thought of as collective subjectivity.[2] The interpretation of the text does not end in shared discussion however; it becomes again an individual matter when the reader writes. There are though collective constraints here too:

---

[2] I described this in an exploration of questions in classroom discourse at A level (see Mitchell 1992a)

often a title or question and a particular form – the essay, and mode – argument. These also shape what is said about a text. A further factor is the use and display of critics, named authorities who reaffirm the text's status as a shared object of literary study. Beyond this, of course, is the process of selection which causes the text to be read and interpreted in the first place and which excludes or marginalises other texts.

Thus there is a network of lived pedagogical practices which shape the meanings attributed to a text and a description of literary study can not really be complete without looking at the complexities they introduce.

Davis and Schleifer describe the humanist tradition as the practice of 'criticism' in order to distinguish it from 'critique'. Critique is self-reflective in that it subjects its own methods to scrutiny – the grounds for knowledge are less secure and so any pedagogy based on critique can not be about what is already known, but about what can come to be known through the application of a certain system or perspective. Critique is both 'institutional' – it addresses historical phenomena in the forms they take – and it is 'transformative' – it aims at changing cultural practice and phenomena (p. 22). The second characteristic follows from the first. (This practice takes us closer to argument). Davis and Schleifer describe the characteristics of many current modes of critique; they

> do not emphasise literary reading as an attempt at a unified 'reading' or even see a text as defined by 'meaning' or 'content'. They see, instead, a process that swings back and forth between textual 'product' and 'production', between meaning/content and reading activity – and never reaches stability or wholeness: the very doubling of critique we have noted and the questioning of the (self evident) oppositions between content and form, subject and object, assertions and method ... (p. 46)

Scholes' definition of 'criticism' – his third activity – apparently comes closer to critique than to the activities of humanist criticism. If humanist criticism precludes questions of grounds other than interpretive potential on which is valued, then criticism as 'text against text' offers a way out of – and since his activities are hierarchically arranged, *beyond* this situation. The hierarchy, of course, leaves the value of the reading and interpretive activities in themselves unchallenged – which would imply that the predominant approaches at, say, A level, are satisfactory and indeed necessary foundations. Retaining these foundations, it might be argued, undercuts the radicalism of what is proposed in 'criticism'. The same contradictory dilemma exists in introducing a course in current critique or theory alongside courses in which the unreflective practices of humanist criticism are still being carried on and rewarded.

Criticism, in Scholes' definition, is performed from a position of generality and collectivity 'some viewpoint beyond the merely personal - and the merely literary' (p. 23). It takes criticism, of course, to show that the personal and the literary are neither of them 'merely'. Scholes states that 'any group that has identified its interests as a class can mount an attack on a story's codes and themes from a position of its own system of values'(p. 23). By identifying with a collective position the reader is able to achieve a distance from the text and this suggests a potential for argument (as opposed to the description and paraphrase referred to earlier). The generation of argument depends structurally upon a separation of voices, two at least, not identical nor necessarily in direct opposition but in some relation to each other. The simplest model of communication can effect this necessary separation and recognition of difference. The reader as well as the author is now named and situated. This simple act can be enormously powerful if it is carried over into the critical writing that students do. The communication model is also a way of moving away from – or enriching – character study by looking at narrative structure and then at conventions such as realism.

The collective position which – by Scholes' definition – the critical reader adopts, corresponds to the identification of themes and codes within the text and from which it has been constructed. Criticism is aimed at the abstractions, generalities and principles of a text; these are the versions of reality, society, culture, ideology with or through which it operates. (Beyond this though is the 'reserve' of language, what is unassimilable by the position that has been taken).

Occupying a critical position becomes possible for undergraduate students with the introduction of theory: explicit method, system, principles for acting upon texts and for examining the literariness of a text. The inclusion of theory in English Literature courses at undergraduate level has taken place relatively recently and there is still uncertainty about its role, rationale and relation to other aspects of courses. (Theoretical perspectives have perhaps been accepted more easily in polytechnics and newer universities which have no historical legacy?) An article by Rowland Wymer (1992) entitled 'What do we want from theory and how do we get it?' is a useful focus for thinking about the impact of theory since it is concerned not so much with the intricacies of theories themselves but with the practicalities and objectives of teaching. It is with these 'muscular matters' (Geertz 1993 p. 153) that I am most concerned.

Wymer suggests that there might be a philosophical aim for theory which involved the questioning of students' 'most basic assumptions'(p. 276).[3] Yet this approach raises questions about what the student's most basic assumptions are taken to be. Or, to put it another way, whether assumptions are made about what their assumptions will be? It seems to me that assumptions are, and to an extent probably legitimately can be, made. The teaching I observed began with such questioning and led neatly to an 'exposure' of the historical context out of which the students' belief in the mind-broadening effect of literary studies had developed. The students were thus assumed (rightly as it turned out) to hold assumptions rooted in the humanist tradition. Inexplicit and unexamined these assumptions take on an untheoretical status; what Catherine Belsey (1980) describes as 'common sense':[4]

> Common sense assumes that valuable literary texts, those which are in a special way worth reading, tell truths – about the period which produced them, about the world in general or about human nature – and that in doing so they express the particular perceptions, the individual insights of their authors (p. 2)

> It is the 'obvious' mode of reading, the 'natural' way of approaching literary works. (p. 2)

As Belsey sees it the common sense view is founded upon a conception of language as transparent and as representing a world. The break with the commonsensical only really occurred with Saussure, whose work introduced the notion that language was itself a complete system of meaning (challenging students' basic assumptions then involves the question not only of 'What is Literature?' but also 'What is language?') Saussure becomes then a bench mark in the teaching of theory. When students have questioned their assumptions what status do they then take on? Are they seen as pre-theoretical, the results of ideological duping, false consciousness?

---

[3] See also chapter 6 where Wymer's discussion is used as a way of thinking about 'ground rules'.
[4] See also chapter 4 for a discussion of common sense argument. Also Gee's (1989 p. 10) contention that primary Discourses (which would certainly include 'reading' and probably 'interpretation') cannot be liberating.

If humanistic assumptions – within the context of a course on theory – are in some way culpable, in other parts of the degree course they are, as I've noted already, still sufficient. The question raised by this disjunction is an important and insistent one: 'What value – educational or cultural – have these common sense ways of operating had so far? And do they have any residual value after the introduction of theory?' Whilst theory shows up that

> common sense itself is ideologically and discursively constructed, rooted in a specific historical situation and operating in conjunction with a particular social formation (Belsey p. 3)

the question of how to value particular social formations remains.

In a sense the theory course must construct its opposite in order to argue its case: it gets going by using the pre-theoretical. The operation of production and construction would seem to be an essential starting point for the activity of criticism (or critique). Interpretation, because it does not make assumptions in reading explicit or the subject of investigation, cannot get beyond the commonsensical.

Students' Writing

I now want to look at some of the students' writing, undertaken at the end of the course. I see the writing as a means to reflect on the impact of the course and the realisations of its aims. There are two different forms of writing represented in the extracts that follow: one is the essay form and the other responses to a questionnaire I devised to accompany the writing. The differences between the two forms of writing are, I think, instructive.

What might be expected from a critical essay which involves the application of one or more theoretical perspectives to a literary text? The theory has a discursive or 'thetic' structure, whilst the literary text is non-discursive. The non discursive aspects of a text are perhaps those which give it its status as Literature or Art; that which is 'in excess'. The theory then does not stand in for the whole of the text or a complete reading – it is always partial. A critical essay would have neither simply to evaluate the theories nor to elucidate the text; it would have to evaluate the theories *through* an elucidation of the texts. The adequacy of the theory, then, is measured against a reading of the text which is more than (in excess of) a theoretical one. The theory treats the text thetically; it looks for what it can state positively about it, what it means, what it refers to; but, being nondiscursive the text always exceeds this in some way: it keeps the thetic in a state of 'suspension' (Derrida 1992).

It is perhaps this which students are talking about when they say that a text can be talked about in any number of ways: there is no right or wrong. One version of this results in the right to one's own opinion, whilst another (more Derridean) results in the escape of the text and further pursuit. A further effect can be destabilisation: an awareness of being somewhere between, seeing possibilities open up and being caught within a defining structure. The theory tutor sees this as one of the primary functions of the introduction of theory. He describes it as an experience of the 'uncanny': a momentary glimpse of how one is both identical and different. It is this kind of experience that he hopes the introduction of theory will give rise to. One of the students put it this way:

> Fully appreciated (not just heard it said) that no one can say what is a good/bad piece of work, or literature. Realised it's all a bit of an intellectual figment: at once have more and less reality to myself as a student (despite not going with this idea). (*Vanessa, questionnaire*)

139

Through the introduction of theory Vanessa becomes conscious of herself as a student and is simultaneously more and less free.

The tutor gives as an example an occasion when, in explaining Althusser's view of education as the site of ideological indoctrination, he was challenged by his students on the grounds that were it so he would not be able to make such a claim. In this instance, experiencing the 'uncanny' is related to the tutor's view that teaching theory must be linked to the related concepts of discourse and the institution: naming oneself within an ideology is a momentary escape from ideology, though necessarily only momentary. At the same time recognising oneself within ideology makes a return to 'innocence' impossible. The Althussarian definition of ideology is, in this way, as all embracing as ideology itself – and could be seen as foundational to all forms of cultural study – as ideology is foundational to culture.

The contextual political/institutional angle would seem to be an inevitable part of enquiries into what literature is, though it can also be understood as – and is – a partisan or inessential view. In any case, I think it is right that, as Wymer suggests, understanding the purpose of the theory, the context out of which it has developed as a critical tool is likewise important to the enquiry, since 'what literature is' is as much concerned with the theory that has provided the answer as with any so-called intrinsic qualities. The theory and the literary work are bound up in a cultural relation: ideology. When one is working within that relation, it perhaps takes an experience of the uncanny to recognise it.

Or perhaps what is needed is what Geertz calls 'an ethnography of the vehicles of meaning' (p.118) something of which I am doing here in considering the essays written by students.[5] Using the essays as a means of insight into the students' thinking about issues, such as the relation of the text to the theory, is complicated by a range of other factors. The wording of a title and the form of the essay (the structure it offers and requires) also shape and constrain what that thinking is – or what we know of it. Student response to the questionnaire often shows up that what 'can' be written in one place, in another, 'cannot'. It is important to bear this in mind: that the shapes and development of thinking are not independent from the opportunities offered in a formal task and by a formal genre.

The essays discussed represent the first occasion on which the students wrote on theory in any developed way. The essay questions the students were given almost all suggest that the theory should be applied to a text but this 'technical' aspect is accompanied also by a need to offer some sort of context, in which comparison (the consideration of similarity and differences) offers the basis for critical comment. For example:

- Compare and contrast a Marxist and Psychoanalytic reading of Katherine Mansfield's short story 'The Garden Party'.

- Feminism offers potentially the most concretely useful theory of literature: it not only provides new readings of texts, it also questions the whole way literature is taught in university institutions.
  (suggestions: you could take the Mod. Lit. course – offer a feminist reading of one Hardy or Lawrence or Conrad text – then reflect on how it has been taught etc ...)

How far the students' writing realises the evaluative potential of the questions is variable. The compare and contrast question, for instance, is the most popular probably because it offers a straightforward structure for the writing. As one of the students comments:

---

[5] This is perhaps an example of a meta-language, the need for which is discussed in chapter 6.

[I] try to avoid doing 1 side of argument and then another, but often do anyway as it's easier/less complicated writing structure (*Vanessa*).

This less complicated writing structure – in which, for instance one theoretical application is dealt with and then another – can lead to no more than the presentation of a contrast and comparison without an evaluation on the basis of this. Thus the straightforward structure can be deceptive. It takes the writer towards fully evaluative argument but falls short of its full realisation. As an invitation to argument (or critical judgement) the essay title perhaps requires a supplementary part directing the student towards judgement.

What does the introduction of theory (accessed through the essay form) allow in terms of cognitive operations; that is, what kinds of learning seem to be going on? The writing certainly seems to function for the students as a way of consolidating understanding. They comment on this in questionnaires which accompanied the essays:

> Really, only by the time I'm writing an essay do I feel confidently knowledgeable enough to argue. In tutorials it's a little more tentative …

> To have to write an essay though, does further your understanding of the theory. It certainly made me appreciate "Heart of Darkness" more. It's good to have actually *used* the theory. (*Neil*)

> Writing an essay is definitely the time where a pupil formulates an argument within himself or against critics. It sometimes helps to verbalise arguments in tutorials, but arguments in literature often need careful consideration. (*Cathy*)

Cathy's comment reflects what seems to be the prevalent attitude and behaviour amongst students of English that writing rather than speech is the place for the formulation of ideas. The reticence of students in tutorials is frequently commented upon. In the theory course this is perhaps partly a reflection of the difficulty of much of the material, yet groups made up of Joint Honours students, who study, say, Drama as well often make far more use of the spoken medium.

Vanessa records that she 'Can't stop thinking of theory but at the same time prove incapable of using it', yet having written her essay her feeling of incapacity is diminished:

> It's a lot more rewarding having done something applied with it and not having come unstuck. I'm more heartened.

The writing process seems to have a definite value in consolidating what has been covered on the course. For Vanessa it is associated with the marshalling of an argument:

> …found 2 theories difficult to connect in one argument first time round. A lot better a day later and 1 fresh start later. Found you had to sacrifice some content which could not fit into structure of argument.

For others, it is grasping the arguments which themselves constitute the theories, which is the main achievement of their essays. Thus, many of the essays offer a detailed account of the Marxist or Psychoanalytic theory.

Many such accounts are excellent: lucid and comprehensive in setting forth difficult ideas. The writing seems to have a dual function: formulation and display. Formulation of course requires more cognitive skills than just knowing: comprehension, interpretation and synthesis are necessary in producing a new narrative which describes the theory. The result is though not an argument but rather a narrative of an argument: the theory is not tested, though its formulation is undoubtedly important to the writer. A move towards argument takes place with the application of the knowledge to a particular text. This represents a more difficult task as the thetic arrangement of the theory confronts the athetic particularity of the literary text.

Here is an example, where the statement from Freud is brought into relation with a reading of 'The Garden Party':

> Laura differs from the other Sheridan women; she has not been totally conditioned by society as her mother and sisters have. She is more of a freethinker like her father. Freud talks of the baby born *"polymorphously perverse"* with *"social orientation"*, *"Its drives are shaped into socially acceptable forms"*. Katherine Mansfield creates the impression that Laura is the youngest of the Sheridan women and there is still an element in her character which has not succumbed to this social conditioning. She is at the stage where she has not fully realised her social position. Through the death of Mr Scott she sees the reality of life and then returns to the security of her class. Laura's elated behaviour at the beginning is an indication of her need to convince herself of her own happiness ... (*Becky*)

The main tendency in this writing is the exploration and interpretation of character. The link between Freud's theory and the action of the text is suggested here rather than worked through explicitly. Reference to the theory, contained within a single sentence, guides but does not contain what remains essentially a 'character study'. The theory, that is, works for the writer to a certain extent, but does not become an essential vocabulary for her. Compare this with another student's feminist analysis of *Tess of the D'Urbervilles*:

> The phallic imagery of pricking, piercing and penetration described above satisfy the narrator's fascination with the interiority of Tess's sexuality and even his desire to take possession of her. Similarly, the repeated images of Tess awakening to violence, and the repeated interweaving of red and white, blood and flesh, sex and death, provide structuring images for the violence Tess suffers, but also repeat that violence.
>
> Obviously the one thing that the narrator desires more than anything else is to capture Tess's sexuality. However in so doing he risks turning her into an erotic object denying her spirituality and instead viewing her as a being whose most great quality lies in her sexual attractiveness. This idea is reinforced by a quote taken from the moment Angel Clare enters the room without Tess realising and there follows a passage of physical description, emphasising her sleepy appearance: "She had stretched one arm so high above her coiled up cable of hair that he could see its satin delicacy above the sunburn; her face was flushed with sleep, and her eyelids hung heavy over their pupils." The narrator continues, "It was a moment when a woman's soul is more incarnate than at any other time; when the most spiritual beauty bespeaks itself flesh and sex takes the outside place in the presentation"
>
> It is very revealing here that the language is destablised by the physicality of the woman's soul together with the brimfulness of her nature that it seeks to represent. Interestingly the incarnate state of Tess's soul appears to be as close to sleep, or to unconsciousness as is possible without fully entering that state. It is significant that here, as elsewhere, and particularly at moments of such erotic response, consciousness is all but ruled out ... (*Lucy*)

This student writes about the text from a distinctly feminist perspective and it is apparent how empowering that perspective can be. A strong textually embedded critique develops. The descriptive passage is looked at 'suspiciously'; that is in terms of questions, such as 'What point of view is this written from?' 'What is being said (argued) about womanhood behind this narrative?' These questions are made possible by the feminist perspective on the text rather than raised by the text themselves: they are critical rather than interpretive questions. Lucy also includes in her reading an acknowledgement of what the text itself explicitly argues: 'a sense that Hardy is making a moral point via Tess's experience, an outcry against the way she is treated for her nature' – so that her reading works both with (Scholes' 'upon') and 'against' the text and shows how Hardy's sympathetic aim 'backfires'.[6]

Lucy goes on to offer an account of the various versions of feminism within institutions and to offer criticisms of these at a general discursive level. As her tutor comments it is a shame she didn't try to connect her immediate experience of this institution to her reading of *Tess*. Her feminist reading might then have become a double edged sword, showing (if indeed her teaching was of this kind) how the institution is complicit with the way texts are read and valorised.

The merging of application into evaluation and argument, as occurs in Lucy's essay, is not common within the essays I have read. This is to a degree a result of the theory that is being used: the feminist perspective is used here to argue against a text and so the positioning is clear, but it is less so in the case of a psychoanalytic reading and though Marxist theory may have the same political aim it is not wielded in the same way as the feminist perspective is. In the essays which deal with 'The Garden Party' or with *Heart of Darkness* the relation of the theories to the text is less clear: how far does a psychoanalytic reading reveal structures which are hidden in the text and how far does it impose its own structure? These questions are not raised by the students, but the way they write frequently suggests that the latter is the case:

> Throughout the text there is much evidence to suggest the presence of the ego. For example, consider the substitute narrator's comment about Marlow: "to him the meaning of an episode was not inside like a kernel but outside, enveloping the tale which brought it out only as a glow brings out a haze." As is written in the study *An Outline of Psychoanalysis,* the ego arises as an intermediary between the id and the external world. Further evidence is available in *Heart of Darkness* of the existence of the ego as a means of self-preservation. For example, Marlow exclaims: "I don't like work – no man does – but I do like what is in the work – the chance to find yourself, your own reality – for yourself, not for others – what no other man can ever know." This acts as an illustration of Freud's theory that the ego is able to modify its action in the external world to its own advantage. (*Lynne*)

It is evident here from the way the student expresses it that the text is being used as a means of explicating and illustrating the theory. The relationship is an instrumental one. The approach results in a conclusion which compares the approaches of the two theories: feminism and psychoanalysis, by stating the differences between them at an unapplied level. Their effectiveness in elucidating the text is not dealt with and in this sense there is no argument.

> It is apparent throughout the two readings that the material dealt with and the considerations made differ tremendously. For example, the feminist reading of *Heart of Darkness* concentrates on the cultural exclusion of women, their material conditions and both social and political formations. Much of the study revolved around the direct presentation of women as well as the implied gender inequality. The aim has been to show how Conrad corresponds to the ideology of femininity. However the psychological approach differed in that the examples presented were much more abstract, as virtually everything in the text could be viewed with a psychoanalytic stance. My presentation of

---

[6] There is an interesting comparison to be made here with essays students wrote on Hardy as part of their Modern Literature course. Amongst the students I observed there, there was little close reading and no satisfactory way of thinking about or showing how the text argues against itself.

examples has concentrated on the theories which I consider to be most prominent in the text. However it must be said that both approaches were concerned with the literature as a totality of literary experience. (*Lynne*)

This concluding paragraph is adequate as far as it goes but it says little about the text to which the theories were applied and therefore little about their critical usefulness. The theories are not evaluated through the text.

Looking at the essays brings out the different ways in which the theories can be oriented argumentatively towards texts: to undermine the authority of the text, to create a layer of meaning which was submerged in the text. The more political the theory the easier criticism in Scholes' sense becomes. Yet psychoanalysis too can be used in this way. One of the students writes in her questionnaire:

> Psychoanalytical readings of novels and horror genres offer a severe interpretation of the text. It leaves little to the ingenuity of the author and rather sees his work as a failure or 'short coming' in dealing with unconscious works of art. Sometimes it offers an extremely limited view and 'cripples' the potential of the text to develop. Not all texts are as easy to read in this way as horror fiction or the classic 'Sons and Lovers' (*Cathy, questionnaire*).

In this description psychoanalysis is seen as undermining, not the text so much as view of the text in which the author is in control and reading is a commonsensical act of narrative progression. In this sense psychoanalytic theory has a similar goal to feminism.

Notice that this comment on the limitations of the theory does not occur in Cathy's essay which is a thorough descriptive account of how a psychoanalytic reading works, synthesising the work of a number of critics, but not dealing directly with a text herself. It seems that the essay is not used for the expression of doubt or critique – as experienced by the students themselves.

For several of the students, nonetheless, it was the writing of the essay (rather than reading or discussion) which realised the power of theory to produce a particular reading:

> I think writing the assignment has made me appreciate just how differently a text can be interpreted. I did realise this during the course, but actually doing a feminist reading of a text really showed me how you can almost manipulate the text to mean what you want it to mean. (*Joanna, questionnaire*)

It is not clear quite how Joanna feels about this 'manipulation': how far does she believe in a 'real' meaning? Is she just surprised that the reader can take so obviously an active stance in making meaning? Her essay – on feminism – certainly shows how she develops a position from which to argue which was absent before. In it she takes up the invitation to reflect on the teaching she has had so far, noting among other omissions:

> The only sentence I found in my lecture notes [on the *Heart of Darkness*] where a woman is mentioned is "He says he hates lies, yet at the end he actually tells the Intended a lie. Contradiction glares out from story." One can see from this that, in the practice of teaching too, the woman has been used by the lecturer to exhibit some feature of the story, or an action of the male hero. (*Joanna, essay*)

Whilst Joanna's may not be a very sophisticated analysis it clearly signals the kind of reflection that Wymer advocates and which leads, in Scholes' terms, to criticism. It doesn't matter which theory achieved this reflective appreciation of the discourse of which she is part – though feminism is undoubtedly particularly empowering because it is still marginalised within the institution and therefore an easy perspective from which to see the familiar as strange. It can also clearly be seen as having personal relevance for many students.

There is a sense in Joanna's essay that she has switched from the passive to the active and authoritative. In my view this is in no small part due to the use she makes here of her own experience (signalled by the personal pronoun). It is rare for the essay form and the conventions of academic writing to allow for this and Joanna is the only student in this group to take the opportunity offered in the question on feminism. I would suggest that the injunction to be 'impersonal' in academic writing[7] is likely to have a very real effect on the extent to which students are able to engage actively in the kinds of self-reflexive questioning said to underpin the theory course – and which would take them beyond simple 'compare and contrast' towards judgement. Judgement here is not based upon external criteria, but upon the successes and failures of the theory in relation to the text, which can be determined in effect only by a reading and interpretation of the text. Reading and interpretation here count as the student's own experience – a basis from which to critique the theory, undermine its authority. And the power to critique is also dependent on the confidence to make oneself heard.

The convention of impersonality seems to me to inhibit the 'Transformation' process by which the student takes from the public domain and makes difficult the differentiation which takes place in 'Publication' (see chapter 2, Harré's model).

McCormick (1990) has similar observations to make:

> To be told one cannot say "I" in a culture that continually emphasis the significance of the individual subject can cause the student to become alientated and disoriented. In "innocently" moving the child into the public sphere by instructing him or her not to use "I", the teacher may be simultaneously (and contradictorily) cutting the child away from this sphere: on the one hand, to be "public" the child learns that he or she cannot say "I"; on the other, the public sphere, from its advertising to its disciplining practices, is continually interpellating, in the sense used by Louis Althusser, of "summoning" or "calling out to", and defining the child as an individual. (p. 197)

As they move in the public sphere of literary theory (in contrast to the 'private' readings of common sense), the students' ability to name themselves is perhaps diminished rather than enhanced. The theoretical texts offer them a chance to realise their own ideological positioning, but at the same time, as authoritative texts within an academic context, they reassert the dominant ideology.

Many of their essays fall short of evaluating the theoretical reading, of showing where there is lack in the explanation and excess in the text: showing, in Derrida's terms, an awareness of how the thetic and nonthetic interplay – how literary experience is 'a nonthetic experience of the thesis, of belief, of position.' (1992 p. 46). The students, that is, do not recognise or have recourse to an authority which is nonthetic. If the text is in excess of the theory, it is equally the case that the individual reader is too: she may take a theoretical position, but not be taken in by it – at least not entirely. The extent to which she can develop and give expression to this excess is dependent, however, on her authority. If the aim is that the student be in dialogue with theoretical positions rather than simply conforming to them, then it is also necessary to think about the power relations which condition dialogue and

---

[7] See chapter 7 for the advice given in the university English induction.

ask whether the student writer can actually do this when she is not given a voice. Self-reflexivity is a process of recognising oneself.

Students appear to recognise that theory, whilst empowering in some respects, is also constraining when it comes to individual pleasures in reading:

> I've seen the value of the course, however on the other hand, whilst it may encourage the student to deal with the text more deeply there is also an increased sense of the need to impose a meaning on a text, a feeling obligation to drag some sort of theory from every text. This can reduce personal pleasure in reading a text. *(Becky, questionnaire)*

> It's really the first terminology that the subject has of its own...
> You haven't got your own personal approach anymore. In my Joyce essay I was conscious of looking for ideologies in his biography and in *A Portrait of the Artist*. *(Neil, questionnaire)*

The students still regard the pre-theoretical as somehow personal and the adoption of theory as a move away from this way of understanding what they do. In terms of learning we might see this as a transitional stage where the new material has been appropriated but not transformed. In this case the true development of argument – as a making new, making one's own through a process of differentiation – is not yet possible. The students are rehearsing the arguments of others rather than acculturated to the extent that these arguments are their own. The comments raise a question about the status of the assumptions that the students use in their personal response and the value in terms of pleasure and confidence that these have for them.

One can sense from Becky's comment that criticism is not a sufficient goal for reading if it effaces pleasure. I would want to suggest that pleasure does not have to be found prior to critical reading, but can be found after it if Scholes' hierarchy – reading, interpretation, criticism – be thought of rather as a circle in which one returns to reading with a richer set of codes and conventions upon which to draw. Criticism is thus not the end point of a process which begins as pleasure but rather a stage through which one passes. At this stage, however, Becky thinks of theory as a technical operation and more obviously institutional than her pre-theoretical reading.

I don't believe it is too far fetched to link the failure to go beyond (or back) – into reading to the marginalisation of personal experience from the essay form. I do not mean here the 'commonsensical', since the function of the theory is to move beyond this, but rather the experience which is post- and despite the theory. Having no legitimate place to name herself the student has no *authority* with which to address the theoretical reading. If the introduction of theory is about creating the conditions for difference (argument) then the student must be able to situate herself in relation to it – identical or otherwise.

At A level, I sensed that what students needed was to develop a way of differentiating their reading selves from the text (Mitchell 1992b). At that stage criticism seemed to provide an answer to the confusion between the source of reasoning and effect, since it created two distinct voices making it is less easy to confuse one's own position with that of the text. Yet now it seems that another stage is necessary. Learning, as the Harré model suggests, is not linear but circular – always involving a return to and movement out of the private/individual quadrant. The nature of this area of identity is, of course, always changed by previous learning, so that 'personal response' is never intrinsic or identically reproducible, but always open to social process.

Once the theoretical position has been tried out a collective position to which the reader has allied herself – 'criticism is always made on behalf of a group' (Scholes p. 24) – the reader needs to differentiate herself. It is no good to find a collective position and remain there – this is little better than ventriloquism. If this happens the theory becomes another form of suppression. Perhaps it is better to express this as a return to the person, rather than to the 'personal'. To be authoritative the person needs to set herself apart, to name herself – as Joanna does. The enterprise is a symbiosis of collective allegiance and individual judgement and transformation – it is this which is described by Harré's model. It is also what occurs in argument: the use of tension between positions of difference (thesis and antithesis) to arrive at a new position from which the process eventually begins again.

Unlike the students who felt that theory was somehow manipulative or reducing of personal response, Cathy feels empowered, rather than constrained by theory. Her response is close to what I am describing as a hoped-for eventual role for theory in reading:

> A text now presents itself as an enigma waiting to be discovered. Sometimes this removes the initial enjoyment of a text, but it enables you to feel you have got much more out of it. Re-reading a text is no longer a 'deja-vu' experience but a delight at finding things you missed in the first reading .... The student is better equipped at deciphering language and studying a text from his/her *own* opinion. (*Cathy, questionnaire*)

Theory empowers because it opens up possibilities, which Cathy sees herself as having a personal stake in. The element of choice is very important: the multiplicity of theories (named and therefore authoritative) makes manifest the status of the text as open to interpretation, in a way that the discourse of personal response and subjectivity does not. The operation of subjectivity is grounded on a collective view of the text. This clearly isn't an inevitable response to theory, but it may well be a more advanced one. As I pointed out before though there is less evidence of the enabling aspects of theory in the essay Cathy wrote than in her questionnaire response.

The academic form and academic training are themselves ideological, concerned, as Meyer (1993) described, with the portrayal of the 'illusion of mastery' and the playing of a 'confidence game'. The power that the theory course gives to the students on the one hand is taken away or at least suppressed by the other. Meyer's phrase, 'the confidence game', describes in effect thetic ways of making sense: in order to move beyond the technical use of theory it may be precisely a lack of 'confidence' that is needed: the entertaining of questions, a new receptiveness in reading.

It should be clear that the use or avoidance of the personal pronoun is more than a matter of style. It is quite possible to write as a critical 'person' without using the pronoun, but it is equally true that at certain stages in learning the licence to write about what 'I think ...', 'What I perceive ...' gives direct access to an area of thought and experience which might not otherwise be expressed or explored and not, therefore, valued. The students' comments in the questionnaires are significantly different in this respect from those in the essays. Teachers might reflect on the reasons they find student feedback in this form so useful and enlightening.

In a way I have been suggesting that the personal pronoun can act as an object, a basic structure against which the conditions of sameness and difference can be developed. In the next two chapters I develop the notion of structure, looking at some ways in which argument can be structured and conversely ways in which structure can produce argument. This leads me to some suggestions for alternatives to the essay form.

11. The Imposition of Structure: Narration and Argumentation

> Complexity in most areas of cognition is handled through the imposition of structure.
> (Applebee 1978, p. 56)

In this chapter I want to look at the way organisational structures contribute to or work against the development of argument in writing. I will start by looking at two A level history essays in which their different degrees of success in terms of argument can be traced the different structuring of material. One essay is organised so as to preserve the coherence of individual accounts; the other to draw out the difference between accounts. I characterise these as narrative and argumentative stances respectively (see chapter 2) and show how their structures can be represented visually. I want to suggest that the successful adoption of the essay form – in terms of its rhetorical features of style and *overall* organisation (the macro-pattern of beginning, middle and end) does not necessarily result in or reflect successful argument. To put this another way, argument is generated by ways of organising and operating upon material which are not intrinsic to writing in the standard form. The separation I am making is between 'mode' and 'form'. 'Mode' describes kinds of processes rather than types of product. It does not refer to the logical rather than, say, chronological organisation of a piece of writing, but rather to the possibilities for meaning which are actively raised by organisational decisions. For instance putting two ideas together, rather than keeping them separate, can create the conditions in which a third, perhaps more inclusive idea is generated.

As a follow-on to the discussion of the two History essays I introduce some other visual representations of argument and suggest that these might be used as a basis for generating and planning argument. I include two specific practical exercises which use patterns to develop argument. In chapter 12, the idea of structure carries over into dialogic forms of written argument.

This present chapter might usefully be read in conjunction with the account in chapter 7 of the induction module on argument. The module involved different ways of organising and reorganising material so as to move from summary towards argument.

Narrative and Argument Structures: Two Essays Compared[1]

At 16 the transition to academic status brings with it an increased expectation of the student's ability to argue. The nature of the school subject may itself change so that students are

---

[1] This section is largely taken from a chapter by Richard Andrews and myself in Freedman, A. and Medway, P. (eds.) *Teaching and Learning Genre* , Heinemann-Boynton/Cook (forthcoming) where a fuller analysis occurs.

dealing with more complex materials and ideas. To state the case crudely, for History there is a move from the teaching and learning of historical narrative and facts to a form of study which addresses the construction of historical accounts as a problem and foregrounds the diversity of interpretations of the past. History becomes in the final two years the subject of historical analysis and, since analyses differ, of historical debate. To put it another way History is less concerned with subject content than with actual and possible ways of acting upon that content.

Writing and argument come together almost exclusively in the essay form in History at A level and in practice therefore any distinction between mode (argument) and form (essay) is blurred. Students commonly have some notion of what it means to develop argument but when it comes to actual practice the task does not seem so easy. Learning the differing views of others – or that others hold views that differ – and that the world can be interpreted in different ways does not in itself mean that the student is able to argue or to operate in the argumentative mode. It is perfectly possible to show evidence of arguments learnt, whilst at the same time revealing no evidence of the ability to argue.

The two essays discussed below were written for the Cambridge History Project (CHP) syllabus which emphasises modes of operating in the discipline rather than subject content to be covered. The ability to argue is particularly highly valued (see chapter 2).

The two essays draw on the same source material and are written in response to the same question:

> On the basis of the available evidence how far would you be prepared to accept that the First World War marked a turning point in the development of the position and role of women in English society?

The question requires argument: the writer must process the 'available evidence' and subject it to scrutiny in relation to the analytical category 'turning point'. The case is unlikely to be a cut and dried one as the phrase 'how far' suggests, and whatever degree of agreement or disagreement, it must be justified by a weighing up of the evidence. The phrase 'turning point' is taken from a repertoire of vocabulary and conceptual characterisations which are supplied by the examination syllabus: others are 'false dawn' and 'continuing trend'. These tie in with the principles by which the course is organised – around themes, such as 'cause and motive' and 'change and development' as well as types of disciplinary behaviour, such as using sources as evidence. The course, that is, supplies a discourse which has a significant role in aiding the development of argument.

From the opening paragraph of each essay it is not easily possible to predict which will be the most successful in these terms:

> *Mike*
>
> The question of how far would you be prepared to accept that the First World War marked a turning point in the development of the position and role of women in English society can be answered providing that it is kept in mind that there are many different aspects which could judge whether it is a turning point or not. Such as the kind of evidence an historian concentrates on, the different perspectives used, spatial or temporal, or the different strands of women's role in society, for example, their Economic or Political roles. If all these elements are taken into account then it can be shown that the First World War is both a turning point, trend and false dawn for women.

In order to answer this question it is necessary to recognise that within the development of the position and role of women in English society there are many different strands – for example VOTING RIGHTS, JOB OPPORTUNITY RIGHTS and EQUAL PAY claims. Each of these strands are affected at different rates over the passage of time and any analysis of a turning point must take account of this. We must in other words explore the full complexity of change.

Both students show an awareness of the task, acknowledging that the claim for World War One as a turning point for women is open to debate; similarly with the conclusions, both of which are credited by the teacher as displaying good argumentative evaluation:

Mike

So it has been shown that using the right evidence, strands and perspectives the First World War with regard to women's role in British society can be seen as a turning point trend or false dawn.

Taking all these aspects into account the evidence tends to lean towards the idea that the war had very little effect on women politically or socially and that it was part of a continuing trend, especially when it is taken into account that progress was first made for women in these areas decades before the war, and that throughout the twentieth century women's role in society has moved ahead only very gradually, rather than the massive step forward that has been suggested took place.

Robert

What we must draw of importance here is that the development of women in relation to men is a very ongoing thing. It is by no means resolved and it by no means started only in 1914. The First World War doubtless has had a lot of influence on the rights and position of women in society. What we have to recognise is that change is not always constant and in all directions. It can affect different strands at different times and to different extents. I have attempted to integrate the strands and demonstrate that change is an ongoing thing. It is fair to comment that some of the modern day changes had their roots in the First World War, but by no means all. I regard the First World War as an accelerator not a turning point.

There is a difficulty with these introductions and conclusions as evidence of argument in that they seem at least to a certain extent to be rehearsals of the discourse supplied by the syllabus and laid out in the highly explicit mark-scheme, which accompanied the essay question. In that scheme, for instance, it states that in the highest level of response 'The full complexity of change will be explored' and this is echoed by Robert who states his intention to explore 'the full complexity of change'. Responding to the surface cues supplied by the syllabus can then produce impressive introductions and conclusions: the correct analytical phrasing disguises the presence – or absence – of reasoning itself. Nonetheless these two essays do not display equivalent levels of reasoning. If the introductions and conclusions are excluded, how can the difference be detected? The answer lies in the organisation and treatment of substantive material in the middle sections of the essay.

In the introduction to his essay Mike made mention of the various ways in which the impact of the First World War on women could be characterised: not only as a turning point, but also as a continuing trend or false dawn. These characteristics become the means by which he structures his essay. Paragraphs 1-4 contain evidence which suggests that the war is a turning point; paragraphs 5-10 consider the war as a continuing trend and paragraphs 11-14 use the idea of a false dawn. Each possible interpretation is conscientiously covered and in each section, taken separately, the evidence could be considered plausible, since conflicting evidence is structurally and therefore temporally separated. The organisation of the material is represented in the diagram below:

MIKE'S ESSAY

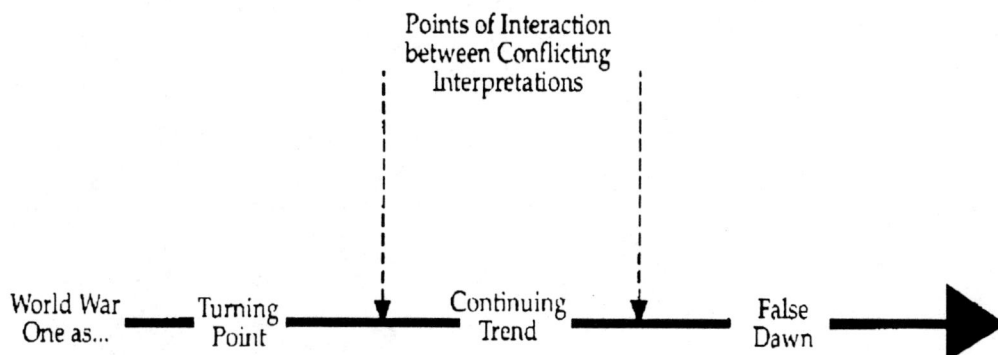

As a result of Mike's decision to treat the interpretations in a compartmentalised way he rarely demonstrates more than comprehension. In dealing with one narrative account of the war at a time there is no complication or integration of viewpoints. When a transition occurs between one narrative and the next, however, the two alternative interpretations are juxtaposed and a spark of argument is generated. Moments such as this are rare though: the material is organised *in such a way as to minimise contrast and comparison*.

Whilst Mike could be said to be operating in what Ricoeur (1970) called the positive mode of interpretation, under 'a vow of obedience' to each interpretation as he deals with it, it is to the negative mode – characterised by a 'willingness to suspect' and a 'vow of rigour' – that Robert's essay tends. He seems to recognise that the argumentative potential of the material lies not so much in the substantive issues themselves – which in the terminology of the course are referred to as 'strands' and which he instances as voting rights, job opportunity rights and equal pay claims – as in the different interpretations that can be offered of these. He therefore organises his essay around his three chosen strands. Presented as complex yet complete bodies of evidence these become the still points around which argument rages. Another way of putting this would be to say that for Robert the discourse is dialogic; it contains competing interpretations which are activated by being brought to bear on each other through the source material or 'content areas'. The discourse is also in this sense given priority over the content.

The 1918 Voting Reform Act, for example, which took place just at the end of the war, is presented by Robert as the cause of contention between historians, who disagree as to whether the war was the decisive factor in bringing about the vote for women. Robert weighs up these issues in his own words:

> It is certainly fair to comment that women had been striving for the vote well before the war; therefore we should judge the impact of the war in relation to this. Having said that, the immediacy of granting the vote seems to suggest that the war was of some considerable impact.

151

Robert also places this debate within a longer term context, by considering subsequent improvements in women's rights and insisting that the issue of voting rights cannot be entirely divorced from the issue of equal pay – this point effects a transition, of course, from discussion of one strand to discussion of another.

The essay's structure is depicted here:

ROBERT'S ESSAY

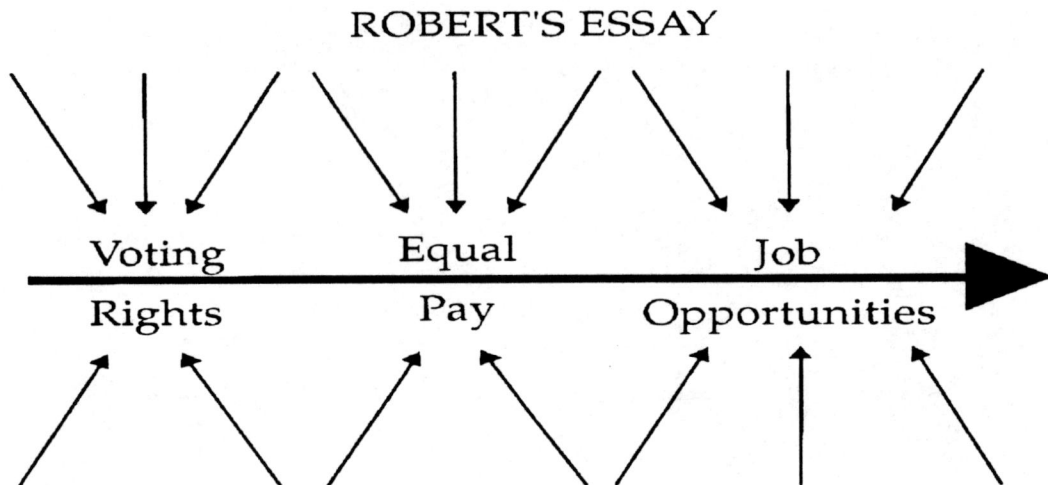

Each arrow represents a different possible interpretation of the substantive material. Looked at from the language point of view this kind of structural arrangement creates a great deal of opportunity for the use of argumentative diction of the 'however', 'nevertheless', 'on the other hand' variety. These articulate the changes of direction, the taking of different positions (in a way that is reminiscent of the mathematical definition of argument). In fact in Robert's essay there are not as many alternatives as the diagrammatic representation suggests. Robert has a tendency to reject the idea of a turning point without fully considering the arguments in its favour.

In another way, too, the diagram is not an accurate representation of Robert's essay since it suggests too neat a division into sections. In fact the organisation is more complex than this: there are other factors at work. The essay begins, for instance, with a consideration of the debate about women *before* the war and tends towards the end to deal with present day evidence in the form of statistics: so there is a kind of underlying temporal structure. In addition there are occasions when Robert steps back from the material to justify or clarify his approach – as when, for instance, he comments that women's position can only been seen as relative to men's and that he has no 'control' group against which to measure his conclusions. He is explicit too in monitoring the progress of the argument, pointing out where gaps in the configuration of evidence still lie. Here, for instance:

> So we see that the role of women within society was already under debate. We must now examine what happened during the War and also afterwards to women in order to determine what impact World War One had on the role of women in society. On this impact there are two distinct camps ...

And so on. Even though both writers achieve a similar degree of argumentative strength at the conclusions of their essays, Robert displays a greater degree of rhetorical skill, employing a style which allows retrospective and prospective control and suggests an awareness of overall patterning.

Ostensibly the theme of these two essays is the same: the effect on women of World War One. In Mike's essay (to generalise) three versions of this theme are offered and brought together at the conclusion to suggest that no one version is satisfactory in itself. In Robert's essay, however, it seems that the theme becomes something more than the effect on women of World War One. Robert in a sense takes argument itself – that is, the exploration of difference – as his theme. He anchors his activity in three major strands and uses these as sites for the attribution of different significances. *Bringing different views of the same phenomena into contact with one another like this generates argument.*

Models for Generating Argument: Some Suggestions

I noted above how knowledge of discourse involves having a repertoire of concepts that are related to one another. They are substitutable in that they perform similar types of function; so, for instance, in this History syllabus, the concept of 'false dawn' bears a similar classifying relation to a given historical event as 'turning point'. The categories of Class, Race, Gender which I noted (chapter 4) as significant in the discourse of Sociology are similarly interchangeable. Again, one of the aims of Literary Theory (chapter 10) might be to provide a repertoire of approaches to texts which can be used in place of one another and so become the basis for comparison and argument. The 'crits' in Fine Art (chapter 3) were also most sustainable and successful where the participants shared a discourse through which to extend their initial perceptions of the art work. Having a range of discursive concepts which have equivalent functions but alternative meanings is, evidently, an important part of engaging in disciplinary argument.

The CHP can be used to provide an example of how discoursal underpinnings might be exploited as a way of generating argument. The emphasis it places on 'understanding of history as a form of knowledge' and on 'explicit reflection on the nature of the discipline' means that the conceptual underpinnings on which the practice of History rest are exposed and named as part of learning. For instance, the historical significance of events is determined by 'the context of prior and subsequent developments' and the nature of that significance depends on 'the amount of change that takes place and the nature of that change'. There are, as I've noted, a variety of terms by which types of change may be manifested: turning point, trend, false dawn, and when one of these – 'turning point' – was used in the essay title it brought others into play.

The starting point of the strategy to generate argument is to locate a general and inclusive idea underlying a topic or an essay question. Locating such an idea is not equivalent to formulating a thesis, but can be an important stage prior to it. The chosen idea or concept is a stable common factor around which the material can be moved – organised, integrated and differentiated – whilst the thesis represents an eventual configuration of material expressed in propositional form (see Applebee's model in chapter 9). Choosing an idea like this tends to create a hierarchical rather than linear arrangement of ideas and examples. (In a hierarchy, a large overall pattern subsumes smaller less inclusive ones, which can be combined and connected in a variety of different ways). This reminds me of the hot-air balloon metaphor for argument and the development of higher order concepts. When the balloon is on the ground, its passengers see only the people standing around and the hedges of the field, but as they go higher they see how the field is connected to other fields, divided, perhaps, from houses by a road, deep in a valley surrounded by hills. As they go higher the passengers can see beyond the hills to other, perhaps previously unsuspected, terrain. All these elements are held together by the perspective attainable from the hot-air balloon. The passengers are not, however, seeing the world as it is in some pure and lucid sense, but rather are engaged in interpreting the connections and separations they see laid below them. It has been pointed out to me too, that the people in the balloon may employ different modes of vision (various spectacles, perhaps a telescope, binoculars): the sense they make of what they see will then be determined by the methods they employ and the way they are themselves constructed.

Identifying wider conceptions and categories for use in the service of the particular task is an important way of enhancing argument. In the case of the Cambridge History Project these conceptions and categories are explicit: the course offers descriptions and diagrams of the concepts upon which it rests. An example, which bears closely on the essays we have been discussing here, is given below:

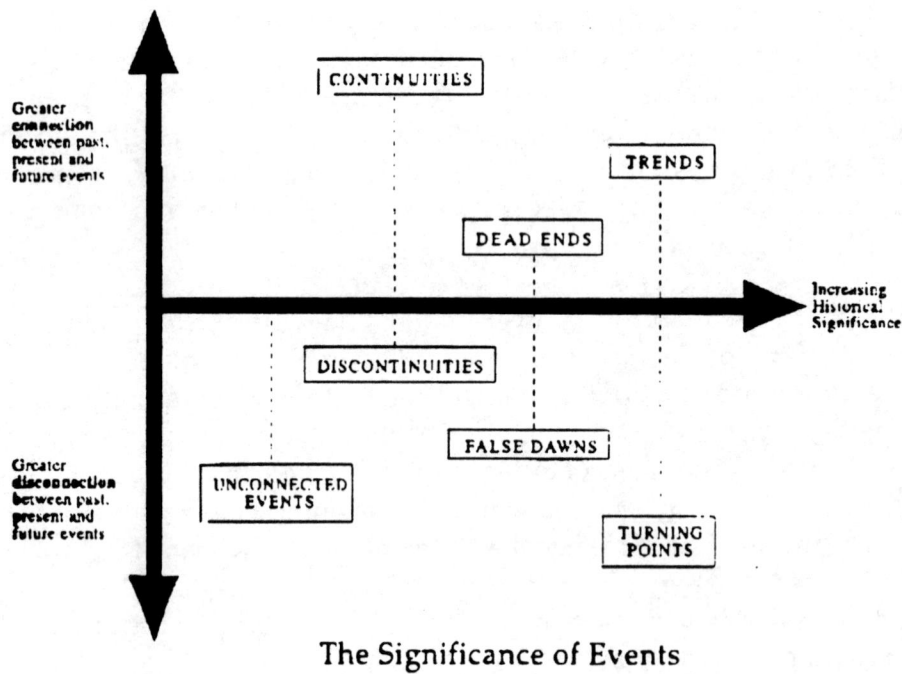

The Significance of Events

This diagram is based upon concepts of relative continuity and discontinuity and of historical significance. Students could be encouraged to use and adapt such a diagram for the generation of argument since it provides a structure against which actual accounts or interpretations can be matched and evaluated. More usefully though they could create diagrams of their own which address their specific purposes and tasks and which have space for the substitution of actual events. The following diagram would be an example:

A WORKING DIAGRAM FOR GENERATING ARGUMENT

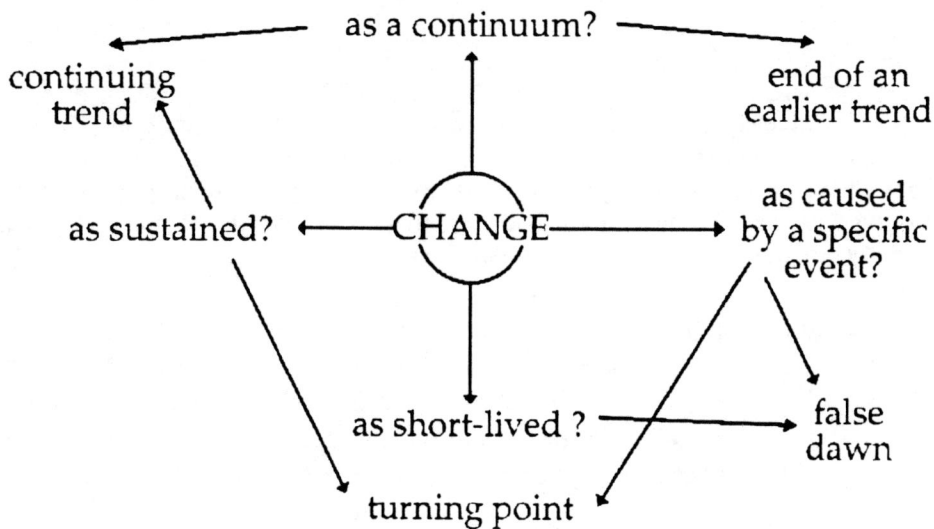

The stable factor was chosen as 'Change'. Possible ways in which change manifests itself are then arranged around the central idea. These possibilities can be combined to produce further ways of characterising change – the arrows drawn are not exhaustive. The labels can be thought of as representing condensed questions by which the event or account of the event can be evaluated or considered as historically significant. The diagram does not address the specific material, but could be applied to any strand that had been identified. The strand of 'Voting Rights' for instance could be examined with regard to the various aspects in the diagram, which would be a means of interrogating the evidence: Where does so and so stand on this issue? How does her view differ from his? Have all the possible interpretations been considered?

The last diagram differs significantly from the official CHP one. It is less coherent, authoritative, abstract and there are inconsistencies in the historical thinking it displays. Its function too is different: it is a working diagram to be drawn on and adapted; in it, meaning and understanding are emergent not developed. The difference between using a given model and generating one of one's own is important. The aim is to alert students to the organising and generative potential of wider concepts and hierarchical patternings, rather than to impose a sense that there is any one inclusive idea to be discovered. The use of such diagrams does not generate an order or sequence for material to be put down in the essay form – that remains the function of the essay plan – but rather it represents an important preliminary step in which 'raw' material is dealt with in an argumentative mode.

A further way of structuring an argument or rather of structuring ideas so that they can generate argument emerged from essays in A level Sociology (see Mitchell 1992b). In the essays the students largely organised their discussions around the learnt opinions of sociologists making these the subject of individual paragraphs (discrete narratives). An argumentative move was implied rather than explicitly made by the juxtaposition between paragraphs. It occurred to me that an alternative method of organisation (which the most successful essay employed to some extent) would be on the basis of significant sociological categories, such as Gender, Age and Class. The resulting structure would be more complex, since the views/narratives of the various sociologists would be divided up into relevant thematic sections. The material would be being worked into an hierarchical structure, where a general idea forms an anchor from which related sub-ideas or illustrations proliferate. An indication of this kind of structure occurs in the following paragraph from one of the students' essays:

> An important factor concerning health is class. In very simple terms, as in Black's materialist explanation, poverty leads to ill health. Poor people are the ones who are likely to be ill and suffer more health problems rather than the majority of middle and upper classes. The variations in health are due to inequalities, in this case the social class of a person. While everyone presumes that health care is increasing it does not for the working class – according to Townsend it has in fact deteriorated compared to the general improvements for the rest of the population.

The most general concept here appears in the middle of the paragraph – 'inequalities'. Social Class becomes a subcategory of inequalities; one means amongst others by which inequality is manifested. The idea of Class divides three ways. Points of comparison are generated between the classes, via their relation to the overreaching concept. In the same way Class could be compared with the other subcategories, such as Gender and Age, if their connection through the more general concept of inequality were acknowledged.

These relationships are represented diagramatically below. Combinations can be tested across the diagram, so that the inequalities of Class, Age and Gender can be seen to contribute, for instance, to the high rate of teenage smoking amongst working class girls – information from a source which the students refer to in their essays. The diagram offers a means by which an individual source such as this can be brought within a structure that applies to all the sources and organises them around concepts and categories. The limitations of a particular source can be easily identified by tracing their relation to the diagram. For instance it would be possible to see that a particular Marxist theory addresses only the inequalities of Class and has nothing to say about Age or Gender. This creates a space within an evolving argument to bring in another example which is more satisfactory in that particular respect, but which may in its turn be faulted. The sources mesh together not by virtue of their similarities, though these may be important to point out, but through their differences and incompletenesses.

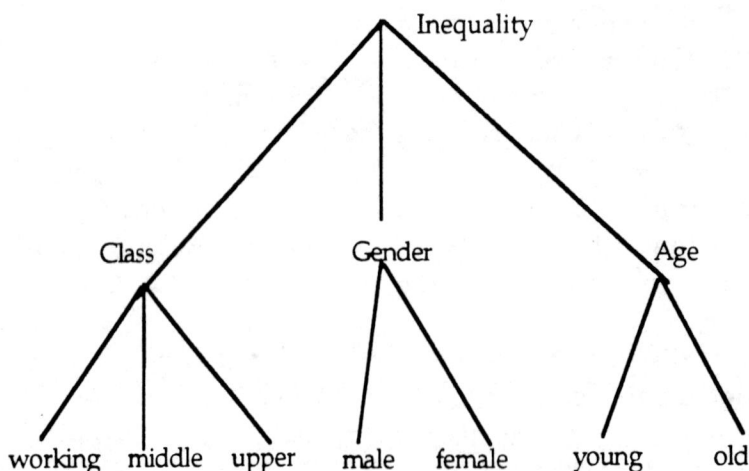

Once again, the diagram is not an essay plan, but a point of reference in transforming static and sometimes disparate material into argumentation. It is a process model, which allows movement between a set of different but relatable categories.

Other Visual Representations

In this section I want to introduce some other visual representations of argument structure, which again, it seems to me, have generative as well as heuristic or descriptive potential.

A very straightforward, but also rather useful one is that reproduced in *Genre Analysis* (Swales 1990) to describe the 'hour glass' structure of research articles. Although the diagram might be used as a way of thinking about the macro-structure of the essay as well as report, there are important differences. The middle section of an essay can not be said to represent a 'procedure': this is precisely the narrative that students need to be encouraged away from. The structure, then, between the focusing and widening of attention is more complex for a discursive argument than the diagram can suggest.

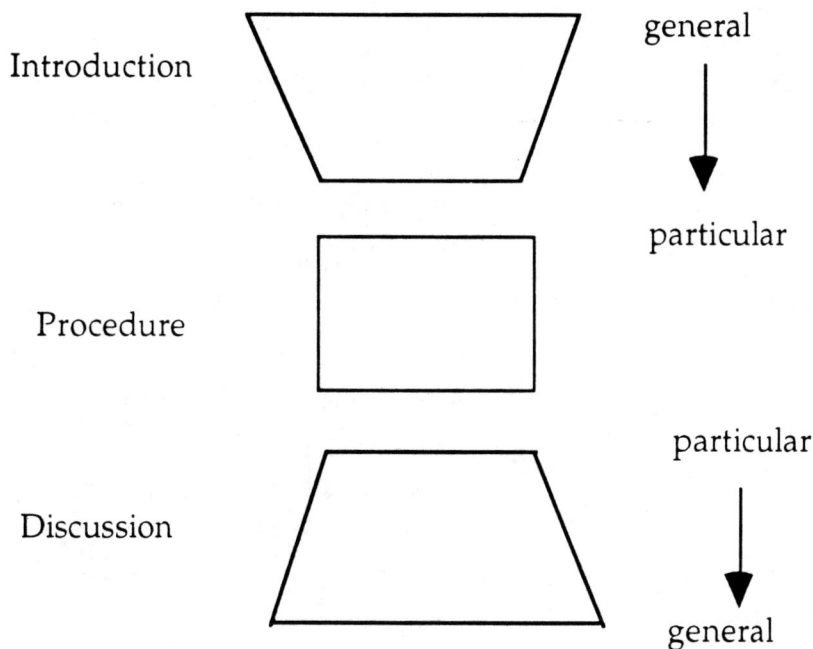

Introduction   general

particular

Procedure

particular

Discussion   general

(Hill et al. in Swales p.133/4)

The diagram functions perhaps more usefully as a tool for reading and making use of actual research articles. In a Sociology tutorial I observed, for instance, students were unsure of how to select appropriate material from a text to incorporate it into their notes. As first year undergraduates they were unfamiliar with the genre of the journal article, having been more used to reading text books. When this became evident in the tutorial the tutor pointed out the tendentiousness of the literature section, the way it differentiated between what was important in earlier studies and how and where it proposed that the research findings were different from these and therefore worthy of consideration. He directed the students towards the end of the literature section to find the specific claims the authors would make. In effect he was alerting them to the hour glass pattern and introducing this might have helped his explanation and taken it further to cover the likely trajectory of the whole text.

Swales offers a more detailed break down of the way such sections tend to function: the CARS model – Create A Research Space – which outlines a number of possible typical moves made by writers who are seeking to create a convincing context for their own original contribution to the field. Again introducing students to this kind of model might benefit their reading and note-taking skills, so they come to see texts as strategic devices for making claims, rather than as straightforward and undifferentiated receptacles of knowledge.

Move 1	**Establishing a Territory**	
	Step 1	Claiming centrality
		and/or
	Step 2	Making topic generalization(s)
		and/or
	Step 3	Reviewing items of previous research
		Declining rhetorical effort
Move 2	**Establishing a Niche**	
	Step 1A	Counter-claiming
		or
	Step 1B	Indicating a gap
		or
	Step 1C	Question-raising
		or
	Step 1D	Continuing a tradition
		Weakening knowledge claims
Move 3	**Occupying the Niche**	
	Step 1A	Outlining purposes
		or
	Step 1B	Announcing present research
	Step 2	Announcing principal findings
	Step 3	Indicating RA [Research Article] structure
		Increasing explicitness

(p. 141)

A second use for such a model (as with the 'hour glass' diagram) might be in influencing the students' own writing and development of argument. The idea of active purpose and of 'moves' indicates the teleological nature of much written argument, both in terms of what is said and how it is said – persuasively, with a view to convincing the reader. Thinking about the essay form in this rhetorical way, in terms of moves, might lead to a more active, manipulative engagement with material than is often the case. In a sense the essay might be thought of as making a number of the moves described above: say, a mixture of Move 1, Step 3 (the display of selected knowledge) with Move 2 (establishing a niche) by a series of counter-claims, indications of gaps, questions – and ending with Move 3 (the outlining of purposes), in this case the establishing of a position of opinion.

The sense in which argument is teleological but also oriented towards other voices as part of its rhetorical goal is conveyed also by the diagrams that Kaufer and Geisler (1991) have drawn to represent the structure of a Philosophy article. These again seem to me to succeed in communicating the sense in which purpose and structure in argument combined. Kaufer and Geisler invite us first to 'Imagine an author's line of argument as a sequence of claims moving readers forward on an issue' (p. 112). This is depicted as follows:

The arrow is not sufficient, however, to represent the whole of what occurs in the text:

> Whereas authors use main-path claims to offer the reader a positive course to take in exploring an issue, they rely on faulty-path claims to identify detours and deadends along the way. Authors present faulty paths as claims that readers need to understand if only to avoid. Faulty paths mark the perceptual boundaries and increase the perceptual clarity of the main path. (p. 114)

Diagramatically, faulty paths are pictured as below:

Faulty Paths

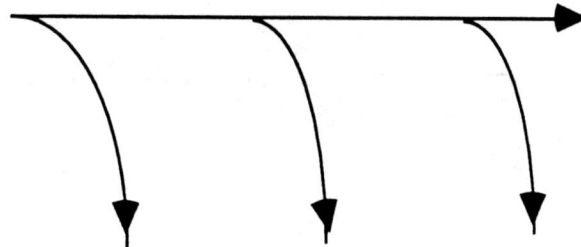

Again this does not complete the representation, since as Kaufer and Geisler explain:

> ...an argument is not a chorus of perspectives. Rather it is a tightly sequenced set of directions controlled by the author's perspective. Authors decide to include other perspectives for self-serving not democratic reasons. They include other perspectives when these perspectives can make their own more clear or fair-minded or persuasive by way of background or contrast. (p. 117)

Authors therefore use return paths to the main argument to show the limitations of the faulty paths and to reinforce the main path. The diagram now looks like this:

Return Paths

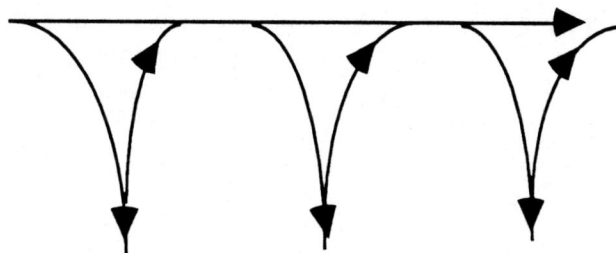

The diagram neatly represents the way in which the monologic purpose and form can integrate dialogic features. At the same time it suggests how this kind of dialogue does not have the discovery and the making of new meanings as its purpose, but rather the construction of a position *as* new.

It is interesting to think of possible variations of this diagram. The faulty and return paths are represented here as of equal magnitude, but this is unlikely to be the case: some arguments used negatively by writers will be carry more weight than others, some may dismissed entirely, whilst others may be agreed with in all but a few minor details. Thinking this way can change the look of the diagram:

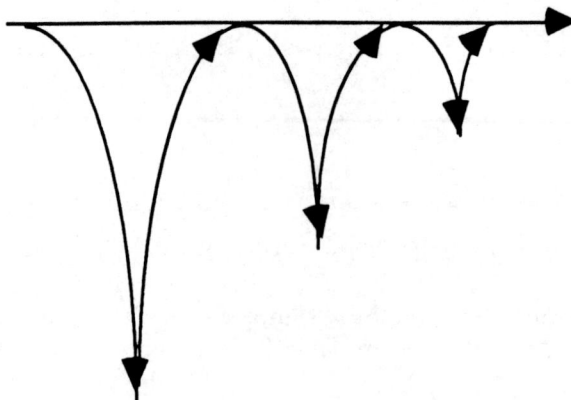

In this version of the diagram the writer can be imagined as putting aside at the outset a major rival position and then moving through positions which are progressively closer to her own. An alternative strategy might be to build to a crescendo:

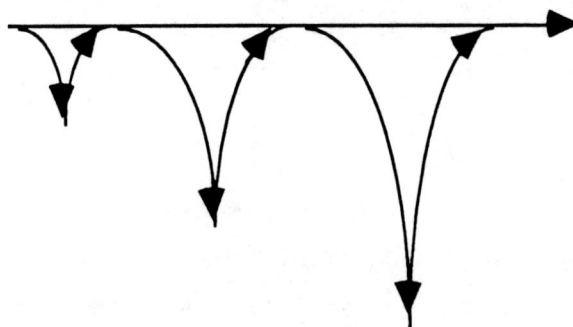

What these versions of the diagram do is introduce a sense of the rhetorical choices that writers can make: do I play my trump card at the outset or reserve it for the final round? Shall my game gather momentum or become more finely tuned? The possibilities are extensive. Students could be introduced to such models as these as ways of thinking about the way they structure their argument. They are playful heuristic devices and can be modified and reinterpreted. They can be used both to map an existing argument and to plan the shape of one that is still emerging. Below is another playful example, in which the ribs represent discrete positions, such as a unified theory, a narrative, a claim by an author. The ribs could be the sources used. (In the case of Mike's essay, discussed earlier, they would be the 'turning point' theory, the 'continuing trend' and the 'false dawn'.)

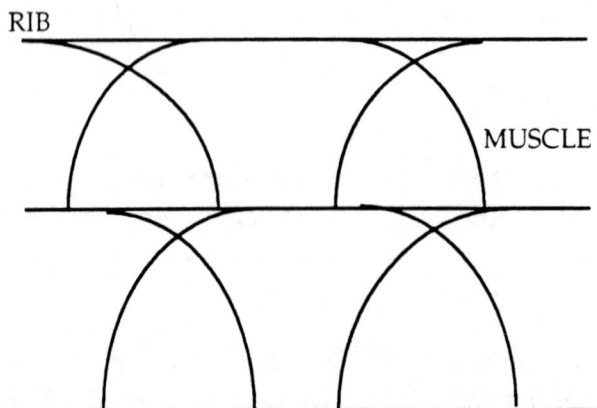

The muscles represent the connection made between the sources. They might be, for instance, questions asked of one text and answered by another, a critical commentary on gaps or weaknesses, a link made in order to compare, a reversal of one statement by its connection with another. It is the muscles which make the ribs work. They represent types of argumentative behaviour both connecting and pulling apart. Each rib on its own is static and without use; only by being connected with others is it put into action as part of a functioning whole. I like the idea of argument as *muscle* here since it resonates with Ricoeur's use of the word 'rigour' to describe the negative mode of interpretation and also with Kress' idea that argument brings about change, it metabolises.

Exercises in Using Structures

To end this chapter I include two activities which use the notion of imposing structure as a way of generating and exploring argument. They both use visual material as these are easier, more immediate 'sources'. Nonetheless they could be adapted with other material.

A. Making Patterns

Rationale

The principle here is that arguments can be developed from the configuring of material in different ways so as to emphasise certain aspects. Identifying similarity and difference (categorisation) is the basis for discrimination and argument. Students can learn ways of doing this by making patterns with a selection of pieces of information. Because they make the patterns and identify the criteria they are using they learn that argument is a matter of interpretation and also that the criteria on which certain things are seen to be similar and different from others need to be made explicit. This also moves them beyond narrative sequences of material towards more complex ways of ordering. The exercise can involve both speaking and writing.

The students first address the question 'What is Art?' in an unstructured way, drawing on their opinions and experience. They are then given six postcards of paintings or other art objects, representing a variety of styles and subject matter. The selection they are offered will influence what the students discover. For example, including a photograph, a piece of ancient art, or an installation will each raise different questions about what art is. Each card is numbered. They are used to complete the worksheet reproduced here:

What is Art?

1. Write a paragraph in response to the above question. These supplementary questions may help you: What do you think Art is? What are your reasons? Do you have examples? What do you think Art is not? Or, what is *not* Art? What are the criteria you are using in your definition?

2. You have been given six examples with which to pursue your investigations further. Each is numbered. Arrange the cards according to the patterns given below: write a number in each box. Below the boxes write your reasons for the order or pattern you have made.

A. (sequence)

Reasons:

B. (two groups)

Reasons:

162

C. (three groups)

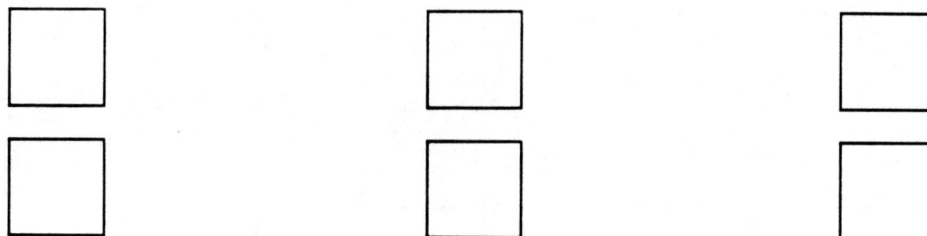

Reasons:

D. (one exception)

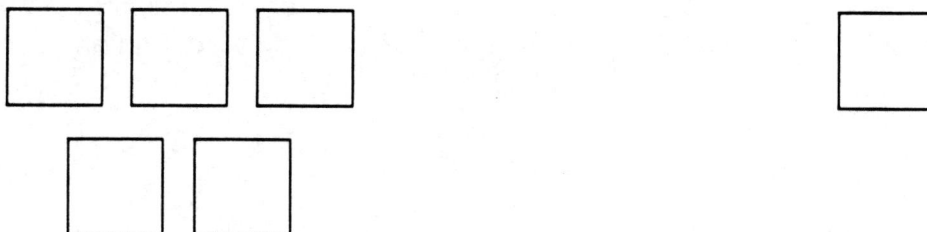

Reasons:

E. (hierarchy)

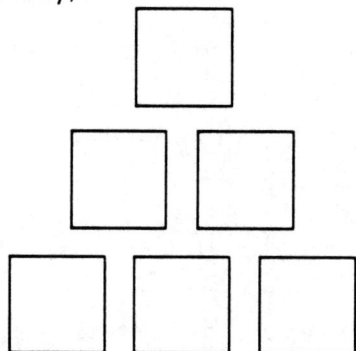

Reasons:

F. Try another patterning of your own here and give your reasons:

3. Try to identify as clearly as possible the criteria you have been using in grouping the cards and list them here.

4. Now look again at the question 'What is Art?' Go back to what you said about Art before you looked at the cards. Do any of your groupings represent what you said? Are there any groupings which don't fit your definition? If some of these groupings aren't Art, what are they? What other definitions of Art are possible besides your own? Could Art be a way of challenging definitions of Art?

5. Write a further response to the question 'What is Art?' You might like to use one or more of the following quotations as a starting point or to guide your thinking.

- 'The greatness of art is not to find what is common but what is unique' (I.B. Singer 1904-1991)

- 'Art of any profundity can be appreciated only slowly, gradually, in leisurely contemplation.' (Daniel Gregory Mason 1897-1953)

- 'There are more valid facts and details in works of art than there are in history books.' (Charlie Chaplin 1889 -1977)

- 'Art is the imposing of a pattern on experience, and our aesthetic enjoyment in recognition of the pattern.' (Alfred Whitehead 1861-1947)

- 'But the Devil whoops, as he whooped of old:
  "It's clever, but is it Art?"' (Rudyard Kipling 1865-1936)

- 'The Devil whispered behind the leaves,
  "It's pretty, but is it Art?" (Rudyard Kipling 1865-1936)

B. Creating Significance / Making Connections

Rationale

Again, this exercise uses pictures as units of information. Students are given a selection of photographic images in no particular order. They must use them to create an argument. This task involves them in thinking about what ideas or themes the pictures could represent and in making connections between pictures. They will need to make these connections explicit. They may decide to group certain pictures together as representing different aspects of a certain idea or to contrast them as representing opposing points of view. Again, they will be making patterns. An additional potential might be exploited by looking at the type of images and grouping them by photographic style or intent.

The same pictures can be used to construct a narrative. If students do both, they can compare the strategies they have used and the different significance of the images in each case.

The exercise can be undertaken collaboratively or individually. There is scope for both written and spoken work. Students can present their argument or narrative solutions to the class, giving rise to discussion of who has been most ingenious or effective.

12. Diversifying Written Argument

In the preceding chapters two points have emerged which are worth noting here. One is that argument can emerge from organisational decisions and the structuring or patterning of material. The other is that the forms conventionally used for the expression of argument are culturally determined and underpinned by assumptions about advanced cognitive development. These two points both play into each other and need to be kept separate. Certain structures, in their unity and coherence, can seem to reflect higher order thinking (see Applebee's model, chapter 9) and, I would think, almost certainly do. Yet the value placed on unity and coherence is also mediated by a particular ideological conception of texts and of writers' and readers' positions in relation to those texts. Recognising this introduces the possibility of alternative, or, better perhaps, greater diversity of structures and forms of argument.

For this project objectives have been two-fold; on the one hand to understand the difficulties experienced by students in using conventional forms and to find ways in which they may improve; on the other, to subject these forms to scrutiny, to see both what they make possible and what they exclude – and as a result to explore alternatives. This second objective is not easy to carry through. As Williamson (1988) has argued, whilst it is recognised that 'the use of academic discourse is a systematic norm imposed by the social and historical conventions of post-secondary education' individual teachers are hindered from introducing greater diversity in writing if 'Failure to master academic discourse must finally result in failure in the academic context because of the unpredictable responses of other members of the community to nonconforming discourse' (p. 95). Thus within the normative conditions of institutions such as schools and universities, diversity paradoxically can be permitted only through some form of consensus.

Nonetheless there is a continuum, rather than an absolute divide, between the uniform and the diverse[1] and in an increasingly pluralist society, with widening access to post-sixteen education, previously excluded voices and ways of operating will need to be explored, valued and used for the possibilities they offer. In addition, we are now in an electronic age in which new kinds of text and new ways of communicating are rapidly developing. On a very basic level, it is now possible for writers easily to change the look and arrangement of text on a page and to introduce, for example, visual elements to areas which would previously have been regarded as the domain of writing. These developments all have implications and possibilities for argument. So though traditional forms may in some ways continue to be seen as necessary, I'm not sure they can be sufficient. Difference is one reason for suggesting alternatives; another is continuation the better writing of academic essays, enlivened by

---

[1] It was for this reason that the study of Fine Art was an important inclusion in research, the main focus of which would be on 'traditional' academic practices and enculturation.

experiments with other forms. Both reasons share one motivation: a shift from blueprinting to creativity.

Dialogic Forms

Both argument and dialogue involve, whether explicitly or implicitly the expression or possible expression of more than one view point. Argument is, like the participant in dialogue, oriented towards the other, seeking to persuade, even in such an apparently neutral sense of supplying reasons in support of statements or proof in support of claims. In addition, as has been explored elsewhere, academic written forms of argument involve the writer in manipulating multiple sources and authorities (other voices), in order to point out how they are aligned or how they differ and thus to show her own positionality and argument in relation to theirs and to the question that has been set. Writing an argumentative essay, then, is as much to do with exploiting multiplicity as it is with the teleological task of developing a thesis. Yet the teleological and the dialogic often conflict with each other, the one cancelling the other out. The need to put forward a thesis can function to constrain and close down the insistence of multiple voices, by rejecting what is distracting or problematic; alternatively the multiple voices can take over, forcing the writer into obedience to each one in turn. In this case dialogue as well as thesis is lost in a sequence of monologues.

Below I explore a number of possibilities for writing argument which foreground the dialogic aspects of argument.

Dialogue and Questions

The Philosophy students whose discussions with their tutor have been quoted several times in this report, appeared to experience a conflict between their learnt sense of an essay as a coherent rhetorical product and their growing perception that the philosophers they read would often write by raising and refuting questions. Was it permissible for them too to raise questions or would that interfere with the structured flow of their writing? As nascent philosophers themselves they wanted to 'stand outside themselves' and comment on their own comments, yet surely the essay was not the place for such behaviour?

The uncertainty of the students seemed to me to reflect the low status of (students') questions in educational contexts, particularly in writing and the far higher status of answers and questions that imply answers (frequently teachers' questions) (see Mitchell 1992a). Yet one very successful way of generating thinking amongst students is to ask them to come up with a number of questions about a text, a topic or an issue. It is questions that very often which provide the clue to meaning and significance and they can be a very powerful means of giving expression to what has not yet been thought or said. They can equally be very powerful in extending, clarifying or undermining what *has* been said. As both generative and critical tools, then, questions have a major role in argument.

So too in dialogue which develops through the use of questions, both those which seek information and those which elicit consent or challenge for contradiction. The questioning approach is implicit in Bakhtin's insistence that the 'activating principle' in creating meaning is in the response (1981, p. 281) In his understanding there are, in a sense, no statements or closure since meaning is always contingent upon the conditions of utterance and reception. Questions demand answers which give rise to further questions. At the same time questions are a kind of answer (a response; they're rarely 'innocent') and answers, a kind of question (Am I making myself clear? Do we agree now?). J. A. Richards (1955) expressed this paradoxical open-closedness of the question from in a piece entitled 'Queries' written entirely as questions (and seemingly as a result of this, very hard to challenge):

> Does a question have to have a direction?
> Can't it go all ways at once?
> Doesn't a question have to have a direction?
> Can it go all ways at once? (p. 134-5)

It's hard to be sure that Richards' queries are not in some way also theories: they are both open to response and objections and at the same time, knowing and intentioned. It is this combination that makes them a particularly intriguing form of argument. Where students do use questions in their writing (examples are given in chapter 7) they are often few in number and signal evasion rather than exploration of issues. Someone who had the courage to employ questions *en masse* as a form of critique was Virginia Woolf. In an article entitled 'Why?' she writes:

> I should explain that like so many people nowadays I am pestered with questions. I find it impossible to walk down the street without stopping, it may be in the middle of the road, to ask Why? [...] Yet what is the point of asking questions of oneself? They should be asked openly in public. But the great obstacle to asking questions in public is, of course wealth. The little twisted sign that comes at the end of a question has a way of making the rich writhe; power and prestige come down upon it with all their weight. Questions, therefore, being sensitive, impulsive and often foolish, have a way of picking their asking place with care. (1992 p. 148)

As she embarks on the two thousand words she has been asked to write, Woolf is continually interrupted by questions clamouring to be heard and taking her descriptions into realms of possibility and aspiration:

> In the old days, when newspapers were scarce and carefully lent about from Hall to Rectory, such laboured methods of rubbing up minds and imparting ideas were no doubt essential. But now, when every day of the week scatters our tables with articles and pamphlets in which every shade of opinion is expressed, far more tersely than by word of mouth, why continue an obsolete custom which not merely wastes time or temper, but incites the most debased of human passions – vanity, ostentation, self-assertion, and the desire to convert? Why encourage your elders to turn themselves into prigs and prophets, when they are ordinary men and women? Why force them to stand on a platform for forty minutes while you reflect upon the colour of their hair and the longevity of flies? Why not let them talk to you and listen to you, naturally and happily, on the floor? Why not create a new form of society founded on poverty and equality? Why not bring together people of all ages and both sexes of all shades of fame and obscurity so they can talk without mounting platforms, or reading papers, or wearing expensive clothes, or eating expensive food? Would not such a society be worth even as a form of education, all the papers on art and literature that have ever been read since the world began? Why not abolish prigs and prophets? Why not invent human intercourse? Why not try? (p. 151)

Far from signalling the ignorance or uncertainty of the writer, these questions very forcibly assert her presence. In an article exploring diverse forms Lillian Bridwell-Bowles (1992) describes how one of her students used questions as an alternative to 'a tightly reasoned argument' in an attempt to overcome what the feminist critic Gearhart calls the 'conquest model of human interaction'. Bridwell-Bowles quotes the following extract:

> Does a voice that tries "to please all and offend none" boil down to the same as Gearhart's voice that refuses to conquer? is a voice that refuses either to please or offend a strong voice? What is a strong voice? What does Peter Elbow mean by a voice so strong it scares

others? What is "Writing with Power"? Is that what feminist rhetoric is attempting? Is powerful feminist rhetoric a contradiction? An oxymoron? Can the rhetoric of consensus building permit strong, powerful, *individual* voices? Can it permit a strong powerful *collective* voice? How is this achieved? If it is achieved, does it contradict the ideology that set it in motion? (p. 364)

She comments that the student 'takes his own opinions out of the paper, except as his questions reveal an underlying position' and, as a result, she does not consider the writing to be argument. I would disagree with this interpretation; the writing is not, I think, unargumentative, nor without persuasive force. The questions are not arbitrary but linked in a way that is developmental though it may not culminate in an explicitly stated position. It is perhaps because it evades explicitness and culminating statement that it is not taken to represent argument, but this suggests a conflation between the form and mode which I don't think is helpful in exploring diversity.

Writing Dialogues

As a dramatic form dialogue enables a range of differing perspectives to be presented, including those which are dissenting or contradictory. As in actual speech, a dialogue may have circular as well as sequential patternings and it may be easier to admit speculation, doubt and divergent thought. Like speech too, the form is less censorious of material from different discourses than much conventional academic argument.

The first example of dialogue is written by a first year undergraduate in philosophy and takes place between Socrates and Schopenhauer on the subject of love. The lecturer for whose course it was written chose the dialogue form as a way of facilitating the interaction between the two men's ideas. He foresaw that a straightforward essay would result in the exposition of one point of view and then the other, with minimal contact between the two. It was in fact possible for students to do this even in the dialogue form if they gave lengthy turns to each philosopher. Where this happens the potential of the dialogic form is not fully exploited, but in the following example it is used with emphasis and pace:

Soc:	I am impressed, sir, by the power of your vitriol. Had a man of lesser intellect presented these ideas I would be inclined to dismiss them for the foul humour they create. But a man of your philosophical bent could not of succumbed to mere bitterness. I think that in another I would suspect that they had fallen for the pose of the dreamy poets, for their sweet descriptions of love and finding reality wanting produced the negative image of these poets' eulogies.
Sch.	Are you suggesting my inquiry is less than philosophical ?
Soc:	I merely allow my mind to wander, your exposition is erudite and precise and worthy of serious consideration. But I declare I see nothing of an enquiry into love in it.
Sch:	Socrates, old man, I do believe you must have dozed off. At the start I made it clear that I believe love is nothing more than the will to life of the next generation, that all this talk of romantic love masks its true nature.
Soc:	Would you say that love can exist only where procreation is the aim?
Sch:	Certainly.
Soc:	Then can love exist between friends?
Sch:	No, only friendship can exist between friends.

Soc:	Then how is it possible that one friend will give his life for another? If the will to live is the supreme driving force surely it would be impossible for an individual to throw his life away when it does not involve the generation of the species.
Sch:	What you describe is indeed a weak form of the will to live, very occasionally a friend will give his life when the will of the species has recognised the value of the other.
Soc:	Then you would agree that the will to live is expressed in more ways than purely sexual reproduction?...

The writer here has recourse to a wider range of imaginative and linguistic skills than is generally required of the academic essay. He has *characterised* the philosophers as well as reproducing their ideas, and this characterisation is a kind of meta-comment, a fuller reading of the work, than a summary or distillation of their ideas into academic language would be. There is scepticism, irreverence and humour in the writing too, which feels confident and positive. A successful dialogue of this kind is not easy to write, because it draws on these unfamiliar skills, but it is, I think, no less rigorous or demanding an exercise.

These philosophy dialogues don't tend to end with conclusions, but with a phrase such as 'etc. etc. until dawn' or 'Here we must leave our two friends quietly musing, always wondering if they ever did resolve this issue'. The open-endedness of the dialogue form reflects in this case the view of knowledge within the discipline. It characterises a style of thinking, rather than capturing and condensing what has been thought. It offers too the possibility of parody, another quality which demands greater understanding than is involved in straight reproduction. These qualities in dialogue might usefully be used, then, to move students away from assuming purely epistemic goals in disciplinary learning.

There are limitations in the above dialogue in that the writer is confined to the actual views of the philosophers and will find it difficult to extend them, or find a voice to challenge them. Any hypothetical criticism is constrained by a need to be faithful to the philosophers as historical figures. This problem might be overcome by the introduction of a further character, the writer herself, who could take on the role of mediator and super-critic. In standard academic forms the writer's role in this regard can be subordinated to the display of authoritative knowledge and surface only in the concluding remarks, where evaluation is as much a rhetorical nicety as an outcome of argumentation in the body of the writing. If, as I think is likely, one of the reasons for the paucity of evaluation and criticism in students' essays is the 'depopulated' nature of academic discourse (see Simpson and Ivanic 1993), then the creation of a commentator figure in dialogue might provide the necessary licence for this to take place.

In this next example of dialogue, the writer, a post-graduate student adopts, as characters, two students on the same course. Their subject is, appropriately, the teaching and learning of argument. In the course of several meetings they review together what the National Curriculum says about argument and the literature they have to hand on the subject, just as they would do in preparing to write an academic essay:

| X: | I see what you mean. On the other hand, there is no indication that the writing of argument *should* be confined to essays. There does seem to be a definite change of approach at Key Stage 3 though, it's as if moving from primary to secondary schooling meant crossing the non-academic/academic divide. They use different terminology. At Key Stages 1 and 2 they define all writing as either chronological |

or non-chronological. Presumably argument would come in the non-chrono-logical category.

Y: And are you happy with that?

X: Well, no, I don't think it's a useful distinction. Most genres fall in to both categories, but I suppose the use of the terms was supposed to broaden the scope of writing in school, other opposing pairs can appear more restrictive: creative/factual, poetic/transactional [...] Teachers are dependent on the examples given. For example, Programme of Study for KS1 AT (Attainment Task) 3,4 & 5, writing, spelling and handwriting (ENG):

> Pupils should undertake a range of non-chronological writing which includes... some at least of list, captions, labels, invitations, greetings cards, notices, posters and ... plans and diagrams, descriptions and notes for an activity.

Y: No mention of argument there, or expression of opinion. In fact what strikes me particularly about this list, apart from a few exceptions, is how uncontentious they are.

X: What's wrong with that?

Y: Perhaps monologic is a better word. Have you read Gunther Kress's chapter in *Narrative and Argument?* (Andrews 1989)

The extract shows how the dialogic form can include an equal breadth of reference and accuracy of referencing as in a straightforward essay. There is an exploratory feel to the dialogue as the characters examine the texts, testing their reactions and linking them with others. Here Y's sense of the neutrality of the Key Stage 1 descriptors begins to emerge into a critical point which is formulated, immediately challenged and modified a little later on. In the next extract, X's question comes after a chunk of quotation by Y and is an invitation to formulate and clarify her use of it – an important move in explicit argument.

X: So what are you saying?

Y: I think I am saying that perhaps they recognise the importance of argument in the development of critical thought, but they do not consider school the appropriate forum for real controversy. As soon as children approach an age where their arguments could be really effective, or influential in the world outside they are expected to focus their energies on simulated situations, or academic essays. They are allowed to engage in sparring, but never the full scale battle.

X: Ha! Do you see it as wholly a political issue then?

Y: It depends what we mean by political! No, I think the issue is one of educational priorities.

X: Well, you may be right to be suspicious of government influence in educational policy, but I think another influence is at work: the community around the school...

The presence of two speaking voices appears to prevent the accumulating evidence being used in support of one conclusion only and to carry the argument forward in the discussion of other possibilities. The form also allows issues to resurface and for the voices to move together as well as apart:

Y: Well, there you are, there's your justification, the APU (Assessment of Performance Unit) said it's important.

X: The government got rid of the APU didn't it?

Y: And you thought *I* couldn't keep away from politics.

X: Well, they are all pervading! But now we're coming to the heart of the matter, the need for alternatives to the formal academic essay.

The form also seems to allow material of an anecdotal or personal kind to be introduced easily without the clash of discourses that can occur in writing:

X: ...Interestingly, Clarke seems to regret the loss of précis from the curriculum, as through the exercise, students had to understand the main ideas and basic rhetorical strategies of the selected passage; they could also see how an argument was constructed via the process of paraphrasing it. He also makes the point that the object of the précis can also be a definition of argument, that is to say, the way an opinion is 'formed, shaped and given force on paper.' (Andrews, Costello and Clarke 1993)

Y: Yes, I find that very convincing. Not my experience, though. I well remember précis at school, and I'm pretty sure most of them were reports not arguments, but maybe I've just forgotten...

In some ways I sense that writing a good dialogue *which is also academic* may be a difficult task, perhaps particularly so for students who have had several years of writing little other than academic essays. Yet the dialogue is, in fact, a form which people encounter daily. I am not thinking only of their own interactions in speech, but rather of the television and radio interviews and panel discussions, which are used to communicate about almost every possible topic and with varying degrees of seriousness and analysis. It seems to me that tapping students' non-academic literacy and using dialogues in a more contextual or situated way – as, for instance, interviews or panel discussions – might be an useful way to develop argumentation.

Peter Medway (1980 p.64-6) gives an example, in his book *Finding a Language*, of a boy who was working on a project on football hooliganism, and who, having interviewed his grandfather and read an article by a sociologist on the subject, decided without prompting to bring these two together in a television programme in which a fictional 'Mr Smith' , 'a 75-year old member of the public who has supported Stoke on Trent since he was 7 years old' was invited to talk to Ian R. Taylor, the sociologist. The interview form was, it seemed, a very obvious and effective way for bringing these two very different view points together and allowing both to be heard.

Dialogues also create the possibility of **collaborative writing**, which makes the most of two or more actually differing perspectives. I have seen book reviews written in this way. Another variant is the **symposium**: a written account of what participants in a discussion have said. This form can effectively act as a bridge between what students say in interactive spoken situations and what they say in 'monologic' writing. As I have noted elsewhere, the move from speech to writing can often result in a disjunction between the two, and a fall-off in writing of what has been argued in speech. The symposium raises the value of spoken argument, making it a necessity for students to listen to what others are saying and to reflect on what has been said in the act of reproducing it. It can be a transitionary stage in the writing of a conventional essay, in which, it is hoped, there will be sensitivity to nuance and a variety of points of view.

A dialogic form of writing, which is increasingly being used and which, again, bridges the divide between speech and writing, is via **computer conferencing.** This is used predominantly on distance learning courses but can also take place between students on conventional courses. Rachel Rimmershaw (1993) has used this on her course in the Department of Educational Research at Lancaster University. This is how she justifies her use of the system: it

recognises that

- collaboration is a common academic practice, which professional academics find useful

- it is also a common real-world practice: lots of people work in teams

and emphasises that

- knowledge is not private property

- in learning encounters (with books, tutors and fellow students) knowledge is jointly constructed

- the acquisition of knowledge is not a zero-sum game, you don't lose any by sharing it with others; in fact you are likely to improve your own understanding.

There are two kinds of 'conference' on the course, one which is concerned with reading subdivided into core reading, further reading and other suggested reading and one which is concerned with topics. In the first conference students contribute comments with the following guidelines:

relevance: 'why the paper is worth reading (for this course)'
message: 'summary of the main points or key ideas'
relation: 'how the reading relates to their own experience'
credibility: 'critical appraisal of what the writer has done/said'.

These guidelines seem to cover a wider range of responses than might be demanded by or included in an essay and at the same time order the responses in a loose way. The activities collectively amount to the components of an argument or critique. They bridge the gap between structured note-making, which is personal and provisional, and forms of writing which are public and final. In this way the computer conference functions rather like an exchange of letters. The pressure to produce finished form is lifted, but the discipline of communicating clearly and interestingly to others is maintained. The students actually enter into dialogue with each other, challenging interpretations and judgements directly and making suggestions, but unlike in spoken dialogue they have the opportunity to reflect on and develop responses. The computer conference thus draws on both the directness and openness of speech and the opportunity for individual consolidation and extension that writing accords.

For the conference on topics a similarly conversational content is encouraged:

Here students talk about the course topics, including saying what the questions are which concern or interest them, sharing their reactions to the activities which have taken place in class meetings, and to the reading they have done. They have agreed a ground rule of a minimum of one contribution to a "topic" conference, and one to a "biblio" conference each week. Some students do considerably more than this.

Dialogic Assessment

What these students are experiencing at Lancaster University leads me on to think of assessment (whether between teacher and student or between peers) as a form of dialogue. This might be put another way as the dialoguing of writing, or indeed, as the dialogic practice of reading. In speech, questioning and dissent are crucial to the continuance of argument, and the same can be said for written argument, too, if the frame in which the text is thought of is broadened; that is, if texts are treated dialogically.

Assessment is dialogic when the reader of a piece of writing responds to what she reads with comments and questions which challenge or seek to further the thinking of the writer. Here is an anecdote from a teacher who habitually responds in this way to his students' essays, writing marginalia or putting numbers in the margins which refer to comments on an additional page at the back. His students were unused to this kind of attention being given to their writing (the way their writing was being treated, in a sense, as speech). On one occasion a student said to him: 'Look I'm having real problems writing this because every time I make a point I imagine you writing a comment like, "What do you mean?". For instance I've just written "Ferdinand moves between possessive love of his sister, the Duchess, and Hate" but then I thought *you* would write "Do you mean *hate*?", so I've put "or rather his obsessive love prevents him from wanting her happiness", but then I thought you would write, "How do you know he wants her to be happy?", so I've put ...' This student saw it as a problem that 'everything I write I imagine you writing a question over it', but was reassured by the teacher that she was showing herself to be a sophisticated writer able to qualify and examine an argument as she writes. For her the sense of an actual reader ('But it's only because I write my essay to *you*') was important at this stage of development. She had made this explicit by writing in her rough drafts for an essay: 'But Mr X, I know you're going to say now ...'. The sense of a reader was very strong for her, though the teacher expects this to become generalised as her questioning processes become internalised. The sense of the writing addressing an attentive and questioning reader means that this student operates with argument as a process of continual slippage (see end of chapter 2), yet ultimately this will not be empowering if there is no safety net, no point of closure which will ensure that the essay gets written, the task completed. This is why Publication is an important stage in the recurring cycle of development.

Below is an example of a student's essay in Philosophy assessed dialogically by a peer. It illustrates that the status of the essay (as process or product) is dependent on the reading and writing practices that are brought to bear on it. The comments on the essay work against its status as closed product and position it in an open-ended conversational frame. For it to be most effective the writer of the essay needs to engage with the comments; many of which, it is interesting to note, take the form of questions.

Even if you accept that there actually is a God there are still many problems involved in tying morality to religion. A religious view of what is good and what is morally correct to do seems to be "what God wills". It is right to do what God wills you to do. Therefore, to act morally you would need to do what God willed you to do in every situation. This seems fairly straightforward on the surface. You can learn of God's will through reading a bible and through other religious teachings which give basic idea of what it is right and wrong to do. However, no teachings can allow for every situation that will occur in your life. How will you know what God wills at every given

(VIII)
Do you here suggest that if there is a God then what you read in the Bible is an "accurate" manifestation of God's will? That in the particular situation (portrayed in the Bible, or whatever religious book with the claim of speaking of the will of God) God's will can be

moment? This would seem implausible. You can know what you think God would want you to do, but you can't really know if it is what he really wants you to do. In respect of this, whatever you do will be what you think is right and what you think you should do, not what God thinks you should do.

Another problem with the idea that it is right to do what God wills is the question of how we know that what God wills really is what is right. If you believe in a God it would seem natural to assume that God is good and actually knows what is good. However you have no way of knowing for sure that God is good, you may believe that what he wills is what is good, but you can never be sure. The only way you can know that what God tells you to do is good is if you know what good is. The problem here is that if you knew what was good you wouldn't need a God to tell you what to do. You would need no spiritual guidance to help you lead a good life.

taken as God's will, since the manifestation of his will is revealed in that particular situation?

(IX)
What do you mean by "really wants to do?" If it refers to what you said in VIII, then how can one be sure that this is really what he wanted the people, in that particular situation to do, since we do not even know anything about that situation, apart from what we read in e.g. the Bible. So how do we "know" that that which they refer to as being the will of God *really* is the will of God? Is there even a question of "knowing" when it comes to the Bible?

(X)
Is the claim of the believer different from "merely" believing? And if that is not so then what significance does that have for claiming something being "true" in relation to belief? And if so, then in what sense?

(XI)
Once again do we *know* what "good" is?

Potentially such a 'conversation' is endless, though in practice it will be a limited exchange. In that the grading of work tends for the student to be a definitive statement it works against the engagement in dialogue. Students often demand to have grades and at certain times they are necessary. But where grading is seen as more valuable than, and a substitute for, dialogue, then its *educational* use is not only limited but limiting. Making assessment criteria explicit to students can be similarly negative if it stands in for dialogue: the actual particulars of a piece of writing are always more complex than a checklist of criteria can do justice to.

Writing Split Texts

A split text is another form of dialogue: the essay and marginalia above suggest what it looks like. The marginalia question divert and extend the 'main' text, making points and objections which are excluded from its argument and the juxtaposition creates a further text: a dialogue across the dividing space. The example below 'compares and contrasts' two films, *Gorillas in the Mist and Aliens*. The student writes 'I see these two films as embodying two sides of the same debate: What *is* natural?'. He then structures the text around four points of comparison, the first of which is 'The Technology of the Look':

... Crucially, early in the film, at a moment when the frame is entirely occupied with the image from a VDU, that image flickers leaving the screen/frame momentarily blank. So, from an early moment in the film, the attention of the audience is drawn to the technologies of communication and how they do not always work.

... Yet this serves to heighten rather than to diminish the sense of realism. The interference comes from the environment represented. It does not arise as part of the technology of communication.

The magic of this realist style of photography arises from the juxtaposition of perfect and imperfect technology: Where Fossey can only make notes, or take (black and white) photos,

176

No one mode of communication is privileged over others within the film. There is no master code into which all information may be translated. There is no possibility of 'perfect' communication: communication is not impossible, yet the appearance of noise and interference in the many technologies within the film indicates how systems are open rather than closed, actual rather than ideal.

A metaphor for this is found in the visual nature of the film. The point of view of the camera is frequently occluded. The colony is an industrial space of artificial lights, steam and smoke, galleries and service tunnels. The extreme chiaroscuro effect created by these light sources means that it is often difficult to see exactly what is going on. The unknown is the unseen, the threatening and horrific.

or where Campbell makes visual but not sound recordings, the cinematic eye/I show us everything (except itself) in a tour-de-force including widescreens, Dolby stereo, and naturalistic colour. It is a master code into which other codes may be translated, showing them to be by comparison, limited and partial.

Filmed largely in the open, the light is 'natural' and falls evenly over the scene. yet to suggest that the lighting of the film *is* natural is another trick of Realism. It belies the way that the effect of 'natural' light was painstakingly achieved – a fact underlined by the inclusion of lighting technicians in the list of credits.

The total illumination of the natural-istic lighting serves as a metaphor for the all-seeing but disembodied point of view. Where the aliens occupy an area on the threshold of the light, the gorillas in the mist bask in the broad daylight which renders them unthreatening – in fact the gorillas are seldom seen in any kind of mist whatsoever.

In the final paragraph in the right-hand column, the two films are brought together in a classic comparative sentence which closes the section. The form is an excellent way of juxtaposing two textual analyses, which in a sequential text would be separated from one another and therefore limited in the extent to which the closely focussed interpretative arguments of one could resonate with those of the other. This way, the narrative tendency of the textual interpretation (critique is as often embedded in the choice of descriptive words as in abstractions and generalisations) becomes argumentative by virtue of its constant contact on the page with an alternative narrative. The 'explicitness' of the argument is visual as much as verbal.

In a later section, 'Same and Different Relationships', comparisons are made directly on a point by point basis between films.[2]

* Ripley is a woman who is not defined within a heterosexual monogamous relationship. Her appropriation of phallic fire-power and her maternal relationship with Newt construct her as doubly gendered.

* Dian Fossey is a woman who is not defined within a heterosexual, monogamous relation-ship. Her scientific abilities and her independence code her as doubly gendered.

It is interesting to note the context which the writer of this piece (an MA student of cultural studies) gives:

> It was unassessed; the tutors on the course got us to write a couple of short essays in between the 'important' assessed work. In them, we were invited to try out ideas, explore new areas, and so on. I think the idea was that these short essays would keep us in touch with the art of writing (- although I did the course on a full-time basis, most of the others were part-timers; I suspect these exercises were aimed at them).

---

[2] This is the kind of approach to imposing structure on material which was implicit in the use of the grid in the module on argument described in chapter 7 and included in the appendix.

The writer goes on to say how much he enjoyed the piece, finding it playful, allowing him to experiment with languages and strategies used by established theorists without taking them too seriously. He notes however that the freedom of the piece derived in part from the fact that it was not assessed:

> It is perhaps significant that the only other adventurous piece of work I submitted was marked down. The rest was occasionally daring in content, but conservative in form.

Ideas for change, including a recognition here of the formative value of experimental writing, are, it seems, in advance of institutional mechanisms for valuing them as product. This, as I noted earlier, is the problem of diversification in essentially normative institutions; it does not mean, however, that change is impossible, rather that it is slow and must be negotiated.

Another way in which a split text may be used is not in juxtaposing critiques of different material, but in juxtaposing different responses to the same material.[3] Different 'lines' of thought governed by different kinds of criteria can be pursued in each column. These 'lines' may be different theoretical stances in relation to the same text or issue: a Marxist analysis or critique, next to a functionalist, next to a structuralist, next to a … the number of columns does not have to be limited to two. In the light of some of the discussions in this report, one column might usefully be taken up with a 'common sense' approach.

Alternatively the split text can be used to explore stylistic conventions, the features of academic discourse and some of the assumptions which frequently underlie and inhibit students' writing. Meyer (1993), for instance, used the split text with her students as a way of getting them to explore the approaches they typically took in writing about texts. She saw this as a 'cocksure' kind of posturing, in which multiple perspectives were 'mastered' by a neatly contained thesis – which often left the writer herself dissatisfied.[4] Her aim was to allow thoughts and approaches which appear tangential or disruptive to successful academic writing to be articulated and used. She notes that having done this exercise her students went on to write 'more traditional, argumentative essays', which she felt were 'less reductive and frequently more energetic. Double Trouble became part of their reading and writing process; addressing the literary text in two different ways fostered revision'(p. 61).

This is her exercise:

ASSIGNMENT: Double Trouble

Fold a piece of paper in half. On one side, tell me what you think the sentences say. Be declarative, stating your reading as though you're sure of yourself and the author's intentions. Begin your writing with a description of the text and what it "means" or represents.

Now on the other side, begin your statements with, "But something bothers me". On this side be hesitant, questioning your assertions and certainties of the "right" side. Think about contradictions, about "what ifs", about what the sentences don't say directly. Explore double meanings and alternative conclusions. Relate what is said to personal experience and to subjective responses. Don't censor the outrageous or the improbable.

---

3 Again this was an idea underpinning the grid in the induction module (chapter 7).
4 See Mitchell 1993a, which looks at the way the demands of the written form can shape the way a reading experience is recorded.

Higgins: Pickering! Nonsense: she's going to marry Freddy. Ha ha! Freddy! Freddy! Ha ha ha ha ha!!!! [He roars with laughter as the play ends]. (Pygmalion 100)

SAMPLE RESPONSE

I know that Higgins is laughing at Eliza and Freddy. Shaw shows that Higgins has not changed at all and is still scornful of others. The tone expresses his continued sense of superiority and Shaw's in relation to other human beings. He is laughing at their weaknesses, compared to his own strength.

(Meyer , 1993, p. 60)

But what if the joke is on Henry? Perhaps his laughter has a slight edge of hysteria to it. Maybe Shaw is suggesting that Henry is not the Superman he thinks he is but is vulnerable to the same emotions such as jealousy as everyone else. I'd like to believe in a more sympathetic Higgins, one who is not fully in control. But then, maybe Shaw has the "last laugh", showing me how much I want a different ending.

It needs to be stressed that the voice of one side is no more 'authentic' than the other, that neither has, in a sense, the greater claim to truth about the text. What the split text does is to offer students the space to explore a variety of different voices and perspectives. They don't discover their true selves so much as discover the different roles they may play and therefore the possibility of distance and critique. This possibility comes both from the opportunity to write differently but also, it seems to me, from the difference itself made visible in the dialogic form. The split text would, for example, be a good way to explore the different kinds of argument and writer/reader relationships which are created by statements on the one hand (literally) and questions, on the other. Similarly a split text would be an appropriate format for the kind of work on 'translating' text I suggested in chapter 4.

In some ways the dialogic forms described above highlight and clarify functions which are performed in academic essays, but which can be obscured or overlooked there particularly by inexperienced writers. It is possible, for instance to imagine a synthesis of the two columns in the 'Aliens and Gorillas in the Mist' text and according to cognitive development models of writing this might be seen as an advance. Looked at another way, however, the act of synthesising might be seen as a way in which the writer takes possession of meaning, closing the spaces in which a reader might interpellate herself and reducing the possibility of multiple interpretations. The text he chooses to write, that is to say, has implications besides cognitive ones.

Recognising this, is, it seems to me, the value of a rhetorical approach. Whichever way one views the relative merits of the different texts, the important point is that students are shown – through experience – the kinds of effects and meanings that different textual organisation can have, and, correspondingly, the ways in which a writer's aims and purposes can be developed in writing.

Writing in Stages

The approach given here uses the idea that the traditional writing task can be broken down into a series of discrete but linked and developmental tasks, and that if students work on the same material from a variety of perspectives, they can build up a richer more complex response. This approach therefore has a rationale in common with that of the induction module reported in chapter 7 and also with the move towards diversification (at least in my interpretation).

Tom Goldpaugh and Evan Rivers[5], who came up with the idea, call them 'writing loops' and explain the process as follows:

1. Begin by identifying one of those tasks we so often ask our students to do, like 'analyse' or 'discuss' or 'interpret'.

2. Define and isolate the thinking skills, breaking the task down into separate components.

3. Organise the skills into a hierarchy based on what skills we can assume students have already mastered and what new skills they need.

4. Develop a sequence of discrete writing tasks to lead students through skills they've already mastered and into more complex and challenging skills.

The writing tasks are done on a daily basis usually with a word limit set.

Two examples are given on the following pages: the first is Goldpaugh and Rivers', slightly adapted; the second, one I have made up; neither has a specifically disciplinary basis, but they could easily be adapted. The sequences they describe are an effective way of moving between discourses; the first days may tap students direct students' direct experiences or observations, whilst in subsequent days attention can be shifted to different ways of considering the issue. The daily tasks are discrete, allowing each approach to be valued, but there is continuity and between them and a gradual process of accretion.

A. Testing a Belief

You are to determine some belief that you hold to be true: human beings are naturally good; human beings are basically evil; people are created equal; money is the root of all evil; democracy is the best form of government; people are androgynous by nature. Don't worry about taking controversial or unpopular beliefs. The only stipulation is that you must believe it.

Day One: *What is this belief? Free write on it. What are your reasons for believing this? How long have you believed this? Is it something that most people you know believe? Minimum 100 words.*

Day Two: *Define the key terms of this belief. First identify them. Check at least two dictionaries, including a specialised one. For example if you claim that 'Democracy is the best form of government', you will need to define democracy and government. At the same time you will have to examine how you are using the term 'best'. If you claim 'Human beings are naturally competitive', that word naturally should be examined very closely. Remember that words have histories. Minimum 150 words.*

---

[5] Tom Goldpaugh and Evan Rivers work at Marist College, Poughkeepsie, New York. They presented their 'writing loops' at the Argument Conference at York University in March 1993.

Day Three: *Find out how others feel about this belief. Interview at least ten other people and find out if they believe what you believe, if they disagree, why they believe what you believe or why they do not. Try to get them to identify the source of their beliefs. Minimum: 150 words.*

Day Four: *Trace this belief back as far as you can. When did human beings start to believe this? Which thinkers have held this belief in some fashion or another? Are there any allied beliefs that can push the idea back further? You must have hard research on this. Minimum 200 words.*

Day Five: *Today there are three questions to consider. First, what hidden assumptions underlie your belief? For example, if you say "people are essentially competitive," what are you assuming is true of people? Second, what evidence do you have to support your belief? Third, How can you counter the objections that your peers raised the other day?Minimum 250 words.*

B. Writing a Dialogue

(This example takes as its subject the issue of single parent families. The students need at least two texts (of any kind: newspaper articles, essays, poems) which represent different points of view on the same issue).

This assignment is concerned with controversial issues surrounding single parent families. These involve such questions as: How is a single parent family to be defined? Are there different categories of single parent families? What are the responsibilities of society towards single parent families? What are the responsibilities of single parent families towards society? Should they be judged by society? What are the consequences for children growing up in single parent families? **You are expected to take an active role in a debate about these issues.**

Day One: *Using the above questions and any others that occur to you, formulate your own views on the issue of single parent families. Minimum 300 words.*

Day Two: *Read the first article that is given to you. Summarise what the writer is saying. Does he address any of the questions above? What does he say about them? Minimum 300 words.*

Day Three: *Read the second article What are this writer's arguments? Does she address the questions above? What does she say? Minimum 400 words.*

Day Four: *Draw up a grid which identifies common points addressed by you, and the two writers:*

	You	*Writer 1*	*Writer 2*
Common point 1			
Common point 2			

You should find at least six common points. N.B. for a point to be common only two people have to hold a view on it. They do not necessarily have to agree with each other.

Day Five: *Imagine you are in a room with the writers of both pieces. Write a dialogue between yourself and them on the issue of single parent families. Try to avoid a sitting-on-the-fence position: remember your views are as important as theirs.*

Writing Emerging From Research

In chapter 2, where Rom Harré's model of personal identity projects was introduced, I first noted how difficult it was for students to develop a 'novel' position within the confines of disciplinary study. Kaufer and Geisler's work (1989a, 1989b, 1991) has suggested ways in which students might develop strategies for newness and this was in part the motivation behind the induction module on argument described in chapter 7. Here, though, I want to give an example of another way in which newness and ownership can be foregrounded – through independent research. The example comes from Fine Art, which as I've suggested before (chapter 3) is something of a special case amongst academic disciplines. Nonetheless the work that goes on there is not without implications for other areas of study. Nor does it have exclusive use of individualised tasks; projects of the kind I describe below occur across the full range of disciplines, though with differing degree of flexibility in terms of subject choice and method used.

The Research Model in Fine Art

In Fine Art, it will have emerged from the earlier account, the art work is driven by a sense of ownership and individual motivation. When it comes to writing a long essay to fulfil the theory component of the course, this pattern is adhered to, though the ways of working and organising material are very different. The students are not expected to work with a blueprint and although some degree of orientation to academic conventions is required this is of secondary importance to the research process itself.

The criteria for the long essay reflect an acknowledged basis in the personal and individual. Just as the cross-section crits (see chapter 3) take as the point of start and return what is concrete and particular so a place for the writer is an acknowledged part of the written theoretical work. The course handbook directly addresses 'The Individual Student's Contribution':

> It is assumed that all students will be continuously and actively engaged in developing their knowledge and understanding of their degree subjects.

> It is important to realise courses do not do it to you. Participating fully on a course you develop yourself.

> To this end tutors expect you to read widely; this should include newspapers, magazines and journals; to watch T.V., go to films, the theatre, lectures, concerts and exhibitions OUT OF PERSONAL INTEREST AND COMMITMENT.

> All of this in turn leads to a sharper, more intense and informed relationship with your course requirements. So that when you are given freedom of choice, it is expected that each student will have an interest in particular things – arguments, themes, works, issues – that may be explored further.

Whilst the research process is important in other subjects – as in an engineering project – here the process is not strictly defined or prescribed by the discipline. The aims are broadly rather than peculiarly academic and therefore discovery of the process is also a form of invention. Again as in the production of an art work, there are tensions between freedom and constraint and also a tension inherent in the freedom of choice. Unlike much work in other disciplines there is little restriction on content and this can range from council allotments, to the work of Alcoholics Anonymous to Bukowski to Polk. This acceptance of diversity really does mean that emphasis is given to the research processes – from the gathering of data to the development of a position or argument. Where so much writing which occurs in academic settings is in response to questions set, here the student has to work to find her own questions. The material is raw rather than mediated via a predescribed angle and the task therefore more demanding. The long essay thus takes students almost into postgraduate academic work, but surprisingly from a background which is less saturated with standard 'academic' tasks than that of most undergraduates – in the Humanities, at least.

The lesson that derives from this for me is that rigorous academic experiences can be had which are rooted in personal interests and motivations, that the ability to conduct research – as a process – is not of necessity the outcome of apprenticeship to a body of knowledge. If this is true for the Fine Art course then it can also be true for other levels and areas of study – with the proviso that other subjects can in fact be defined by their methodology and this must be acquired if the research is then to be valid within that context. By contrast research in Art and Design is often cross disciplinary – drawn upon as and where necessary as the individual student's investigation progresses. Whilst the individual research process may, as a result, be more demanding, the eventual product may be less methodologically coherent. This is entirely consistent however with the theoretical approach adopted by many in this field where the start of any investigation is in the object or data itself. Attention to what is there leads to a search for wider discourses in which it may be implicated.

The criteria for staff involved in the examination of 'long essays' is worth reproducing here, as an indication of what is hoped for the exercise :

Research and Production of the Final Year Long Essay

During the three terms leading up to the submission of the Long Essay tutors concentrate on supervising the research process. Students are encouraged to participate in and understand the functions of the stages involved which would usually include:

(i) identification of topic and parameters of research

(ii) readiness to revise ideas as comprehension of subject area increases

(iii) address to the complexity of designing and communicating argument in relation to research variables

(iv) realisation of the effect of discipline-based attitudes and assumptions on organisational structures

(v) the important role of first hand study in enabling dialogue with 'received' opinion in the form of critical and scholarly material.

Proposal, plan, report and draft stages are monitored and aim to facilitate progression towards the final production.

The research and Working Handbook also supports students by providing general guidelines.

Students are encouraged to 'take charge' of their enquiries and this results in quite considerable diversity of subject and approach.

Staff have an important role in helping to guide research and to provide informed critical commentary on students' work.

There is not a single 'model' which is favoured as a 'blue print'. Many of the essays embody cross-disciplinary or inter-disciplinary features.

Students are expected to be able to defend ideas and present appropriate material to underpin statements. They are not encouraged to work on topics which they cannot experience at first hand or research with some degree of thoroughness.

The description is a good overview of the research process, in terms of what the experience can teach: that the material and argument is limited by the eventual product and by time limitations, that knowledge changes and work must be revised, that different perspectives construe material in different ways, that what is needed is some form of dialogue. The description suggests too that the students reach some form of meta-understanding of what research involves. Part of this comes from the way in which the essay is taught or, better, supervised – in individual tutorials. Here the tutor can monitor the progress of the individual piece of research, feeding back to the student comments about early ideas and first draft writing. This means that though the student is always ultimately responsible for producing the work there is a sense in which the process is shared and can be reflected on. The tutor, with greater experience, is able to take a longer view of, say, periods of despondency and confusion and to suggest routes out and beyond. In the example that follows, the tutor is able to reflect back to the student, after the process is all over, a narrative account of its highs and lows. For the student the research period is validated by the interest shown by the person who to some degree shared it. As with making, the process carries a significance independent of that contained within the final product.

A Look at One Student's Experience

Carol's eventual essay is entitled *The beauty myth and magazines: how do magazines influence identity?* It is an account of the development and changing concerns of women's magazines in relation to the forms of femininity they transmit. Its argument is that the magazines play a formative role in the exploitation of women through representation. This is at least my interpretation and synthesis of what the essay argues – much of this is implicit rather than explicit in the writing. As argument the essay is not fully successful, yet it does represent a significant achievement in terms of the way material is handled and in certain aspects of the analysis.

Researching and writing were not straightforward or easy processes. Carol started out on her long essay with ideas about body image and adornment, which she spent a long time proliferating and at the same time trying to manage until she finally came to focus on the magazines. Her early attempts to write were unsuccessful – she started too early, before she had mapped out ideas and so ended up with continuous narrative. Her writing did not differentiate between the texts she was reading and her own voice and therefore no dialogic or argumentative sense could develop. She was overwhelmed by her reading and the accumulated material – a result of inexperience, underconfidence and the nature of the research itself, both as a process and as content.

As the tutor was aware, the area of Carol's investigation could be approached in a number of disciplinary ways and is also open to general rather polemical commentaries. Her tutor encouraged her to pin down the issues in a material way by collecting copies of *Cosmopolitan* and by focussing on the hypothesis of just one writer. She also strongly advised against writing at this stage, instead keeping the ideas and various aspects separate, though linked diagramatically. This advice integrated a way of working, organising and progressing, with a way of generating ideas. For Carol, unused to the complexity of the task, the postponement of writing was not at first reassuring, since it meant her progress was not obvious. At this time she was in despair that she would ever manage the task, finding it easier to envisage another topic than persevering with the existing one. The tutor offered her a systematic structure to get her past this impasse. She must go back to her main source text and identify the important issues by skim reading chapter headings; to ask herself the questions, is there anything more I need to read, where is the writer successful, where is she fudging the issue, what headings will I use? The bulk of undifferentiated material needed to be captured within 'an arbitrary series of cages'.

The tutor saw these processes as part of the standard research procedure – identification, classification, 'gate-keeping', filtering out whilst at the same time recognising that what is filtered out at one stage may need to be reintroduced at another. As discussed above the role of the tutor in communicating this to the student was very important – Carol was able only to see the mess of her own workings, where the tutor knew, through experience, that the mess was legitimate and she could help Carol to capitalise upon it.

After this Carol made visits to the offices of *Cosmopolitan* in London and was able to find out about the history of the magazine and its advertising and circulation statistics. She also followed some work of the photographer Cindy Sherman for *Vogue*, though this was less forthcoming. These research activities provided Carol with raw material to set in dialogue with the writings of the texts that she had read. This was essential work as it gave her some command over material which had not yet been interpreted. She was able to use her own first hand research to challenge authoritative sources and discover that there is no such thing as objective information – an important step in developing argumentative thought.

Four weeks before the end of term (with the deadline early the next term) the tutor noted:

> She has a framework, has selected visual material and is struggling to retain a grip on the framework of her enquiry. The most valuable role of her tutor at this point is to keep her confident of her capacity to manage the task, to reinforce all her good planning and see her at frequent intervals to minimise the tendency to feel panic stricken.

Carol finished her essay before the deadline and experienced a tremendous sense of achievement in doing so. She testified to the value of the process when she commented that she'd found through writing that the subject she'd now like to tackle was not the one she did – new ideas had formed and the work represented in that sense an opening up rather than closing down.

Reflecting upon the process afterwards with her tutor Carol recalled the surprise she had felt when she realised that she could quote, but that she didn't have to agree with what the quotation said. Her comment is startling but links to points made elsewhere in this report about the way students perceive academic study and its ground rules, their behaviour as novices rather than experts.

A great deal of the trouble which Carol experienced in this work came from a lack of confidence, a long standing dread of writing and feeling of disempowerment. She is according to the tutor not untypical in this respect. The insistence upon a significant piece of research from the student, supported by a close supportive relationship with the tutor is though a valuable part of the degree, complementing the practical work with a different form of experience, no less demanding, but ultimately no less exciting either.

What was impressive about the student/tutor relationship I observed was its independence from judgement in terms of the final product. The work was valid in terms of the experience it had offered; assessment within the criteria for an academic degree is quite a different thing.

The Essay Itself

In the text the struggle to master an argument is still apparent, particularly at a macro-level. So that in the introduction, for example, too much is given too soon. The structural position of the introduction gives it the function of summarising the argument, but in this case, though the diction ('consequently' … 'however' …) signals argument, the assumptions upon which it rests are insufficiently articulated:

> The large number of women's magazines address different areas within the market and tackle a wide range of subjects, and the agenda of women's magazines changes through time and markets, consequently the way in which women's magazines influence femininity is complex. However, their enormous readership makes women's magazines indisputable as a force in the media.

The text is at a surface level largely descriptive and the argument implicit. It is for instance implicit within the structuring of the essay in three sections: Past, Present, Future – suggestive of continuity: the exploitation of women for ideological and commercial reasons – and change: the shifting focus from domesticity to body image and now towards men. But these threads of more abstract critical thought do not emerge within the text itself. At times an argument appears to be expressed, often where a transition is being effected from one section of material to another. Here Carol uses questions as a device to move on:

> The portrayal of beauty in *Cosmopolitan*, the market leader in young women's magazines, is central to the question of how women are represented that Cindy Sherman addresses. What sort of magazine is *Cosmopolitan*? Is *Cosmopolitan* condemned to back the beauty myth or can it break it?

The questions indicate that the descriptive material that follows is selected to demonstrate a particular significance The problem is that this does not happen often enough and the links in the argument are often omitted at least explicitly. An example of such omission is a quotation from the model Cindy Crawford followed by a description of a photograph of her:

> In an interview with *Cosmopolitan*, Cindy Crawford the "supermodel" said "We're too hard on ourselves. Instead of saying we love our eyes, we say we hate our lips or ears or breasts. We focus on the ugliness". Even a "supermodel" cannot live up to the beauty myth. Cindy Crawford is one of the current icons of the beauty industry, she is fundamentally linked with the creation of the term "supermodel". In figure 7 Cindy Crawford is photographed from the top of her thighs upwards revealing her curvaceous figure …

Only the phrase 'Even a "supermodel" cannot live up to the beauty myth' is interpretative here: there is no critical commentary to make the transition between what Cindy Crawford says and how she is portrayed and so it is left to the reader to read either narratively, accepting the descriptions, or to construct an argument about the incompatible messages of the words and images.

Later, the way Carol structures her description helps her to be critical. She conducts a sustained comparison between *Cosmopolitan* and *Ms* at a sentence by sentence level. This makes very successful argument – the two magazines and their differing agendas brought into dialogue with one another:

> *Cosmopolitan* has about 50 full pages of advertisements per issue costing several thousand pounds per page, while *Ms.* does not run advertisements, the cover price just covers the overheads of the magazine. Although similar issues are discussed in both magazines,

such as careers, sex, reviews or health, the range and focus is different according to the angle of each magazine. A typical edition of *Cosmopolitan* is divided into the sections; 'Features', 'Fashion and Beauty', 'Offers', 'Careers ahead', 'Living and Food', 'Travel', 'Fiction', and 'Regular', while a typical edition of *Ms.* is broken down into 'Features', 'Books', 'Arts', 'Sisterhood is Global' 'Home Fires' (American political issues), 'Poetry', 'Fiction', 'Feminist Theory', 'Race and Women', 'Ecofeminism', 'Health' and 'No Comment', although the subject matter of the magazines crosses over, *Cosmopolitan* is dominated by fashion, health and beauty while *Ms.* concentrates on feminism and politics. This difference in style is apparent in the readers' letters .....

This exploitation of the similarities and difference leads Carol eventually to clinch her argument:

The beauty myth's portrayal of beauty is helpful for business. Advertising is the main profit making department of most magazines, and although it tries to cover the feminist angle it is not *Ms.* – advertisers are more dominant in the magazines' make-up than feminism. It is unlikely that *Cosmopolitan* would endanger its huge circulation and profits in order to reach beyond the beauty myth. It is a mainstream magazine and reflects the tastes of its advertisers, consciously or unconsciously manipulating women's insecurities to sell their products. However, *Cosmopolitan* can influence the way in which beauty is perceived, it can portray beauty as less rigid and more pro-women and *Cosmopolitan* in turn influences the way the advertisers perceive beauty.

Carol comes to a strong conclusion here, but also qualifies it with the sense that *Cosmopolitan* can also be an agent of change. There is an implication perhaps that the magazine should be more forceful in this respect, but Carol doesn't go quite that far.

It is worth mentioning Carol's ability to describe the visual images she chooses from the magazines. Her fluency in this suggests that she has grasped the argument at this important perceptual level. It may be that she has adopted the style of her source texts in doing this (the rhetoric of the image type of approach), but in any case her writing is consistently engaging when she recreates the images in words. Her descriptions are distinctly tendentious, inviting us to see the pictures, but at the same time undermining our complacency with what we see. The careful description, moving all the time into interpretation, reveals how carefully the images are constructed:

The woman stands with her arms folded, looking past the camera, emulating the masculine pose of the costume. The model has a stern look on her face, implying she 'means business'. A white chiffon scarf is draped around her shoulders, offsetting the masculine look. Placed on the chiffon scarf is a Sheriff's badge suggesting she is a woman in charge, and a woman in a man's world. The image of the cowboy is reminiscent of the classic advertising icon, the 'Marlboro Man' ...

What I think Carol's work indicates is a process, not fully realised, of developing argument. It is different from the standard academic essay – which often also fails to argue – in that it deals with a greater bulk of material, much of which is in a raw state (the magazines themselves, the statistics) and this means there is further to go in processing it. Here, I suppose, is the difference between research and argument. All academic work requires a degree of research, but this is generally directed by a question and/or by a body of material investigated in a group as 'content to be covered'. In the case of the 'long essay' the journeying is much longer – an important reason for the time spent – the end of the second year to the Easter of the third. The expected length (and breadth) of the work is of course another factor impeding the full development of an argument.

This – as with the idea of independent research itself – I do not see as a bad thing. What Carol's work suggests – and this is work which in academic terms will not receive above a 2:2 – are the emergent stages of argument, a control which is both secure and provisional – which is another way of saying, I suppose, that 'it shows promise'. Though this is a hackneyed academic cliché it is perhaps not inappropriate if it suggests that what students do should be valued in more than terms of full achievement. Teachers have the choice of whether to set and repeat tasks which through practice will come well within their students' control or whether – in addition, perhaps – to offer ambitious tasks the end results of which are beyond the students' (and tutor's) conception throughout a great part of the study, gradually emerging and taking shape.

There are implications here, of course, for what is possible in modularised courses, where a unit of study is begun and completed in a relatively short period of time. It is possible that the practical constraints imposed by such packaging of learning might result in greater standardisation of forms and experiences, but given sufficient staffing levels the opposite might also be true. Provided students had sufficient previous orientation to the subject and that quality tutorial support was available, modules might be devised which were entirely research-based.

13. Two Essays Compared

In this short chapter I compare two essays written by third year undergraduate students for the Sociology of Murder course described earlier (chapter 4). The comparison – an experiment with form – brings out some factors involved in constructing academic argument and is a way of raising again issues discussed elsewhere in this report.

These two essays were written for assessment. The marks awarded to them will go towards the students' final degree (which is examined entirely by coursework). An earlier version of the essay will have been submitted to the tutor as an ungraded requirement for completing the course.

Matthew's Essay	Liz's Essay

Titles:

Analyse the relation between 'righteous slaughter' and 'primordial evil' in Katz (1988)
The title specifies a single *text* and sets out the elements of that text which are to be dealt with. It thus demarcates the field of investigation quite strictly. Is there potential for argument in the relation between the two categories?

Examine the distinctive aspects of 'serial murder'
The title invites the writer to investigate a *topic*. The quotation marks suggest the need for a definition. The 'distinctive aspects' are not specified, so that this also becomes part of the writer's task. Where is the potential for argument?

Setting the tone, preparing the way:

Introduction: In this paper I will be concerned with an analysis of the work of the American sociologist Jack Katz. In his seminal book *Seductions of Crime* (1988) Katz presents us with an intriguing exploration of the dynamics of criminality. My analysis will focus upon the concepts of 'righteous slaughter' and 'primordial evil'. Through these categorisations Katz develops a theory of criminal homicide that has been widely received as a major advancement upon the traditional explanatory schemas.

Studies of criminal homicide have traditionally fallen into one of two camps. In the biogenic/psychogenic perspective, (a perspective particularly favoured by those in

Introduction: A mad, sex crazed beast, stalking the streets, killing repeatedly, randomly, and horrifically for perverse sexual gratification. These are some of the perceived distinctive aspects of Serial Murder which have enabled it to become a mysterious incomprehensible crime, in reality and the genre of horror fiction, giving it a horror status unlike any other category of murder. A recent example of this image of Serial Murder can be seen in the newspaper article in appendix 1. It talks of the killer of killers being 'out there' as if somehow apart from the rest of society, killing randomly and without motive, 'on the loose; like a wild animal' (Gardiner; Daily Mail; Friday, April 30th, 1993) search of populist appeal as opposed to academic insight) homicidal behaviour is deemed to have its origins in particular physiological and psychological defects....

The impression is of control and a straightforward intention. It is not objective or neutral – there are numerous evaluative phrases – rather it is coolly knowing. The text by Katz, is given a positive endorsement and set against two other traditional camps. These are used as 'faulty paths'[1] in the two subsequent sections of the essay. The writer makes no claim of his own, no 'novelty' claim at this stage.

The essay will be situated *within* the sociological domain and focussed on the *text* by Katz; first by showing what Katz is different to and *in advance of* (context), then by showing what the details of what Katz says.

However, as I see it the most distinctive aspects of serial murder are, that *it does not exist* as we perceive it, and in reality *it is not distinctive at all!* ...

The scene is set dramatically. It is declarative and has pace. A contrast is set up between *perceived* and *real* distinctive aspects of Serial Murder. This opposition runs through the entire essay as 'myth versus reality' and in another variant 'folklore versus sociological'. The writer's position is directly signalled and at the end of the introduction she makes a further claim:

I hope to show that the creation of the serial murder myth is a way in which patriarchal society exonerates itself from guilt and responsibility for these crimes and refuses to acknowledge its violent and misogynist nature.

Authorial intention is broadly focussed, unmediated by texts. The essay will operate *outside* as well as within the sociological domain.

Structuring the essay:

Matthew's essay can be depicted with the 'main path, faulty path' model:

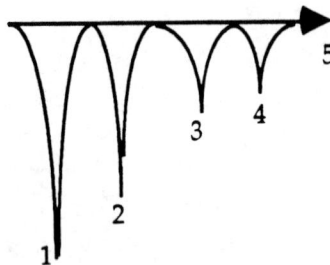

1 – the biogenic and psychogenic perspectives
2 – the cultural perspective
3 – Katz 'righteous slaughter'
4 – Katz 'primordial evil'
5 – conclusion/contribution: both categories motivated by quest for self-affirmation (responds to title by establishing a relation between the two categories – a synthesis)

Liz's essay can also be depicted as having faulty paths leading from off from the main argument:

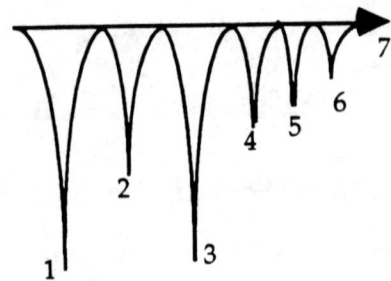

1 – folklore explanations
2 – sociological explanation(text: Leyton)
3 – folklore: example of how the myth is constructed – Yorkshire Ripper
(4–7 concluding section on gender)
4 – folklore concentrates on sexual motives
5 – violence is an accepted part of society
6 – return to Leyton
7 – reiteration of own position: Serial Murder a manifestation of misogyny in society
(uses title to put forward own argument)

---

[1] See chapter 11 for details of this way of describing (and depicting) argument.

This depiction can be turned on its side and viewed as a pyramid shape which moves from broad to narrow.

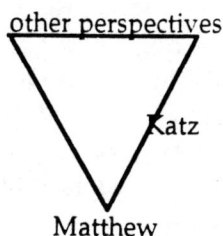

other perspectives

Katz

Matthew

Or, alternatively as a flight of steps, through which Matthew reaches the top (i.e. new) position:

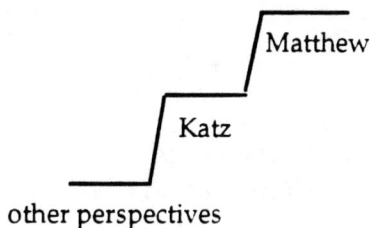

Matthew

Katz

other perspectives

All the perspectives Matthew uses are grouped as 'studies of criminal homicide' and they are all contained within texts.

Matthew's contribution is small – a synthesis of two positions within Katz, whose general position he has carefully endorsed. Using Katz, he constructs a place for himself within the discipline.

Language, focus and evaluation:

The writing is dense with nominalisations and evaluative phrases.

It seems difficult to reconcile Bundy's adherence to normal family behaviour with Norris' persistent claim that the serial killer is in possession of a brain that leads him to sporadic and uncontrollable spasms of homicidal behaviour. The reductive biogenic perspective, of which Norris's work is prime example, displays a profound analytic myopia. What should be clear from the many serial killer case histories that Norris presents in his book, is that situational contingencies have a key bearing over the homicidal act.

The pyramid shape fits Liz's essay less easily. She makes her position clear at the outset and returns to it by various routes. It is less emergent. However, the pyramid shape can be used to show the proportion of the essay given to different discourses:

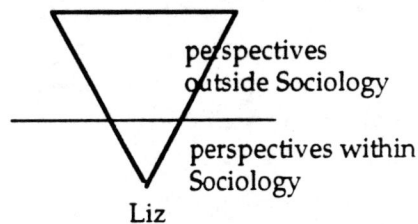

perspectives outside Sociology

perspectives within Sociology

Liz

Liz uses the large-scale categories 'folklore' and 'sociological': under 'folklore' are included theories which describe Serial Killers as psychologically or biologically different. These are placed *outside* the disciplinary field and so reduce it to the single text by Leyton.

Liz sets out to make a large claim about misogyny in the folklore and sociological explanations of serial murder. She uses a number of sources (newspapers, police reports, popular texts) and makes minimal use of sociological texts to *support* her position/belief.

Texts do not form the subjects of sentences; ideas and narratives do:

If once the killer is discovered and he does not fit the characterisation, as is invariably the case, then he is seen as a modern Jekyll and Hyde, disguising his evil under a layer of respectability and charm (Cameron and Frazer (1987) page 40).

Where does the evaluation in this sentence originate? Is it a feature of the text or of Liz' critique of the text?

Norris is characterised as occupying a biogenic position on the spectrum of sociological theory and at the same time is used to criticise that position. The analysis is rooted in a *particular* text, but shows *orientation* to the wider disciplinary field. The field is constituted by texts.

At the end of this section, Norris's account is turned against itself and prepares a 'return path' to Katz:

I hope this brief consideration of the Bundy case reveals that Norris's biologically deterministic account is woefully inadequate in explaining the actions of the murderer. As Jack Katz makes clear in his opening remarks, a comprehensive explanatory model of criminal homicide must be 'phenomenologically grounded'. Only through an enquiry into the foreground factors that shape the criminal experience will we begin to approach what could be called an holistic appreciation of the act of murder.

So, motivated evaluation takes place on both a sentence-by-sentence level as well as the essay's larger structure. When it comes to making his own claim Matthew uses less evaluative language: he wants to distinguish himself but not distance himself from Katz:

However I would want to suggest that righteous slaughterers perceive themselves to be defending something more than simply some abstract eternal moral order. I suggest that in the above case history the killer may have interpreted the visitor's conduct not merely as an infringement of his property rights, but as an attack upon his very sense of self worth.

The sociological perspective is characterised broadly, without reference to textual 'proof':

A Sociological perspective on serial murder concludes that it is not a random crime, without motivation, committed by a mad beast, but rather it is directed at a particular section of the community, its motivation being legitimated by society and the killer being a social actor expressing his frustrations in culturally mediated and legitimated ways; putting the Serial Murder within society's control. It is an extreme expression of society's norms of violence, masculinity and misogyny. (faulty path 2)

By including 'misogyny' here Liz pre-empts the *outcome* of her argument and damages her claim.

Evaluative claims are widely based and are not signalled as part of a developing strategy:

This plea of insanity is society's culturally mediated and available explanation for such crimes. In history they were thought to murder due to possession by evil spirits (Leyton (1986) page 11) rather than as a result of any psychological disturbance. Psychological explanations are today's culture's available explanation for many phenomenon, therefore it is not surprising that the public, psychiatrists and even the killers use it to explain Serial Murder.

When Liz returns to Leyton's sociological theory at the end, she suggests that it has some worth and then differentiates herself from it:

However worthy Leyton's theory may be, by ignoring the relevance of gender, he misses a crucial aspect of Serial Murder, and so is accepting this violence towards women as a normal unnoteworthy part of society.

However Leyton's theory has not been *shown* to be 'worthy' in terms of the essay's structure or the wider sociological field.

The Differences

The task of essay writing was carried out by these two students in significantly different ways. Both perceived the need to argue, though in neither title was this explicitly signalled, but their argumentative strategies are by no means identical. Matthew argues within a closely framed area and 'designs to be new' by orienting to texts. Towards the end he adds an example of his own, but otherwise he uses material from existing sociological texts. Liz, on the other hand, broadly categorises perspectives and puts the niceties of disciplinary texts in a secondary position to what she wants to argue. Her 'opinion' is pre-formed, whilst Matthew's 'position' (I seem to need a more neutral word) is withheld until it can be securely expressed. Nonetheless he is constantly, if prudently, evaluative. The scale at which he works is smaller, more systematic. Liz has some sort of a pattern but it is less controlled and teleological and less hooked into disciplinary nuances. What she wants to argue is, in a sense, more ambitious as a statement, less achieved as a strategy.

What did the established discipline make of the two essays: there were ten percentage points between them; Matthew's received 70% (a First) and Liz's 60% (a 2:1). The difference can, I imagine, be accounted for by such features as I have isolated above. What can we conclude from it and what questions does it raise?

Perhaps the first question to consider concerns the goals and purposes of argument – to what ends do we argue? The two essays suggest rather different goals. Matthew's essay, it seems to me, argues both *within* the discipline and *for a place within* the discipline. Its ends are in a sense professional and result from meticulous apprenticeship to the disciplinary discourse. The discourse is manifested here in particular systematic textual strategies, as well as to a more generalised way of the thinking.

It is this more general sense of the discourse that Liz displays. The ends to which she argues are more individual, more 'amateurish'. Her comments about the use of texts in writing show up this stance:

SM: Do they [texts] help you construct your argument?

Liz: I suppose in some ways in that I've read them already and my ideas have come from them, but I tend to get ideas in seminars that I just write down and I use those and sort of feedback from the seminar. I mean if I've got questions that come up in mind, I'll ask [the tutor] and then I'll sort of use that rather than the text and not – I have to use them for like examples and references, but I don't like to use them. I prefer my own arguments. [...] So I suppose what I do is I have my own arguments. Because I tend to plan my essay before I've read anything more than just for the seminars and then I'll look and see if there's anything in those papers that'll back up what I've said, but I don't tend to use people's arguments and then back them up with my own, it's the other way round.

For Liz learning to argue sociologically is a kind of liberation, but the sociological understanding she manifests is quite different in feel from that which Matthew employs. Although Liz felt that she had become enculturated within the discipline (see her comments in chapter 4), her enculturation seems to be something other than successful professional apprenticeship.

It is interesting to note that, in writing essays, Liz has recourse to the ideas generated in speech (in seminars), rather than, in the first instance, to those which are recorded in texts. The ideas she uses have thus already been processed, subject to interactive interrogation. As the analysis in chapter 4 suggested, in the seminar situation, the text under discussion becomes mutable and fluid as it is taken on by the different voices and as the talk diverges away from and returned to it. As the transcripts in that chapter show too, Liz is one of the most vocal of the students and actively tests her understandings and those of the group. It may be significant that I do not remember Matthew from the seminar situations and it may be too that what I am identifying here is a gender difference; Liz valuing those ideas which are generated communally, Matthew those which have the authority of texts.[2]

Some Implications and Questions

This discussion seems to have several implications for the teaching and learning of argument. Firstly it suggests a need to identify what the aims of disciplinary teaching are; whether they are narrow and professional or broader more liberal ones. It may be that they are both and that the difference between the first and second class degree is a way of separating out those students who will go on with academic training and those who will leave academia for employment in other fields.

Secondly – and related to this – it raises questions about the relations between speech and writing and the undervaluing of speech within academic contexts. What are the purposes of shared spoken discourse? Is it enough to explore content and discourse in speech if the transitions into writing then impose a new set of ground rules? Should these too become the subject for discussion and if so, how? What are the best strategies for, for instance, alerting Liz to the possible drawbacks of her approach to writing? Is it appropriate that assessment should be confined to a narrowly defined written performances? Are the uses of argument more extensive than these and should they be acknowledged?

These questions seem to me to arise not only from the two essays compared here, but from many of the teaching and learning situations that I have observed in the course of this project. In the next pages I attempt to condense and reiterate the main areas and questions that have emerged.

---

[2] The role of gender in argument is suggested as a future possibility for research.

14. Overview

At the end of the three year project and now at the end of this report it is possible to stand back and make a number of observations about the teaching and learning of argument at sixth form and higher education levels.

The project was conducted in nine subject areas at A level: History, Politics, Sociology, Communication Studies, English, Theatre Studies, Biology, Mathematics, and Physics. Teaching and learning in these areas were observed with a particular focus on the use made of argument, its forms and characteristics. It became clear that argument performed a variety of functions in learning; it could, for example, be used as a means of coming to understandings, a form of display, or simply a way of behaving appropriately within the discipline. The function that argument had in learning was often determined by the classroom context and the medium in which it was conducted: speech or writing. In addition differing degrees of emphasis were placed on argument in the different subject areas, so that, for instance, whilst argument was seen as a central activity in Politics, in Biology it was scarcely valued at all.

When the project moved into higher education a smaller number of subjects was selected for detailed study of the processes of teaching and learning: English, Sociology and Fine Art. Visits were also made to a number of other departments to observe and discuss work directly involving argument.

With the interesting exception of Fine Art, the experience at both sixth form and in higher education predominantly constituted an academic training or apprenticeship, a form of enculturation into particular disciplinary discourses. Argument played a significant part in many of these discourses, and indeed its display (in writing) was considered a sign of knowing *in* rather than just about a discourse. To be successful, however, knowing that one had to argue was not enough – disciplinary arguments involved particular kinds of rhetorical and generic decorum, particular understandings of the scope of what could be said and the means for saying it. It required orientation as much as independence, and detachment as much as belief.

I discovered that, broadly speaking, as the student moves from A level to undergraduate study, she is both acquiring a broader knowledge base and an increasingly specialised way of dealing with that knowledge. The world of the discipline, that is, becomes increasingly sufficient as a resource for the conduct of argument: there is more that students can say *within* it; less need to, for example, use first hand experience as a source of contrast or comparison. (As the discourse becomes more inclusive, there may also be stricter rules about what disciplinary argument will *exclude*.) In undergraduate English, for example, the expanding discourse, as well as the increased repertoire of literary texts on which to draw, creates a possibility for critique which was not present at A level. It is not so much an increased ability to argue which distinguishes a third year undergraduate from a sixth form student so much as increased expertise in the discourse and disciplinary culture.

There were certain common difficulties with argument particularly in its written form. These included difficulties with highlighting the thematic, rather than particular, characteristics of material and with structuring it in such a way as to show it as as similar or different to other material; a related difficulty with showing point of view as emergent, strategic or oriented to other points of view; a tendency to avoid contradiction, ambiguity or questions; an obedient rather than suspicious stance towards authority. Many of these difficulties seemed to arise from a conflict between understanding (reproducing) material and acting upon (changing) it.

The complexity – and also the importance – of learning to argue raised questions about how argument might be taught. In very little of the teaching I observed was attention given explicitly to the role, purpose and method of argument in the discipline. Where this did occur it was generally at the beginning of a course with the aim of equipping students with the necessary tools for study. More often the importance of argument was tacit: it might be modelled by the teacher in speech, or signalled by an essay question, or praised as a feature of a 'good essay'. I rarely saw it focussed upon as a strategy at the centre of a learning experience; either in reading, writing or speaking. My sense was that, whilst knowledge, content and understanding were foregrounded as learning objectives, discourse and ways of operating upon content were subordinated, rendered invisible.

The reasons for this seemed, at least partly, to be to do with power and assessment. To be within the discourse, to be able to exercise effective arguments within it, was to be in a position of power. Since teachers, as 'experts', had internalised the discourse, their tendency was to let students know 'things' rather than to put them in charge of the process of knowing. Symptoms of the subordination of discourse (hidden) to content (shared) were the infrequent use of (spoken and written) exercises which break down a task and the correspondingly heavy investment in final forms of writing as evidence of what has been learnt. In addition, speech – the medium in which the discourse *as process* is manifested – was generally not valued in assessment terms.

Yet it was clear that revealing discourse and the grounds upon which successful arguments are made does not lend itself to easy solutions. In this report there are a number of suggestions as to how argument might, on occasions, be foregrounded as a significant as well as a playful and creative activity. Whilst these suggestions hint that the skills of argument can be explored and learnt, they do so only at a crude level. The finer nuances of, say, fully understanding the rhetorical problem posed by an argumentative task still remain to be addressed and still have much to do in determining the efficacy of any particular argument. In important ways, then, argument is not a transferable skill, but specific to context.

One aim of exploring argument with students is to improve their performance, to further their place within disciplinary culture; another is to enable them to reflect upon that culture and its methods. This would be an important reason for introducing opportunities for argument into subjects where it played very little part (ethics into Biology, for example). In other subjects investigating the underlying assumptions and methods of argument might be part of disciplinary study itself. It seemed to me, however, that such an exploration would be incomplete if the forms of institutional learning were not also subject to examination. Breaking the boundaries of disciplinary cultures or talking about what is invisible can become a means by which power structures are undermined – and change initiated. At the same time, however, whilst the element of meta-awareness may have a liberating effect on those who are serving apprenticeships within institutions, it may also be destabilising. Power is not simply wielded by institutions but is contractual; students as well as teachers have an investment in maintaining its conditions – conditions which, for instance, place a low value on the student's questioning role and a high value on orientation to precedent both in terms of form and knowledge.

Complex issues such as these emerged from this project particularly strongly as argument showed itself to be, in turn, a learnt process, a public form, a means of individual differentiation and a force for change. The research was both ethnographic and pedagogic: descriptive and aspiring towards improvement. In combination these approaches led not only to ways in which students might better achieve the goals set by disciplines, but also to a questioning of the goals themselves, whether these were the concrete outcomes of learning (e.g. the essay) or its wider purposes. The dual, but not incompatible, questions of how to consolidate and improve and how to challenge and change have not been resolved by this research. Nonetheless, a basis for further exploration has, I hope, been created.

Dissemination of the Research

In Publications

Andrews, R. Mitchell, S. Costello, P. 'Philosophers of the classroom' in *The Times Educational Supplement*, January 3rd 1992, p 6.

Mitchell, S. *Questions and Schooling: Classroom Discourse Across the Curriculum;* Occasional Paper I, Centre for Studies in Rhetoric, University of Hull 1992.

Mitchell, S. *An Examination of The Teaching and Learning of Argument in Sixth Forms and Higher Education: Interim Report* , Centre for Studies in Rhetoric, University of Hull 1992.

Mitchell, S. 'The aesthetic and the academic: are they at odds in English Literature at A level?' in *English in Education*, Vol. 27 No. 1, Spring 1993.

Mitchell, S. 'Learning to be critical and correct: forms and functions of argument at A level' in *Curriculum*, Vol. 14 No. 1 Spring 1993.

Mitchell, S. 'Not so much a 'trying out' as a handing-in - a challenge to the academic essay' in *CUE News: The Newsletter of the Council for University English*, Vol. 5 No. 2 Summer 1993.

Andrews, R. 'Developing Argument' in *The English and Media Magazine*, 28, Summer 1993, pp. 34-38

Griffiths, Sian 'Essays Under Siege' in the *Times Higher Educational Supplement* 30 July 1993.

Mitchell, S. (1994) 'Room for argument in English Literature at A level and beyond?' in *ETUDE Newsletter*, No. 2 February 1994.

Andrews, R. and Mitchell, S. 'The development of argument in English and Politics in 16-18 year old students' in *Literacy Learning: Secondary Thoughts*, Vol. 1 No. 2, 1994.

Mitchell, S. and Andrews, R. 'Learning to operate successfully in advanced level History' in Freedman, A. and Medway, P., *Teaching and Learning Genre*, Heinemann-Boynton/Cook, (forthcoming).

Andrews, R. *Learning to Argue*, Cassel (forthcoming)

Mitchell, S. 'Argument in English Literature at A Level and Beyond' in *English and Media Magazine* No. 30 Summer 1994.

Mitchell, S. 'A level and Beyond: a case study' in *English in Education* , Vol. 28 No. 2 Summer 1994.

Costello, P.J.M. and Mitchell, S. (eds.) *Competing and Consensual Voices: the theory and practice of argument*, Clevedon: Multilingual Matters (forthcoming)

In Talks and at Conferences

The findings of the project have been disseminated by the project's director, Richard Andrews, on the following occasions:

- Carleton University, Ottawa, April 1992

- Annual Conference of The Association of Teachers of English in Quebec, Montreal, April 1992

- a two-week intensive course on argument and the essay for English teachers from New York City public schools at Lehman College, City University of New York, July 13-23, 1992

- Domains of Literacy International Conference, Institute of Education, University of London, September 1992

- a weekend conference for Heads of English from Croydon LEA at Leeds Castle, Kent, October 17-18, 1992

- 10 seminars on narrative and argument for M.Ed module for University of Hull, October-December 1992

- one-week course on argument across the curriculum at British International School, Jakarta, Indonesia, February 1-5, 1993

- course for Suffolk Heads of English on argument and genre, Ipswich, March 19, 1993

- NETE Colloquium, Adelaide, July 1993

- National Council for Teachers of English conference, Pittsburgh, November 1993.

- Australian Association for the Teaching of English Conference, Adelaide, July 1993 (keynote address)

- 1st International Australian Reading Association Conference, Melbourne, July 1993 (keynote address)

- course for Lincolnshire Heads of English, Horncastle, May 1994

- 3rd International Conference on Argumentation at the University of Amsterdam, June 21 -24, 1994

- USA teachers summer school, University College of Ripon and York St. John, June 26, 1994 (keynote address)

- New York University summer school, Trinity College, Oxford, July 18-20, 1994.

In addition I have spoken about the project and contributed papers on a number of occasions:

- Domains of Literacy International Conference, Institute of Education, University of London, September 1992

- Danish Teachers of English in five Danish towns, November 1992

- Creative Arts M.Ed. group at Exeter University, December 1992

- Postgraduate students and staff, School of Education, University of Hull, June 1993.

- English Teachers in University Departments of Education meeting, University of Leeds, January 1994

- Linguistics Circle and Studying Academia workshop, Lancaster University, February, 1994

- British Association of Lecturers in English for Academic Purposes conference, York University, June 11, 1994

- 3rd International Conference on Argumentation at the University of Amsterdam, June 21 -24, 1994

- INSET for Wolverhampton Girls' High School sixth form teachers, July 1994

- Creative Arts M.Ed. summer school at Exeter University, August 1994

York Conference

A national and international conference on argument was organised by the Centre for Studies in Rhetoric, Hull and held at the University of York, March 29-30 1993. The conference brought together teachers and researchers from Britain, Europe, North America and Australia united by an interest in argument at all levels and from a variety of different perspectives. Patrick Costello and I are editing a book entitled 'Competing and Consensual Voices' containing a selection of the papers presented at the conference.

Finally I should mention that at a reception was held at The University of Hull on July 4 1994 to mark the end of the project and launch this report.

Further Possibilities for Research

It is clear that this project which has been so broad in its scope – cross-disciplinary and roughly spanning the age range from 16 - 23 in sixth forms and higher education – will contain gaps and oversights. There is considerable scope for further research. Some areas which seem to me promising are listed here:

- more in-depth studies of the role and nature of argument in particular disciplines. These could take into account cross-phase developments and/or cross-institutional similarities and differences

- further investigation of the forms and uses of argument in scientific disciplines

- investigation of the uses of argument in modern language teaching

- further exploration of the relations between academic and workplace forms of argument

- exploration of differences between academic and vocational education in terms of argument

- study of argument in post-sixteen education other than A level (e.g. BTEC, GNVQ, NNEB, RSA)

- exploration of cultural and gender variations in argument; within a single educational system or, comparatively, between systems. This might include attention to bi-lingual students

- practical application, testing and development of some of the suggestions that have been made in this report

- exploration of teaching and learning argument with the help of new technologies and multi-media. How do these media change what we mean by argument?

- exploration and evaluation of critical approaches to academic and argument literacy

- an action research approach to improving the ability of students to argue.

Appendix

Below are the student instructions for the induction module on argument described in chapter 7.

STUDY SKILLS: DEVELOPING ARGUMENT

The aims of this work are:

1) to practice basic study skills which are of use in following spoken langauge, making notes and academic writing

2) to make sense of the complexity if the issue of press regulation and the arguments which surrounded it in 1992/3

3) to analyse and be critical of these arguments

4) to use the above processes to arrive at a considered and perhaps original contribution to the debate

SESSION ONE (75 minutes)

1.1 First of all make sure you are aware of the basic facts about the Calcutt Report which appeared in the second week of January 1993 (An article from the *Guardian* is supplied)

1.2 Now spend 5 minutes jotting down your views on the subject.

2 You are now going to hear an audio tape relating to the article. The tape is of Radio 4's "Any Questions"programme where a panel of well-known people are give their views in response to questions asked by members of the public. In the section you will hear asks "Are the press more sinned against than sinning?"

You will have to take some notes SUMMARISING what each speaker on the tape says (not the introducer). It will help you if you have some categories of information that you are looking out for:

2.1 Does the speaker use any evidence or examples to support his/her opinion?

2.2 What is the speaker's opinion?

3 Listen to the tape again, checking on your previous notes and this time making extra notes on the following questions:

3.1 Does the speaker suggest any solution to the problem he/she is addressing?

3.2 Does the speaker express any views about what other members of the panel have said? E.g. "I agree with so and so, but would like to add ..." "So and so is talking nonsense.."

4 As a group discuss the difficulties of responding to audio information, levels of concentration, losing the thread by concentrating on details, no pause/rewind, density, mis-hearing.

5 Now write a short summary of each speaker's position. (One short paragraph each.)

6 You will be supplied with a transcription of the speakers' words at the end of this session. *Make sure you take one away with you.*

THE NEXT PART OF THIS MODULE IS TO BE COMPLETED IN YOUR OWN TIME BEFORE TOMORROW'S SESSION.

7 Check your summaries against the transcription. If there are differences, why do you think they occurred? For example, did you not notice some things? Did you notice them but not think they were important? (Do you think they are important now?) Were there some ideas/words you did not understand at first? Did you hear what you wanted to hear and confuse your own opinion with a speaker's?

7.1 Still only dealing with the important points, make any alterations to your summaries that you feel are necessary.

8 The next task is to tease out the common themes or points raised. Sketch a grid which shows roughly who is in agreement with whom. Identify common points which two or more speakers address.

Draw your grid something like this, with the speakers along the top and common points down the side. (See the completed example in Appendix One.) Viz:

	Mary Archer	Sheila Lawlor	Robin Page	Ken Livingstone
Common point 1 (e.g. privacy must be protected)				
Common point 2				
Common point 3				

(Make your grid much bigger than this – you will probably need more than one sheet of paper!)

8.1 In the spaces summarise what the speakers say in relation to the common point you have identified. You may find that although two speakers agree on a certain general point, the emphasis they place on its significance differs, i.e. there are variations within the same broad idea.

9 Write an account of the different positions on the common poins raised. A paragraph or two on each point is enough. It is the ideas themselves you are particularly interested in so you need not attribute every point you make to a particular speaker. Look at points such as: is there general agreement ? Does one position diverge from the others? In what way?

YOUR ACCOUNT MUST BE READY FOR THE NEXT SESSION IN THIS MODULE

SESSION TWO (60 minutes)

10 Get into pairs and read your partner's account, thinking about how they went about the task. Ask them to clarify any points you don't understand or points that you feel are unclear to you. Remember, their job is to make things clear to you.

11 As a group discuss common problems with the tasks, both those done at home and this one.

12 Now look at the sample grid and compare it to what you have done. Did you identify any common pointsthat are not on the grid?

13 If time allows you will listen to the views of the public who phoned in to comment. Can you see where these people's views fit in to the debate on press regulations? Do they echo what has already been said or do they say something - slightly or totally – different? Use these people's contributions to modify and enrich your existing picture of the debate. You may need to create a new category.

THE REST OF THIS MODULE IS COMPLETED IN YOUR OWN TIME, TO BE HANDED IN TO THE OFFICE BY THE DATE GIVEN TO YOU IN THE SESSION.

14 In order to strengthen your understanding of the arguments you have identified, try now to find examples/illustrations/evidence to support and/or refute them. These could even be from your general knowledge but you should consider carefully the status and value of the material you come up with.

15 Start to prepare for a piece of writing on the issue of press regulation as opposed to the radio programmes you have heard. Using the material you have collected, consider again:

15.1 What is too important to leave out? and what can be used as illustration of points as space permits?

15.2 Are you satisfied with any one line of argument - would you like to challenge or adapt it? How?

15.3 How your initial thoughts on the issue might fit in?

15.4 Whether you have any personal experiences against which you could test the various arguments. What are their strengths and weaknesses?

15.5 Whether you need any more information.

15.6 The status of the speakers. Should you retain their names in your writing or to characterise their views in more impersonal ways. E.g "It is sometimes argued..." "An alternative explanation is..." "Examples given to support this view include..." "This point might be extended to suggest..."?

16 One of your biggest problems will be selection, so have your priorities clear from the start. Also, bear in mind the issue of your responsibility to your reader to be clear and aware of what you're doing. Ask yourself "What am I doing with this sentence/paragraph?".

17 WRITE AN 800 TO 1000 WORD ESSAY ON THE SUBJECT OF PRESS REGULATION. When you write about this issue you should show that you are aware of the varied and complex arguments that it provokes (that is, you should use the work you have done summarising and analysing) and use these arguments to develop a position of your own.

18 Write a short, (200 word max.) account of the problems you encountered doing this exercise.

19 SUBMIT A PORTFOLIO OF ALL THE WRITING AND GRIDS ASSOCIATED WITH THIS MODULE (INCLUDING THE HANDOUT). THE ESSAY SHOULD BE AS LEGIBLE AS POSSIBLE, THOUGH TYPING IS NOT NECESSARY.

Appendix One
Sample Notes And Grid

Here is an example of the grid making exercise where the subject of the original material was food.

Below are some notes made from a recording of a conversation between some students; Anne, Bill Claire and Dave. They have been watching a television documentary about famine in Africa. We have included just the notes made on Anne's contribution to the conversation. On the following page we have reproduced part of the resulting grid. These two together should demonstrate how to use notes like yours to make a grid of common points.

ANNE

She says that the programmme has put her off her food because it showed so many people with starvation.

She finds it disgusting that we eat too much and die of diseases related to eating too much and eating things which are bad for us when people in other countries are starving. (*She's very emotional in her reaction to the subjcet – disgust is emotive.*)

All the colour and additives put in food, especially for kids, is bad for you. It makes you ill and it's addictive. (*Remember how I was really hyperactive when I ate certain things as a child. Used to get in trouble a lot – could have been food colouring allergy.*)

The English have no imagination in food. they must always have their meat and two veg.. Chips with everything and it's mostly tasteless. (*Pot Noodles*)

'I became a vegetarian for six months after that Band Aid thing' (*Guardian report 6.6.87 p.22 says that a survey in schools shows that 13% of young females had become 'wholly or mostly vegetarian' over the previous two years.*)

Her mother used to go on at her to eat her vegetables, but they were so badly cooked, now she prefers what her mother forced on her. She used not to tell her to eat everything in front of her whilst leaving her own, or not giving herself so much. She thinks parents didn't know enough about food and taught their children badly. (*Need for nutrition information, not food marketing – you get it in some schools now. Do eating disorders relate to bad examples at home?*)

There are more notes on Anne's conribution, but those above will suffice to indicate the points in grid construction. 1) Not everything goes in the grid. 2) Some of your own comments (*italics*) will go in thegrid. 3) A speaker's words may or may not go in the notes or grid.

	ANNE	BILL	CLAIRE	DAVE
COMMON POINT 1) We eat too much as a nation whilst others starve.	It's disgusting that we die of eating too much whilst in the 3rd World kids die of starvation *(emotional response)*	There is enough food in the world but it's the wrong sort and in the wrong place.	If we ate less and more nutritious food we would save on health care and could give more aid to others *(type of food is important too)*	We eat loads of meat which is inefficient use of energy. Other nations can't get enough lentils or even beans -or water.
COMMON POINT 2) English food is boring.	English people are obsessed with meat and two veg. Usually it's without taste			Our food all tastes the same, processed meat with stodge. Aisian cookery is much more interesting.
COMMON POINT 3) Were encouraged to both eat for pleasure and to diet.		Went out with someone who couldn't enjoy a meal because she felt guilty -would starve herself next day.	When alone, sometimes the TV chocolate ads really make her fancy some - makes a cup of tea instead.	Watches his weight. As a kid was rewarded by sweets, execises to control his weight.

Appendix Two
Advice On Essay Writing - Some Questions To Ask Yourself

Below are several questions which are related to various features of writing in the essay form for academic purposes. You should these questions as you work to prepare to write and as you write. You may find it useful to write out your responses. You needn't follow the order of the questions.

1. What is the purpose of this writing?

    Writing usually has more than one purpose. Here are some possibilities:

    *   to show knowledge of facts
    *   to show knowledge of debates or issues
    *   to analyse and evaluate facts and/or debates
    *   to argue the case for both sides in a debate
    *   to work out a position for yourself
    *   to provide a convincing argument for one side
    *   to persuade the reader of the validity of your analysis and evaluation.
    *   to point out inadequacies in the arguments that you have commented on.
    *   to make suggestions – for practice, for further research
    *   to answer the question.

    The list is not exhaustive. Some purposes may be more important to you than others.

2. Can you sum up in one or two sentences what you want to say or to argue in this writing? (This is hard but a good exercise to try).

3. Who are you writing for? What kind of register and tone do you want to adopt?

4. What does your reader need to know in order to understand what you want to say or to be persuaded of your argument?

5. If you need to show awareness of various different positions, ask yourself:

    What are these positions?
    What are their strengths?
    What are their weaknesses?
    What evidence can I supply to illustrate or prove these strengths or weaknesses?
    (Evidence includes quotations, sources, facts, illustrations).

6. How are these positions and ideas related to one another? Is it possible to put them in any order? Can you make links between them? Do you want to emphasise certain positions or ideas more than others.

7. How are the positions related to what you want to say or to argue?

8. How do you want to end the piece of writing? Is the end of the piece the end of the argument? Are there questions still unanswered?

9. What do you need to say first? Or, to put it another way, what does the reader need to know first?

Bibliography

Andrews, R. (ed.) (1989) *Narrative and Argument*, Milton Keynes: Open University Press.

Andrews, R. (ed.) (1992) *Rebirth of Rhetoric: essays in language, culture and education*, London: Routledge.

Andrews, R. and Costello, P. (1993) *Improving the Quality of Argument, 7-16: final report*, Hull: University of Hull, Centre for Studies in Rhetoric.

Andrews, R. (1993) 'Developing Argument' in *The English and Media Magazine*, 28, Summer 1993.

Andrews, R. (1994) 'A Rhetorical Perspective' in K. Watson and W. Sawyer (eds.) *English Teaching in Perspective*, Sydney: St. Clair Press.

Andrews, R. and Mitchell, S. (1994) 'The development of argument in English and Politics in 16-18 year old students' in *Literacy Learning: Secondary Thoughts*, Vol. 1 No. 2.

Applebee, A. N. (1978) *The Child's Concept of Story*, Chicago: The University of Chicago Press.

Atkinson, J. (1989) 'Developing Argument at Sixteen Plus' in Andrews, R (ed.) *Narrative and Argument*, Milton Keynes: Open University Press.

Bakhtin, M. M. (1981) *The Dialogic Imagination*, Austin: University of Texas Press.

Bakhtin, M. M. (1986) *Speech Genres and Other Late Essays*, Austin: University of Texas Press.

Barnes, D. (1976) *From Communication to Curriculum*, London: Penguin.

Barnes, D., Britton, J. and Torbe, M. (1990) *Language, the Learner and the School*, Portsmouth, NH: Boynton/Cook - Heinemann.

Barton, D.(1994) *Literacy: an introduction to the ecology of written language*, Oxford: Blackwell.

Bassey, M. (1981) 'Pedagogic Research: on the relative merits of the search for generalisations and the study of single events' in *Oxford Review of Education* Vol. 7 pp. 73-94.

Bassey M. (1983) 'Pedagogic Research into singularities: case studies, probes and curriculum innovations' in *Oxford Review of Education* Vol. 9 No. 2 pp. 109-121.

Bazerman, C. (1988) *Shaping Written Knowledge*, Wisconsin: University of Wisconsin Press.

Belsey, C. (1980) *Critical Practice*, London: Methuen.

Berrill, D. (1990) 'Adolescents arguing' in Wilkinson, A., Davis, A. and Berrill D. *Spoken English Illuminated* , Milton Keynes: Open University Press.

Berrill, D. (1990) 'What exposition has to do with argument: argumentative writing of sixteen year olds' in *English in Education*, Vol. 24, No.1, Spring 1990.

Berrill, D. (1991) 'Exploring Underlying Assumptions: small group work of university undergraduates' in *Educational Review*, Special Issue 23.

Berrill, D. (1992) 'Issues of Audience: Egocentrism Revisited' in Andrews, R. (ed.) *Rebirth of Rhetoric*, London: Routledge.

Billig, M. (1991) *Ideology and Opinions*, London: Sage Publications.

Bloom, B. (ed.) (1956) *Taxonomy of Educational Objectives; Book 1 Cognitive Domain*, New York: David McKay Company, Inc..

Bridwell-Bowles, L. (1992) 'Discourse and Diversity: experimental writing within the academy', in *College Composition and Communication*, Vol. 43, No.3 October 1992.

Britton, J. et al. (1975) *The Development of Writing Abilities*, London: Macmillan.

Burwood, S. (1994) *Essay Writing: an introduction*, Hull: Department of Philosophy, University of Hull.

Davis, C. and Scheifer, R. (1991) *Criticism and Culture: the role of critique in modern literary theory*, Harlow: Longman.

Derrida, J. (1992) 'This Strange Institution Called Literature: an interview with Jacques Derrida' in Attridge, D. (ed.) *Acts of Literature*, London: Routledge.

Devitt, A. (1993) 'Generalizing about Genre: new conceptions of an old concept' in *College Composition and Communication* Vol. 44 No.4 December 1993.

Dixon, J. and Stratta, L. (1986) 'Argument and the teaching of English: a critical analysis' in Wilkinson, A. (ed.) *The Writing of Writing*, Milton Keynes: Open University Press.

Dixon, J. (1989) 'If it's narrative, why do nothing but generalize?' in Andrews, R (ed.) *Narrative and Argument*, Milton Keynes: Open University Press.

Donald, J. G. (1992) 'The development of thinking processes in postsecondary eduaction: the application of a working model' in *Higher Education* Vol. 24 1992.

Fahnestock J. (1993) 'Genre and Rhetorical Craft' in *Research in the Teaching of English*, Vol. 27, No. 3 October 1993.

Flower, L. and Hayes, J. R. (1981) 'A Cognitive Process Theory of Writing' in *College Composition and Communication* Vol. 32 Dec. 1981.

Foucault, M. (1972) *The Archaeology of Knowledge*, London: Tavistock.

Foucault, M. (1984) 'What is an Author?' in Rabinow, P (ed.) *The Foucault Reader*, London: Penguin.

Freadman, A. (1988) 'Anyone for Tennis?' in *The Place of Genre in Learning: current debates*, Deakin: Typereader Publications no.1, Centre for Studies in Literary Education, Deakin University.

Freedman, A. and Pringle, I. (1980) 'Writing in the College Years: some indices of growth' in *College Composition and Communication*, October 1980.

Freedman, A and Pringle, I (1984) 'Why Students Can't Write Arguments' in *English in Education* Vol 18 No.2, Summer 1984.

Freedman, A. and Pringle, I. (1989) 'Contexts for developing argument' in Andrews, R (ed) *Narrative and Argument*, Milton Keynes: Open University Press.

Freedman, A. (1993a) 'Show and Tell? The Role of Explicit Teaching in the Learning of New Genres' in *Research in the Teaching of English*, Vol. 27, No.3 October 1993.

Freedman, A. (1993b) 'Situating Genre: a rejoinder' in *Research in the Teaching of English*, Vol. 27, No.3 October 1993.

Freedman, A., Adam, C. and Smart, G. (1994) 'Wearing Suits to Class: simulating genres and simulations as genre' in *Written Communication* (forthcoming).

Gee, J. P. (1989) 'Literacy, Discourse and Linguistics: introduction' in *Journal of Education*, Vol. 171 No.1 pp. 5-17.

Geertz, C. (1993) *Local Knowledge*, London: Fontana Press.

Geisler, C. and Kaufer, D. (1989) 'Making Meanings in Literate Conversations: a Teachable Sequence for Reflective Writing' in *Rhetoric Society Quarterly* Vol. 19 Summer 1989.

Geisler, C. (1992) 'Exploring Academic Literacy: an experiment in composing' in *College Composition and Communication* Vol. 43 No.1 February 1992.

Giddens, A. (1984) *The Constitution of Society*, Berkeley and Los Angeles: University of California Press.

Gilligan, C. (1982) *In a Different Voice: psychological theory and women's development*, Cambridge, Mass: Harvard University Press.

Giltrow, J. and Valiquette, M. (forthcoming) 'Genres and Knowledge: students writing in the disciplines' in Freedman, A. and Medway, P. (eds.) *Teaching and Learning Genres*, Heinemann- Boynton/Cook.

Glaser, B. and Strauss, A. L. (1967) *The Discovery of Grounded Theory*, London: Weidenfeld and Nicolson.

Goggin, M. D. (1994) 'Situating the Teaching and Learning of Argumentation within Historical Contexts', unpublished paper.

Gorman, T. et al (1988) *Language Performances in Schools: Review of APU Language Monitoring 1979-1983*, London HMSO.

Gubb, J. (1987) 'Discursive Writing – a Small-scale Observation Study' in Gubb, J. et al. (1987) *The Study of Written Composition In England and Wales*, Windsor: NFER/Nelson.

Halliday, M.A. K. and Martin, J.R. (1993) *Writing Science : literacy and discursive power*, London: Falmer Press.

Harré, R. (1983) *Personal Being*, Oxford: Basil Blackwell.

Hillocks, G. (1986) *Research in Written Composition: new directions in teaching*, Urbana Il.: National Council of the Teachers of English.

Ivanic, R. and Roach, D. (1990) *Academic Writing, Power and Disguise*, Working Paper Series, Centre for Language in Social Life, Lancaster University.

Johnstone, H. W. (1978) *Validity and Rhetoric in Philosophical Argument*, University Park Pa: The Dialogue Press of Man and the World.

Kaplan, R.B. and Ostler, S (1982) 'Contrastive Rhetoric Revisited' Paper read at the 1982 ESOL Convention, Honolulu, Hawaii.

Kaufer, D. and Geisler, C. (1989) 'Novelty in Academic Writing' in *Written Communication* Vol 8 July 1989.

Kaufer, D. and Geisler, C. (1991) 'A Scheme for Representing Academic Argument' in *The Journal of Advanced Composition* Vol. 11 1991.

Kelly, G. (1955) *The Psychology of Personal Constructs*, New York: Norton

Kress, G. (1989) 'Texture and Meaning' in Andrews, R. (ed.) *Narrative and Argument*, Milton Keynes: Open University Press.

Kuhn, D. (1992) 'Thinking as Argument' in *Harvard Educational Review* Vol. 62 No.2 Summer 1992.

Lamb, C. (1991) 'Beyond Argument in Feminist Composition' in *College Composition and Communication* Vol. 42, February 1991.

Lewis, C.S. (1992) An Experiment in Criticism, Cambridge, Cambridge University Press.

Lotman, Y. M. (1988a) 'Text within Text' in *Soviet Pyschology* Vol. 26 No, 2.

Lotman, Y. M. (1988b) 'The Semiotics of Culture and the Context of a Text' in *Soviet Pyschology* Vol. 26 No, 2.

McCormick, K. (1990) 'The Cultural Imperatives Underlying Cognitive Acts' in *Reading-to-Write: exploring a cognitive and social process* by Flower, L., Stein, V., Ackerman, J., Kantz, M. McCormick, K., Peck, W. New York: Oxford University Press.

Mathison, M. (1994) Discourse about Discourse: constructing arguments in sociology (unpublished paper).

Medway, P. (1980) *Finding a Language: autonomy and learning in school*, London: Writers and Readers.

Meyer, S. L. (1993) 'Refusing to Play the Confidence Game: the illusion of mastery in the reading/writing of texts' in *College English* Vol. 55 No. 1 (January 1991)

Miller, C. (1984) 'Genre as social action' in*Quarterly Journal of Speech* Vol. 70.

Mitchell, S. (1992a) *Questions and Schooling: classroom discourse across the curriculum* (Centre for Studies in Rhetoric, Occasional Paper No.1), Hull: University of Hull, Centre for Studies in Rhetoric.

Mitchell, S. (1992b) *The Teaching and Learning of Argument in Sixth Forms and Higher Education: Interim Report*, Hull: University of Hull, Centre for Studies in Rhetoric.

Mitchell, S. (1993a) 'The Aesthetic and the Academic: are they at odds in English Literature at A level?' in *English in Education*, Vol. 27 No.1, Spring 1993.

Mitchell, S. (1993b) 'Learning to be critical and correct: forms and functions of argument at A level' in *Curriculum* Vol. 14 No.1 Spring 1993.

Mitchell, S. (1993c) 'Not so much a 'trying out' as a handing-in - a challenge to the academic essay' in *CUE News :The Newsletter of the Council for University English* Vol. 5 No.2 Summer 1993.

Mitchell, S. (1994a) 'Room for Argument in English Literature at A level and Beyond?' in *ETUDE Newsletter* No. 2 February 1994.

Mitchell, S. (1994b) 'Argument in English Literature at A level and Beyond' in English and Media Magazine No. 30, Summer 1994.

Mitchell, S (1994c) 'A level and Beyond: a case study' in *English in Education*

Mitchell, S. and Andrews, R. (forthcoming) 'Learning to operate successfully in advanced level History' in Freedman, A. and Medway, P., *Teaching and Learning Genre*, Heinemann-Boynton/Cook.

Popper, K. (1979) *Objective Knowledge*, Clarendon Press.

Pringle, I. and Freedman, A. (1985) *A Comparative Study of Writing Abilities in Two Modes At the Grade 5, 8 and 12 Levels*, Toronto: Ministry of Education.

Reid, I. (ed.) (1988)*The Place of Genre in Learning: Current Debates*, Deakin: Deakin University, Centre for Studies in Literary Education.

Richards, I.A. (1955) *Speculative Instruments*, London: Routledge Kegan Paul.

Ricoeur, P. (1970) *Freud and Philosophy* , New Haven and London: Yale University Press.

Rimmershaw, R. (1993) 'Collaborative Study in a Computer Conferencing System' in *Nexus Magazine*, Information Systems Services, Lancaster University, Spring 1993.

Ross, G. MacDonald (1994) 'Socrates versus Plato: the origins and development of Socratic thinking' in *Aspects of Education* No.49 1993.

Scholes, R. (1985) *Textual Power: Literary Theory and the Teaching of English*, New Haven: Yale University Press.

Schuster, C. (1985) 'Mikhail Bakhtin as Rhetorical Theorist' in *College English*, Vol. 47, No.6 October 1985.

Sheeran, Y. and Barnes, D. (1991) *School Writing*, Buckingham: Open University Press.

Simpson, J. and Ivanic, R. (1993) *Putting the people back into academic writing* Working Paper Series, Centre for Language in Social Life, Lancaster University.

Spivey, N., Mathison, M. A., Goggin, M. D. and Greene, S. (1992) *Writing from Academic Sources: acquiring discourse knowledge for writing and learning (Final Report)* Berkeley: Centre for the Study of Writing at University of California, Berkeley, and Carnegie Mellon University.

Street, B. (1984) *Literacy in Theory and Practice*, Cambridge: Cambridge University Press.

Swales, J. (1990) *Genre Analysis: English in academic and research settings*, Cambridge: Cambridge University Press.

Toulmin, S. (1958) *The Uses of Argument*, Cambridge: The Cambridge University Press.

Vygotsky, L. S. (1962) *Thought and Language*, United States: Massachusetts Institute of Technology Press

Vygotsky, L. S. (1978) *Mind in Society: the development of higher psychological processes*, Cambridge, Mass.: Harvard University Press.

Ward Jouve, N. (1991) *White Woman Speaks with Forked Tongue: criticism as autobiography*, London: Routledge.

Wersch, J. V. and Smolka, A. (1993) 'Continuing the dialogue: Vygotsky, Bakhtin, and Lotman' in Daniels, H. (ed.) *Charting the Agenda: educational activity after Vygotsky*, London and New York: Routledge.

Williams, J. M. and Colomb, G. G. (1993) 'The Case for Explicit Teaching: why what you don't know won't help you' in *Research in the Teaching of English*, Vol. 27, No.3 October 1993.

Williamson, M. M. (1988) 'A Model for Investigating the Functions of Written Language in Different Disciplines' in Jolliffe, D. A. (ed.) *Advances in Writing Research Volume Two: Writing in Academic Disciplines*, New Jersey: Ablex Publishing Corporation.

Womack, P. (1993) 'What are essays for?' in *English in Education* Vol. 27 No.2.

Wymer, R. (1992) 'What do we want from theory and how do we get it?' in *Critical Survey* Vol. 4 No.3.